IMAGES
of Rail

Treasure Valley's Electric Railway

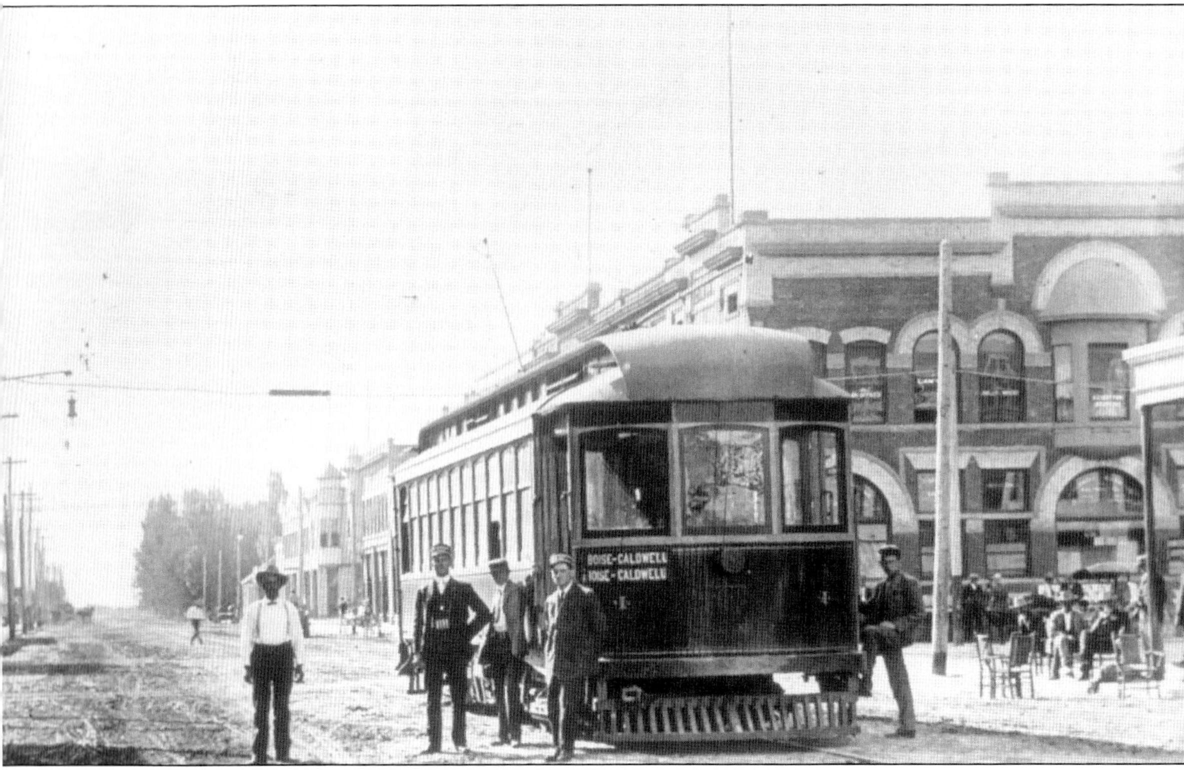

On the Cover: Boise and Interurban Railway Car No. 4 is pictured in Caldwell, around 1907.

IMAGES
of Rail

TREASURE VALLEY'S ELECTRIC RAILWAY

Barbara Perry Bauer
and Elizabeth Jacox

ARCADIA
PUBLISHING

ISBN 978-978-0-7385-9633-4

Published by Arcadia Publishing
Charleston, South Carolina

Printed in the United States of America

Library of Congress Control Number: 2012944064

For all general information, please contact Arcadia Publishing:
Telephone 843-853-2070
Fax 843-853-0044
E-mail sales@arcadiapublishing.com
For customer service and orders:
Toll-Free 1-888-313-2665

Visit us on the Internet at www.arcadiapublishing.com

This book is dedicated to our children—Jordan, Nick, and Ellen.

Contents

ACKNOWLEDGMENTS

This book could not have been produced without the support and enthusiasm of the many people who have willingly shared their time and their knowledge about the electric railway in the Treasure Valley. Thanks go to John Aguirre and Worth Montgomery for their help in unraveling the complex route of the electric railway and for their expertise in all things railroad related. John also allowed us to use images from his vast collection of railroad photographs. No project about the electric railway can be done without acknowledging the late Jim Witherell, who was an expert on the system.

We want to thank Erica Flitton and Virginia Vaught of the Idaho State Historical Society for their assistance in identifying and scanning images. The Idaho State Historical Society holds the largest collection of images related to electric street railways in the state, and we have made extensive use of it. Unless otherwise noted, images in this book were provided by the Idaho State Historical Society.

Shane Baker, senior archeologist at Idaho Power Company; Jan Boles, archivist at the College of Idaho; Wendy Miller, former director of the Canyon County Historical Society; and Lila Hill of the Meridian Historical Society all made special efforts to locate images and answer our questions. Sharon Fisher suggested we contact Arcadia Publishing and started us on the path to this book. Our husbands, Martin and George, have patiently provided support and encouragement through all of the ups and downs of research and writing.

Introduction

The first electric street railway in the United States began operation in 1887 in Richmond, Virginia. By 1891, only one year after Idaho achieved statehood, businessmen in Boise were initiating construction of the first street railway lines in Boise. Before the advent of affordable automobiles in the 1920s, a 44-mile electric interurban railway system connected communities in Ada and Canyon Counties, providing both passenger and freight service.

The city of Boise was established in 1863, when a US Army fort was built at the crossroads of the Oregon Trail and the road to gold mines located in the surrounding mountains. Boise became the major distribution center for mining supplies and food for the immigrants and gold-seekers. By the time Idaho became a state in 1890, settlements stretched west along the Boise River to the Oregon border. People lived in railroad towns, such as Caldwell and Nampa, as well as in small farming communities like Star and Middleton. While it was originally identified as the Boise Valley, local booster Peter Olesen came up with the name Treasure Valley in 1959, reflecting the abundance of natural resources, agricultural production, and recreational and business opportunities available in the area. At the end of the 19th and beginning of the 20th centuries, the electric railway system and irrigated agriculture were two important factors in the growth and development of the region now commonly known as Treasure Valley.

The Treasure Valley electric railway era lasted for almost 40 years (1891–1928). During that time, a number of companies were chartered, including the Boise Rapid Transit Company; the Boise Traction Company; the Boise Streetcar Company; the Boise Valley Railway; the Boise & Interurban Railway, Ltd.; the Caldwell Interurban Company; and the Caldwell Traction Company. Eventually, after many mergers and splits, the separate companies were organized into a single system, operated by the local power company. The electric railway provided recreation and entertainment opportunities, inspired the creation of local parks, and encouraged the growth of neighborhoods and communities.

Today, there are few remnants of the electric railway. Evidence is buried under modern streets and sidewalks, rediscovered when street repair or utility work requires destruction of the modern surface. Buildings have been converted for other uses—for instance, the Warm Springs carbarn in Boise has been transformed into a restaurant. Visitors to Caldwell can stop to see "the Hat," a shelter station on the interurban loop that, though modified, has been preserved as a landmark on the College of Idaho campus.

One

First Tracks in Boise

Boise had a banner year in 1890. On July 3, Idaho was admitted to the union as the 43rd state. Boise, the capital city, was on the brink of a decade of growth and prosperity. The electric streetcar boom in the East quickly spread to the West, and Boise initiated its own streetcar system in the summer of 1890 with the incorporation of the Boise Rapid Transit Company (BRT). The company initially planned a 20-mile route. Tracks would cross Boise, east to west, and run south from the city center to the bluffs, or benches, across the Boise River. The following summer, the BRT began operating on a two-and-a-half-mile line that extended east from downtown Boise to the site of a proposed hot springs resort on Warm Springs Avenue. The construction of the electrical railway, combined with the commercial development of geothermal springs east of Boise, opened up that side of town to development. Warm Springs Avenue soon attracted wealthy residents, who built new, elaborate homes, heated by geothermal water and lit with electric lights.

Early street railway operations in Boise began at the mill of Boise pioneer merchant Cyrus Jacobs, who invested in the BRT. His water-powered flour mill was remodeled to provide the power for the electric trolley. Because the BRT did not have the means to build the railway or the electrical apparatus, the company signed a contract with the Edison Company of New York to complete construction. Once the project was finished, the Edison Company operated the street railway for 30 days in order to work out any problems before transferring the system to the BRT.

By 1903, when the BRT was dissolved and reorganized under new investors, the company had established a streetcar system that extended over six miles through Boise, connecting downtown to emerging neighborhoods.

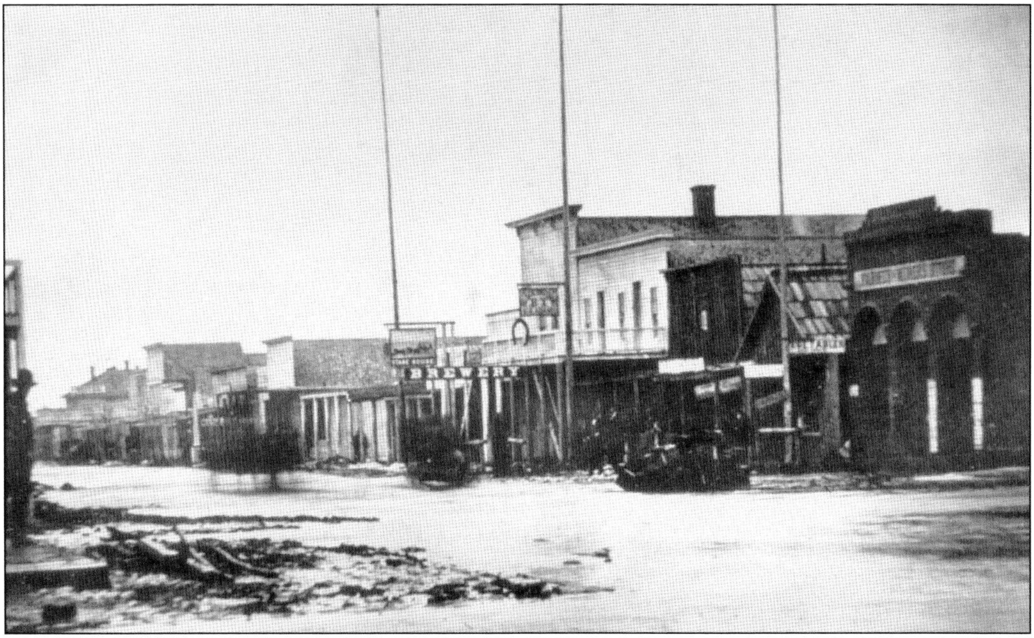

This photograph shows Boise's Main Street around 1867. Note the dirt streets and wood sidewalks. Transportation was horse-powered until 1891, when the Boise Rapid Transit Company was organized to provide local electric streetcar service.

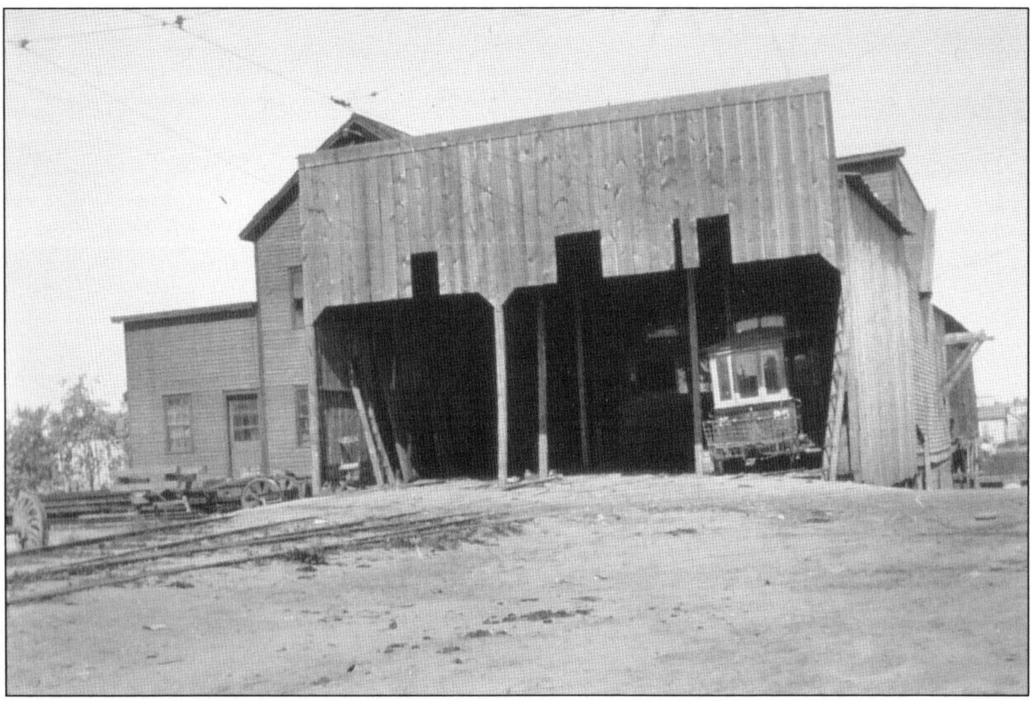

The Cyrus Jacobs flour mill at the intersection of Fourteenth and Idaho Streets was remodeled in 1891 to house the office, depot, powerhouse, and carbarn for the Boise Rapid Transit Company. The building was used until 1904, when a new powerhouse was constructed.

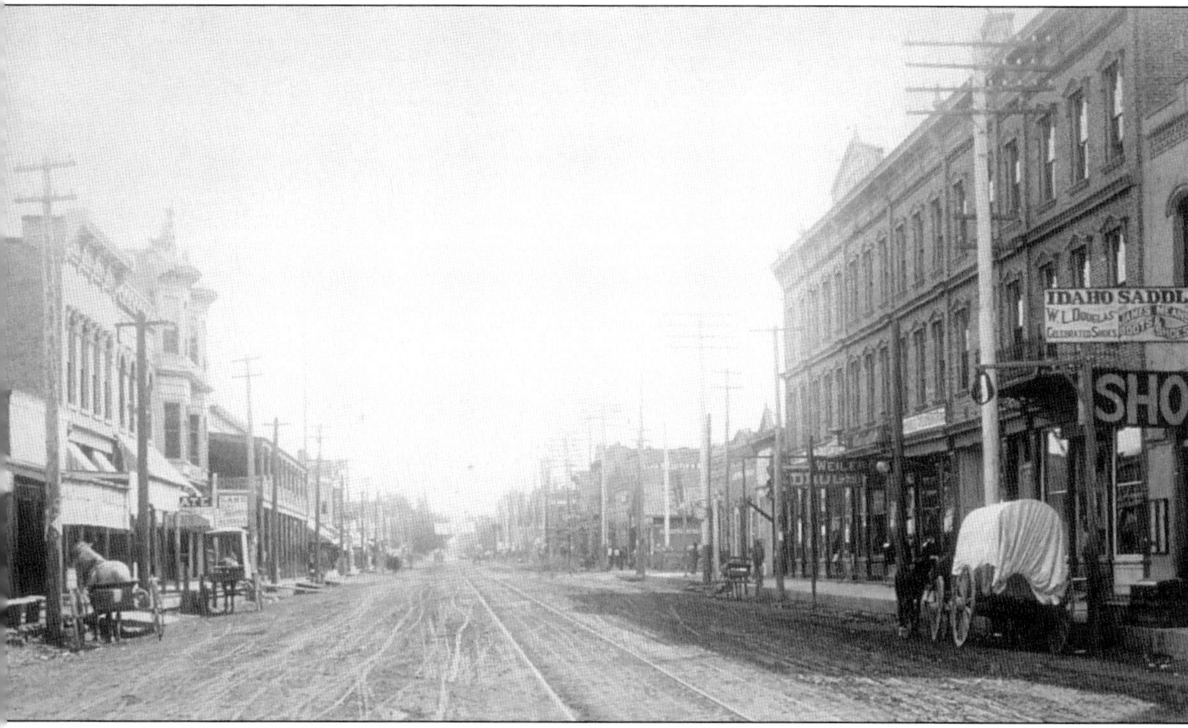

During the summer of 1891, workmen began laying rails for the electric streetcar in Boise. The line began at the powerhouse on Fourteenth and Idaho Streets and went one block east to Thirteenth Street, then south to Main Street. The tracks visible in this photograph were laid in the center of Main Street, heading east to Warm Springs Avenue.

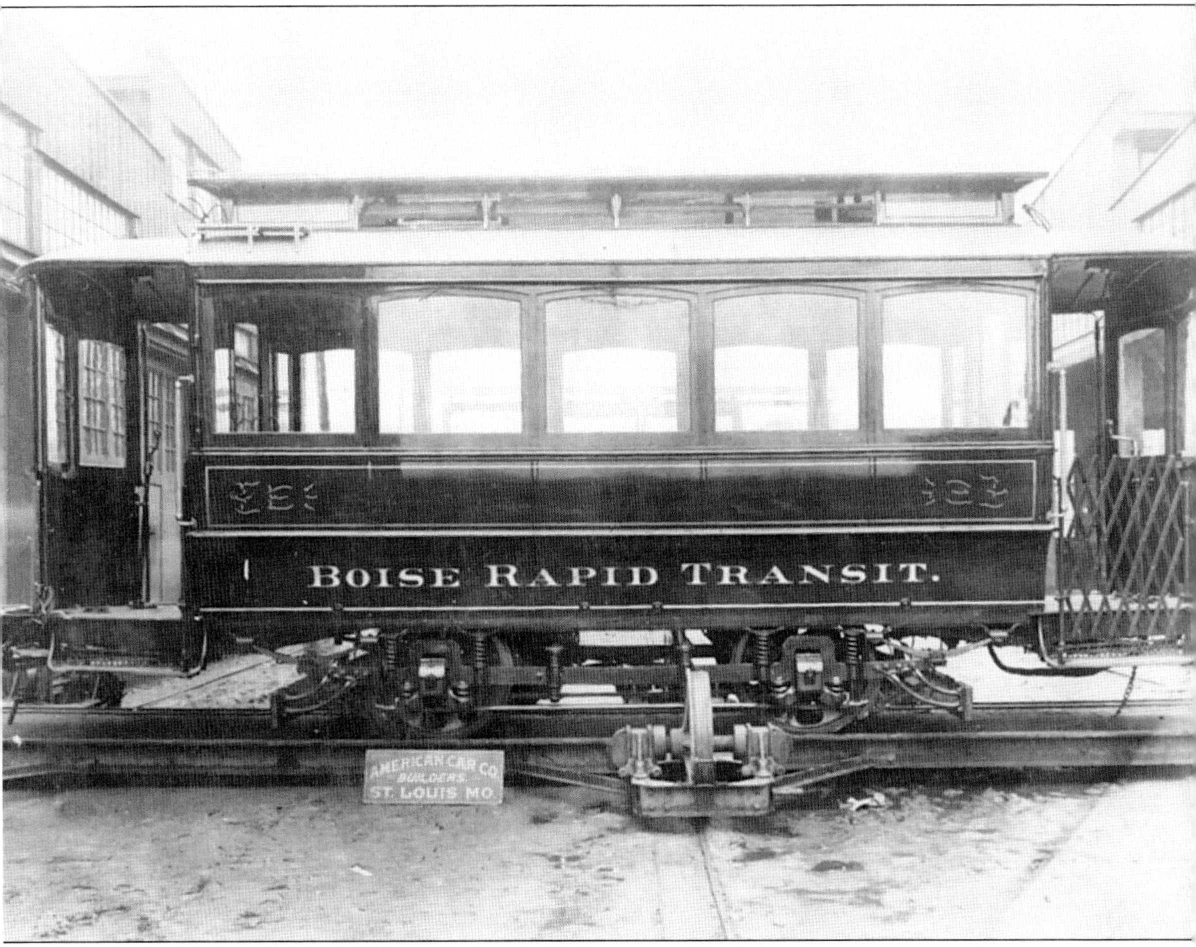

This undated photograph shows a BRT car at the factory of the American Car Company in St. Louis, Missouri. The cars were brought by rail to the Boise depot, located on the bench above the city, and were then transported downtown on freight wagons.

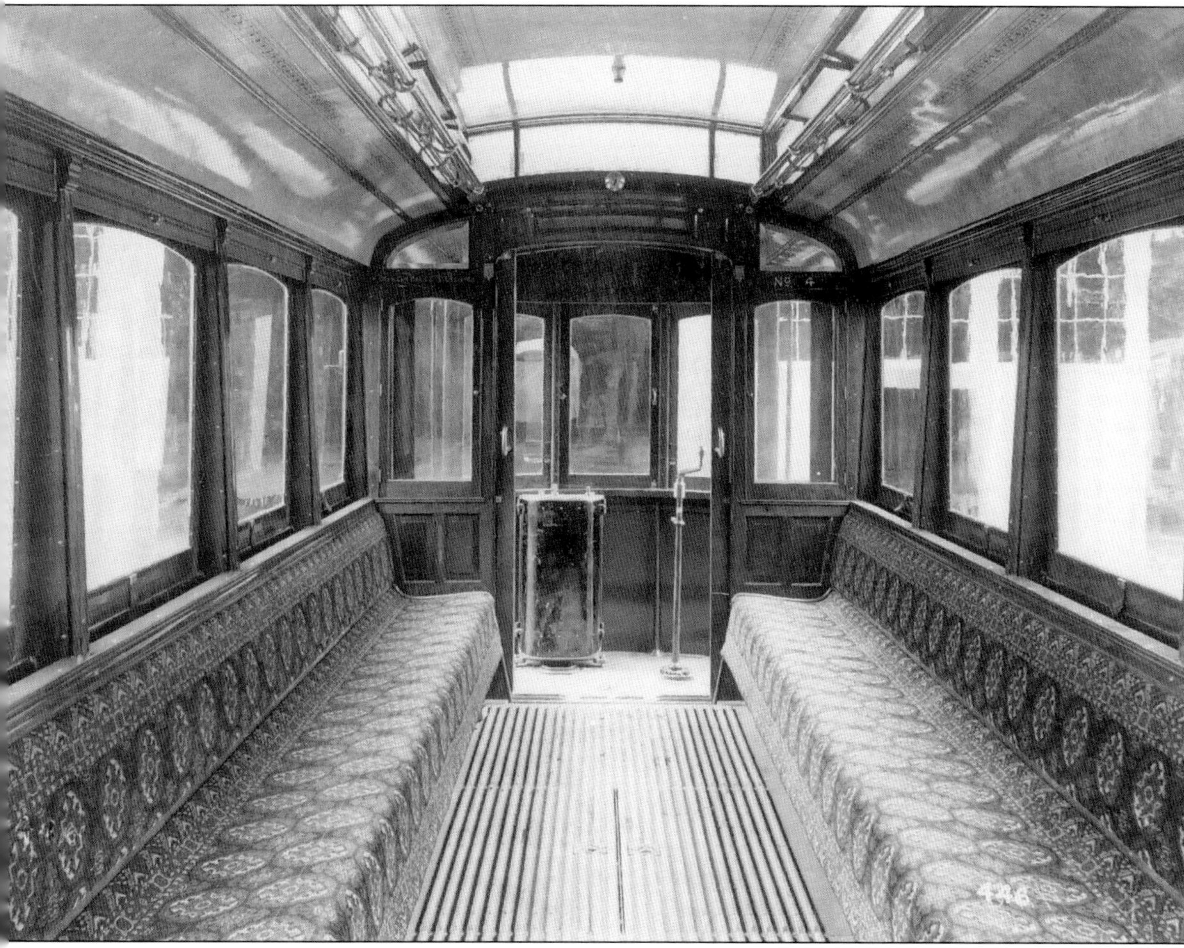

This photograph of BRT American Car No. 4 shows the interior, with fabric-covered bench seats and wood accents. The wooden slats on the floor replaced hemp matting that was used previously in trolley cars. The slats could be removed and cleaned, and most dirt fell between them.

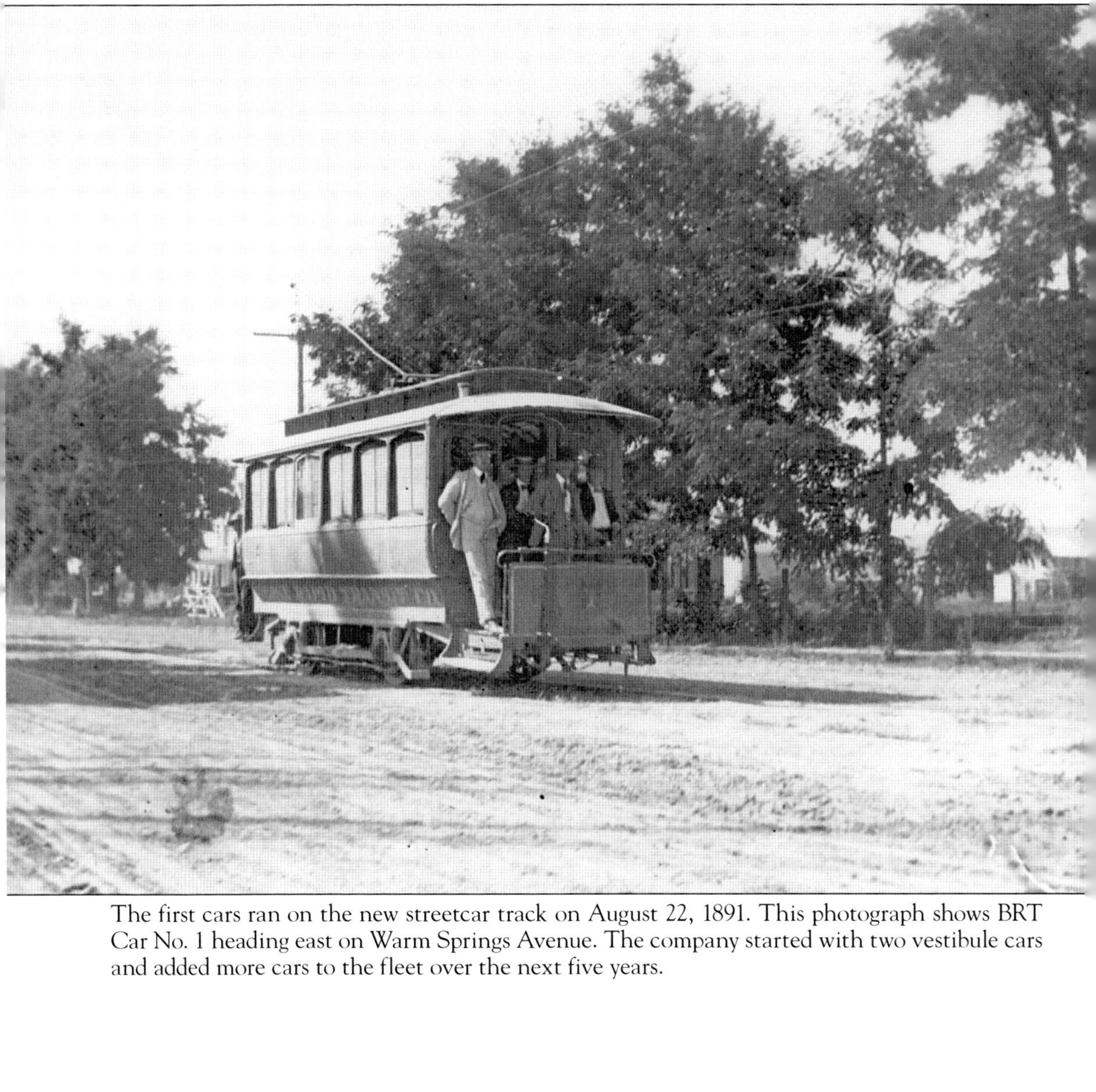

The first cars ran on the new streetcar track on August 22, 1891. This photograph shows BRT Car No. 1 heading east on Warm Springs Avenue. The company started with two vestibule cars and added more cars to the fleet over the next five years.

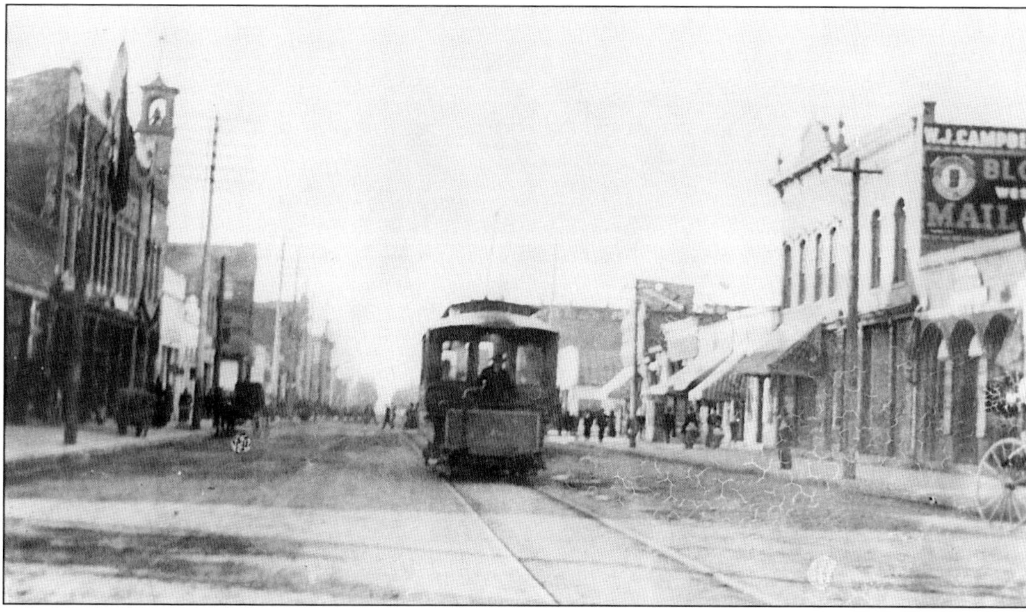

This c. 1895 photograph was taken on Boise's Main Street, looking west from Sixth Street. The streetcar, heading east, has passed the old Central Fire Station (with its bell tower) and the Masonic Hall on the left. The streetcar operator stands in an open deck with no protection from the weather.

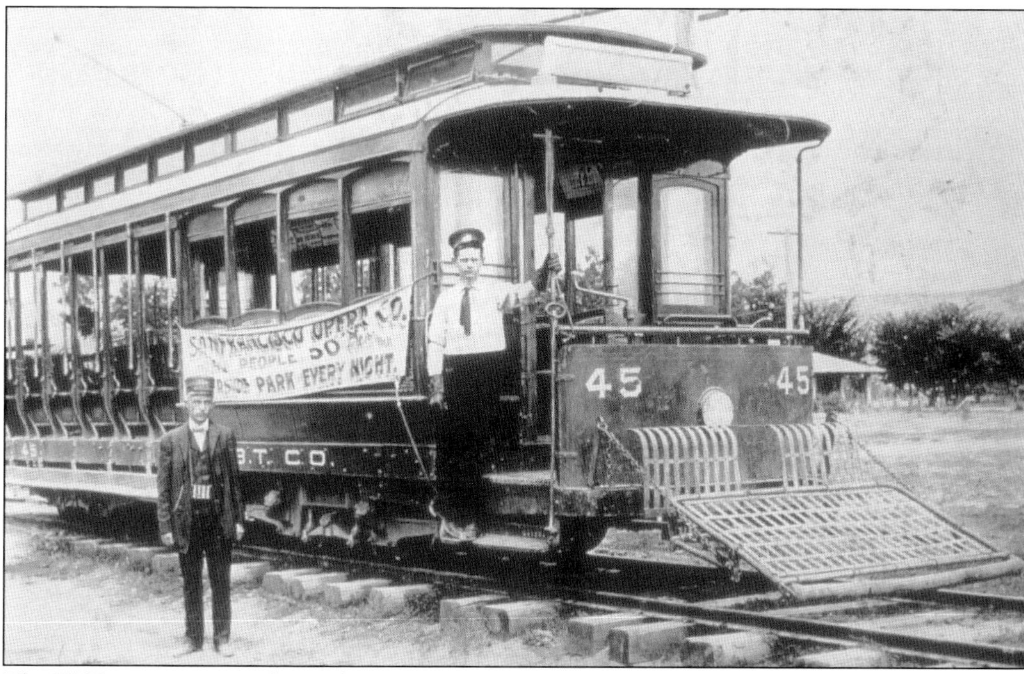

The BRT was reorganized into the Boise Traction Company (BTC), and additional rail lines were added outside the downtown core. The San Francisco Opera Company stopped in Boise after the disastrous earthquake and fire of 1906. This photograph shows an unidentified conductor and motorman posing with Car No. 45, which transported passengers to Riverside Park for the opera company's performance.

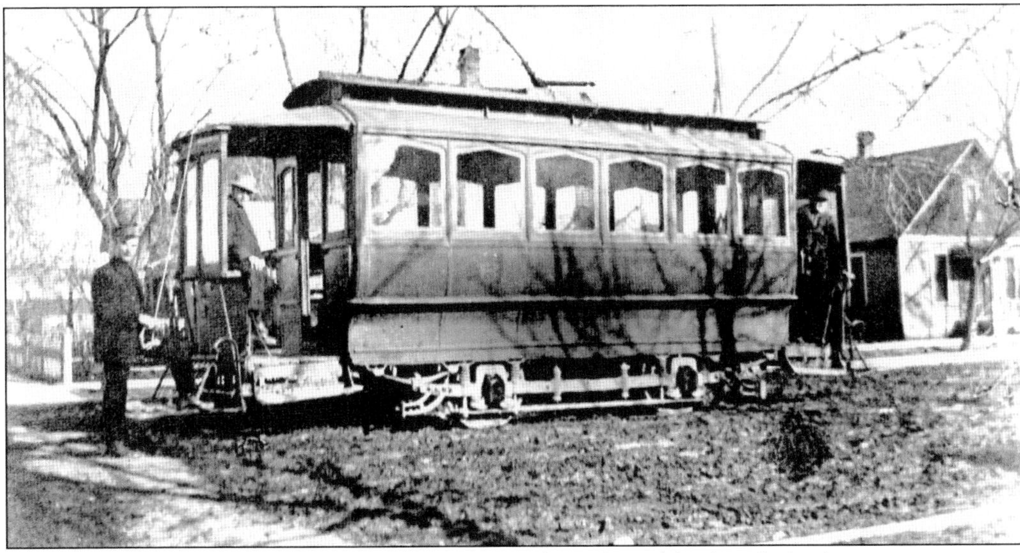

Away from downtown, the trolley lines went to residential neighborhoods. In this view, motorman George Clayville is shown in a car stopped at Fourteenth Street and Grand Avenue.

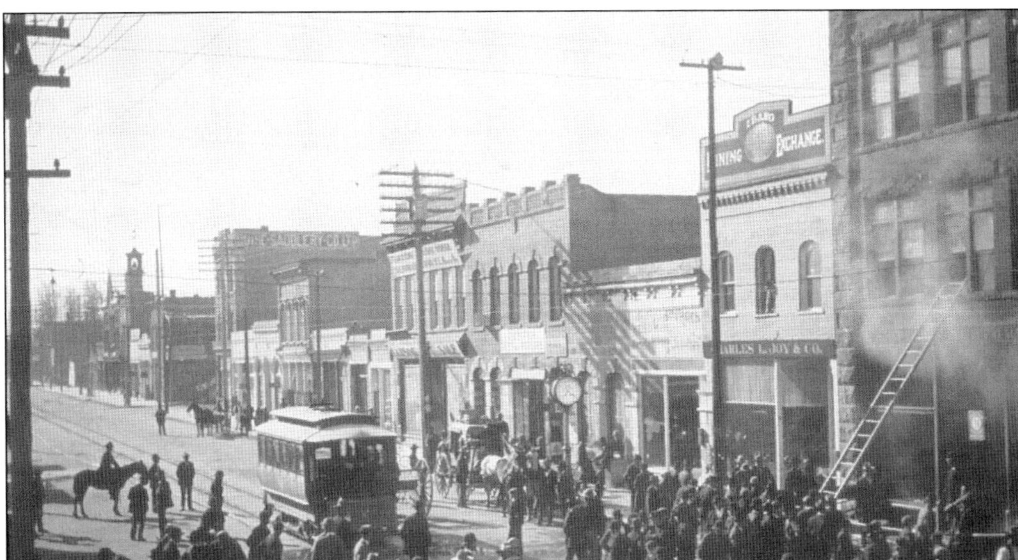

This photograph of Boise's Main Street was taken on April 20, 1899. BRT Car No. 2 has just passed a fire at the Coffin-Northrop hardware store in the Pioneer Building. The disastrous fire destroyed the store and severely damaged the building. This streetcar has a monitor, or deck roof. The trolley pole, which conducts electricity from the overhead wire to the car, is visible at the center of the roof.

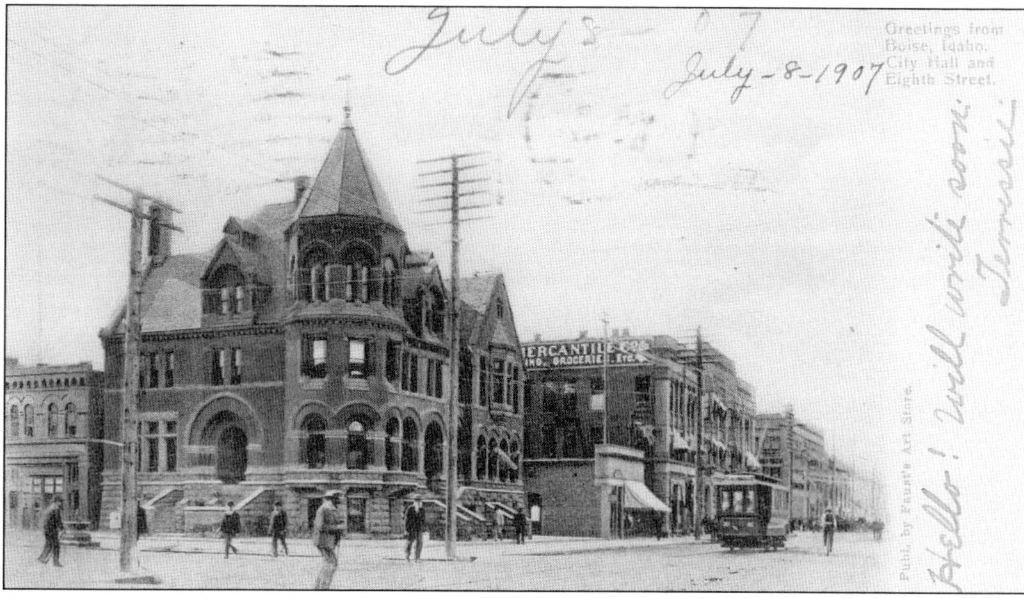

A postcard view of Boise shows the streetcar heading west on Idaho Street. On the left is Boise City Hall. The redbrick-and-sandstone building, which stood on the southeast corner of Eighth and Idaho Streets, was designed by architect John C. Paulsen and built in 1893. It was torn down in 1953. (Courtesy of John Aguirre.)

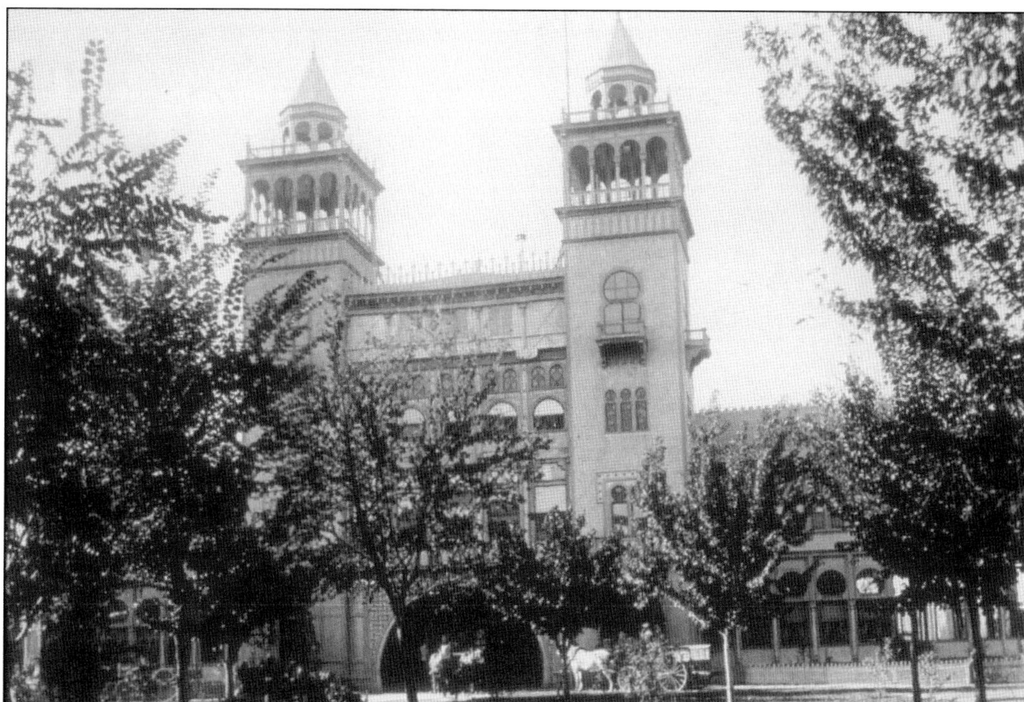

The BRT line extended two and a half miles from the powerhouse east along Main Street to the site of the Natatorium on the Warm Springs Avenue. "The Nat," as it was called, included an indoor natural hot-water swimming pool, billiard rooms, card rooms, Turkish baths, and a bar.

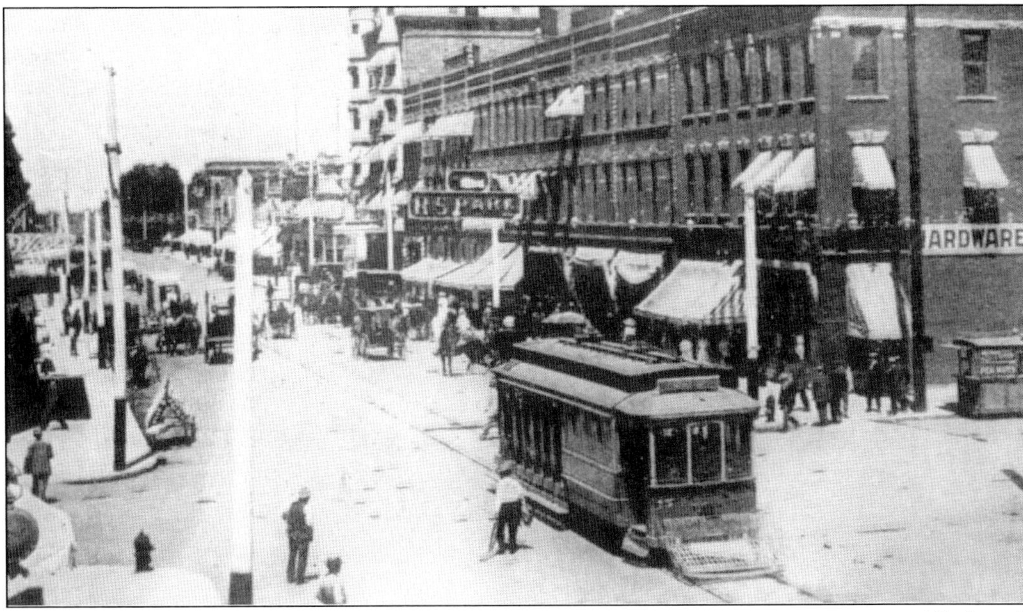

On the midsummer day documented in this undated image, Boise's Main Street is filled with pedestrians, buggies, and bicycles. Car No. 13, heading east, has just passed the Idanha Hotel (at the corner of Tenth and Main Streets) and the Sonna Building (at Ninth and Main Streets). Note the cowcatcher on the front of the car. (Courtesy of John Aguirre.)

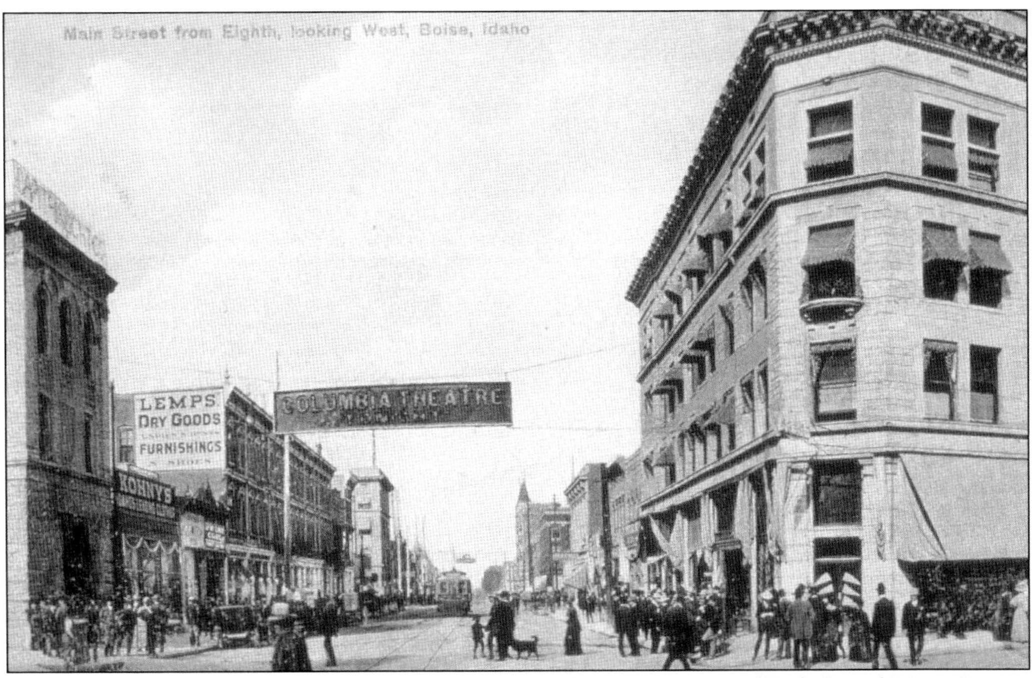

This postcard view shows the streetcar approaching the intersection of Eighth and Main Streets beneath an advertisement for the Columbia Theatre. The Columbia Theatre was built by James Pinney, a leading Boise businessman, in 1893. Boise had grown from a small mining town to a bustling urban center and was ready for an expansion of the existing streetcar line.

Two

Rival Companies

The golden age of American electric street railways fell between 1892 and 1904. Across the nation, street railways experienced rapid expansion, and Boise was no exception. A booming local economy and growing population encouraged local entrepreneurs to establish competing electric street railway lines. The BRT, reincarnated as the Boise Traction Company (BTC), was promoted by local residents Harlan P. Ustick and Watson N. Donaldson. Financial backing came from Eastern investors Cyrus Pierce, W.F. Butcher Jr., and Isaac N. Anderson. These investors had also invested in street railways in other western communities, including Spokane and Walla Walla, Washington, and Aberdeen, South Dakota. A few short years later, in 1907, the BTC was sold to the Boise Railroad Company, Ltd. (BRC). The investors and promoters essentially remained the same. Ustick and Donaldson envisioned expanding the street railway throughout Boise and began to negotiate for an interurban line that would run to Nampa, a town 20 miles west of Boise, in Canyon County. In their book *The Electric Interurban Railway in America*, historians George W. Hilton and John F. Due define an interurban as a railway that shares four characteristics: electric power, primary emphasis on passenger service, cars heavier and faster than city streetcars, and operation on streets in cities but at the sides of highways or on private rights-of-way in rural areas.

The Boise Valley Railway Company (BVRC), organized as an interurban line between Boise and Nampa, was an offshoot of the BRC. Boise developer Walter E. Pierce organized a competitor, the Boise & Interurban Railway Company, Ltd. (B&I), in 1905. The B&I planned an interurban line from Boise to Nampa and other towns in neighboring Canyon County. By 1912, the BVRC extended to Nampa on what was known as the Southern Division and the B&I built lines to Caldwell on what was known as the Northern Division.

Caldwell, the county seat of Canyon County, also developed an interurban system. In 1906, the Caldwell Interurban Company (CIC) was organized by several Caldwell businessmen to build a seven-mile street railway line. In 1910, Walter Sebree and others organized the Caldwell Traction Company (CTC). By 1912, interurban lines in Ada and Canyon Counties linked communities and provided a convenient mode of travel for residents.

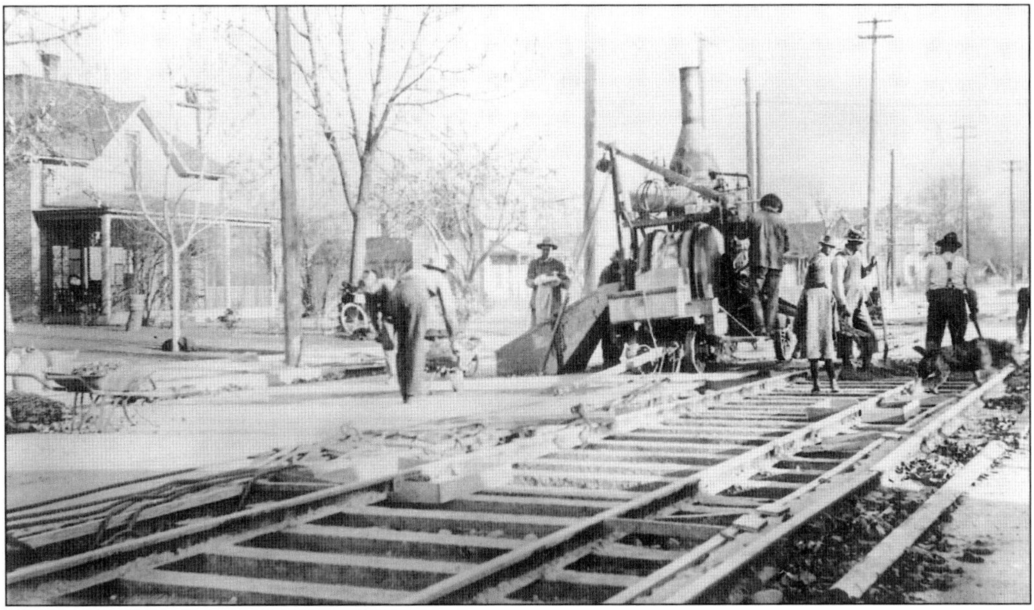

The BTC made several improvements to the old streetcar line, including the replacement of old and worn tracks. Here, unidentified workmen replace tracks on Warm Springs Avenue. The apparatus they are using is a concrete mixer.

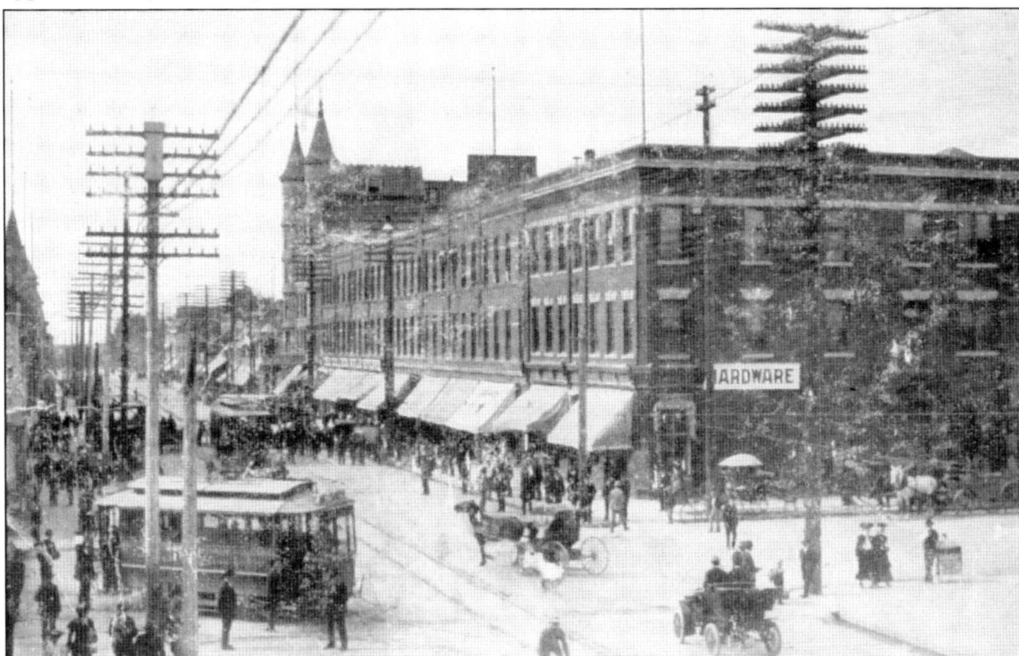

The new extensions of the BTC allowed the streetcar to provide better service and increased the rail mileage to seven and a half miles within the city. This photograph shows a BTC car turning north from Main Street to Eighth Street, heading to new subdivisions in what is now known as Boise's North End neighborhood. The round trip from Eighth and Alturas Streets on the north side of town to the junction at Fifteenth Street and Grand Avenue took 24 minutes. (Courtesy of John Aguirre.)

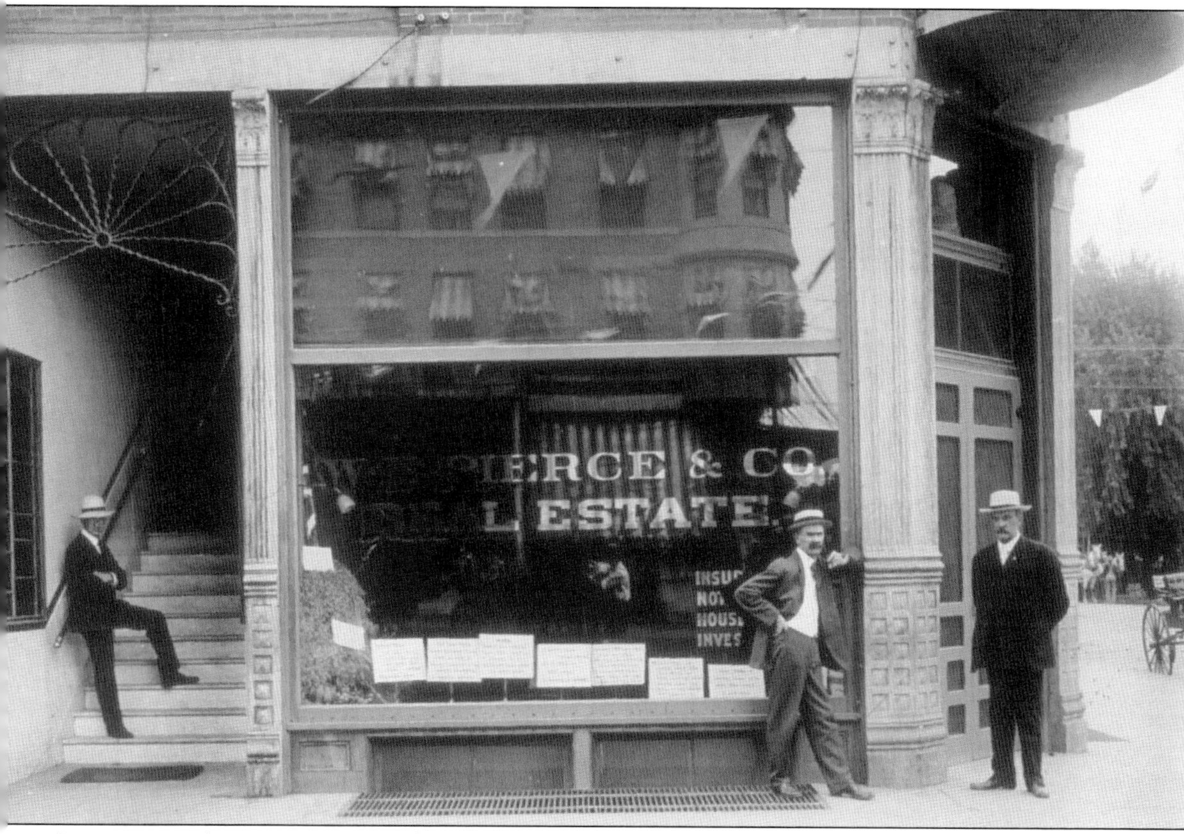

A creative and energetic group of entrepreneurs was behind the development of Boise and the Treasure Valley. This group included Walter E. Pierce (left), Lindley H. Cox (center), and John M. Haines (right), who arrived in Boise in 1891. These three partners were active in many businesses, including the streetcar and interurban systems.

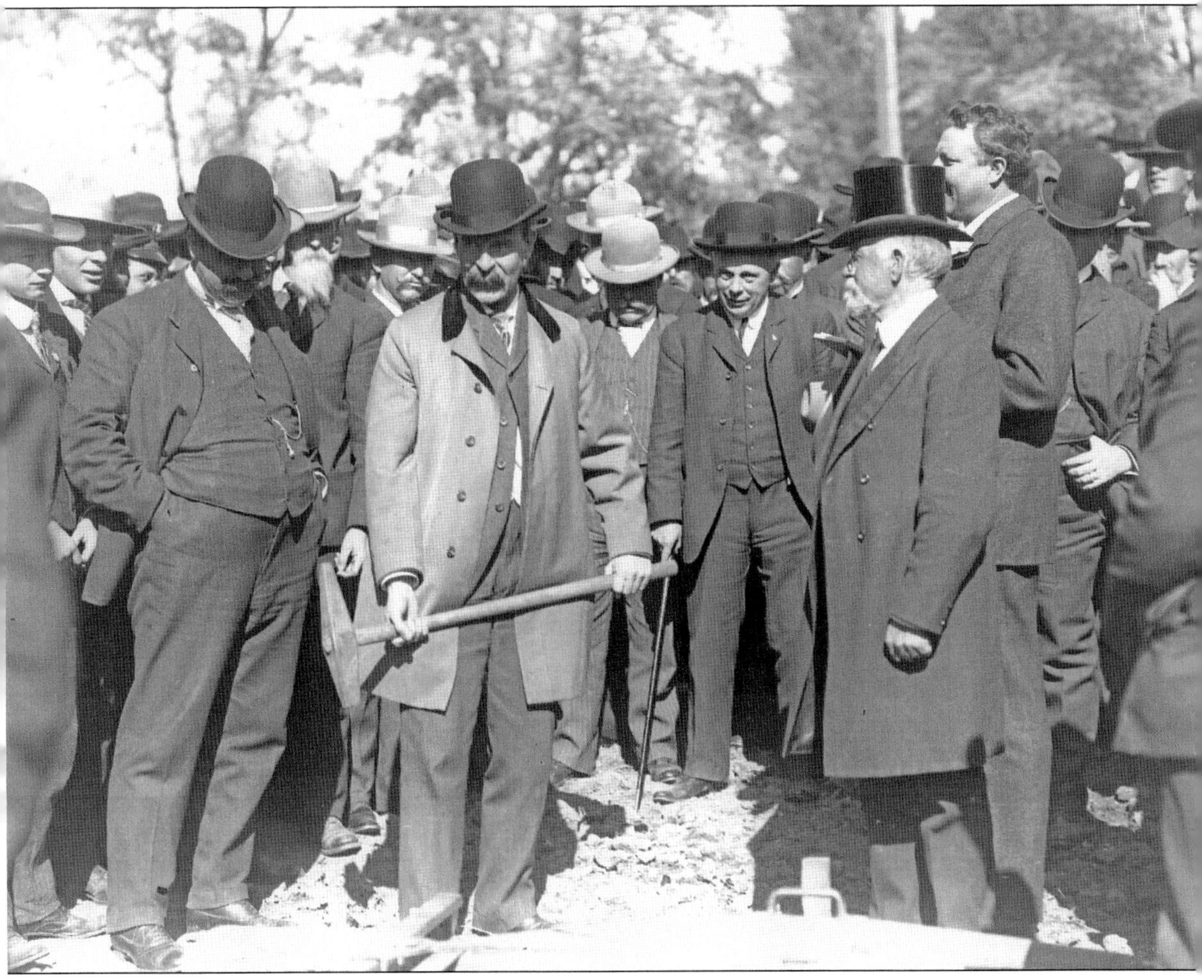

The Boise Valley Railway Company (BVRC), organized as an interurban company, developed plans to route tracks from Boise to Nampa. On October 24, 1905, the BVRC drove a silver stake in anticipation of the construction. Harlan P. Ustick, one of the company's promoters, is pictured in the top hat.

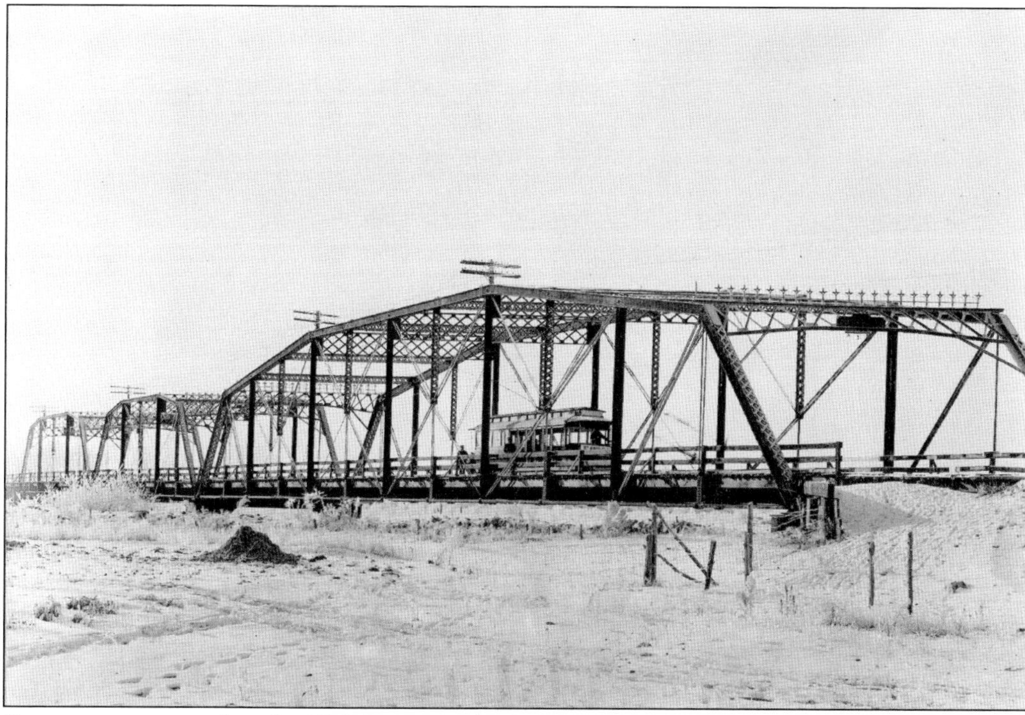

On a snowy winter day, the BVRC crosses the Boise River to the village of South Boise. These tracks were laid about three miles out from downtown Boise, ending at Garfield School.

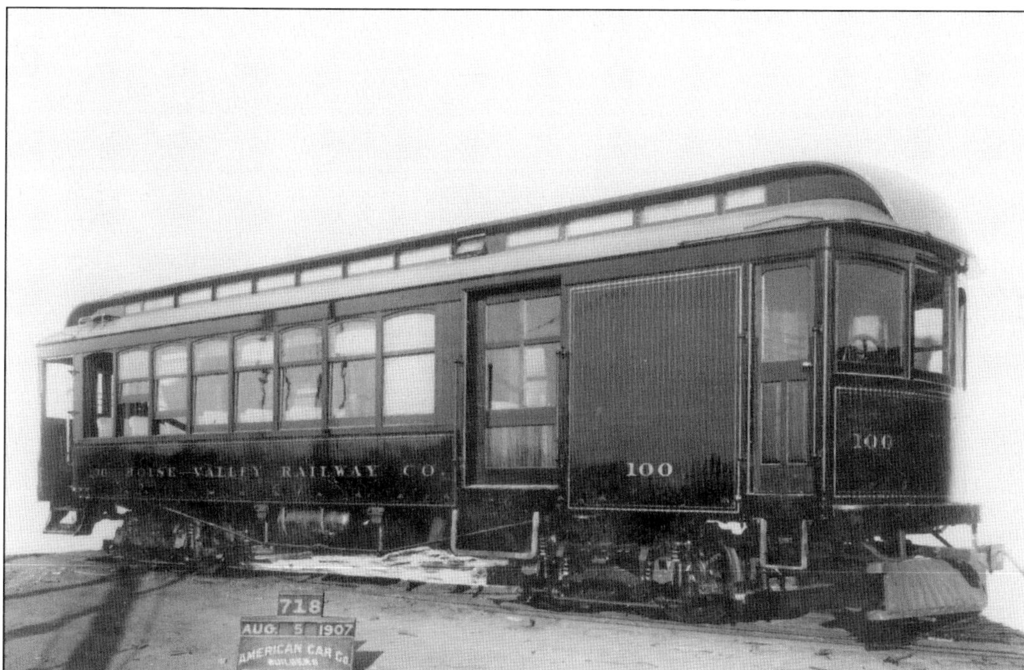

BVRC Car No. 100 is shown at the American Car Company factory in St. Louis, Missouri. The BVRC purchased new cars, including passenger cars, baggage cars, freight cars, and combination (passenger and freight) cars. Car No. 100 was a combination car.

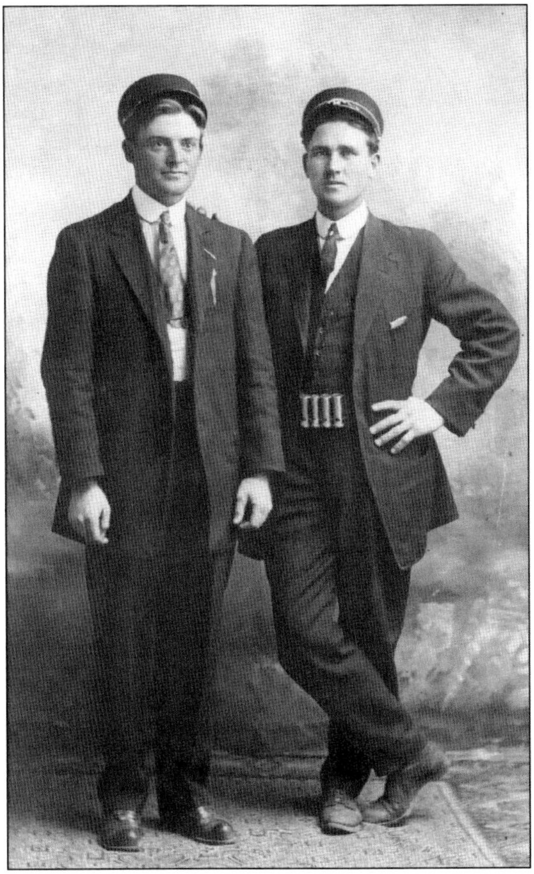

Two unidentified young electric railway employees pose proudly in this undated studio shot. The man on the right is the conductor. Note the hand-change machine around his waist and the packet of tickets in his coat pocket.

BVRC Car No. 201, manufactured by the American Car Company, was a passenger car. The sloped roof was called a "bull nose" roof. The raised portion of the roof with the small rectangular window panes is the clerestory, which provided light and/or ventilation for the interior of the car.

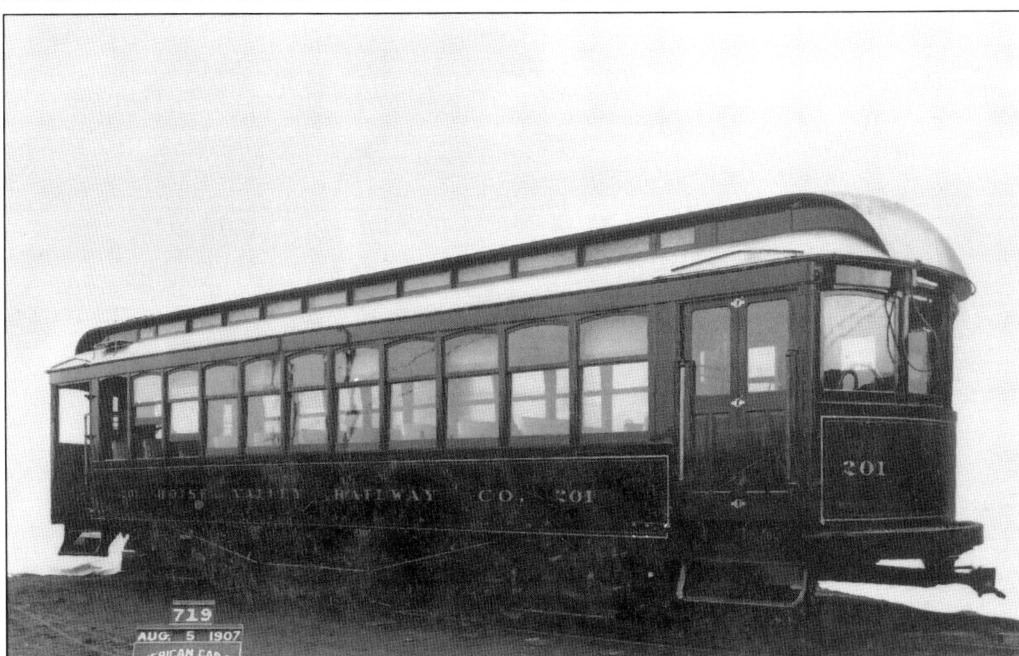

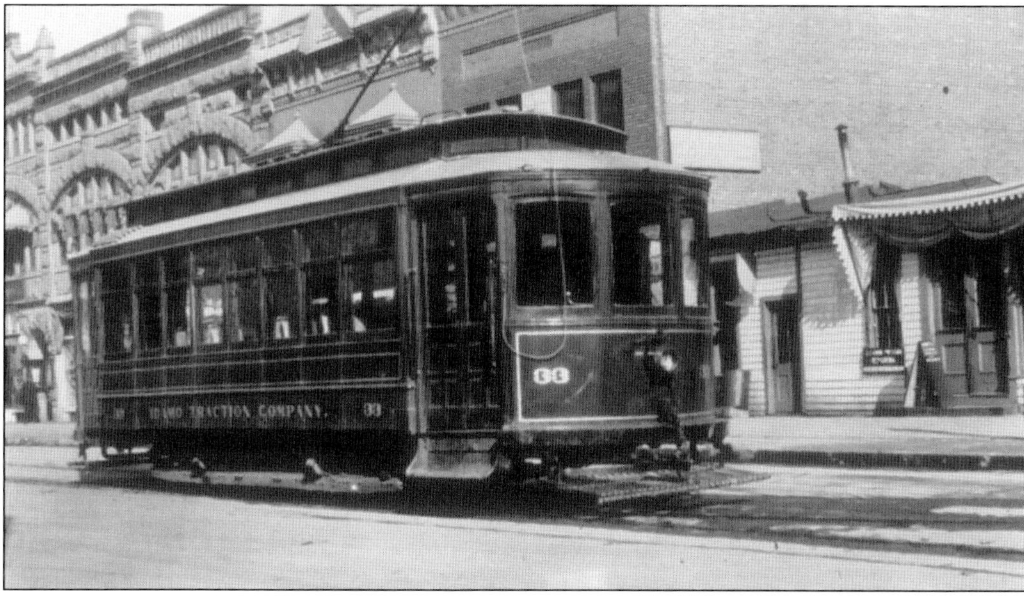

BTC Car No. 33 is shown heading east on Idaho Street. The cars were painted distinctive colors: BTC cars were green and yellow, and the B&I cars were green and red.

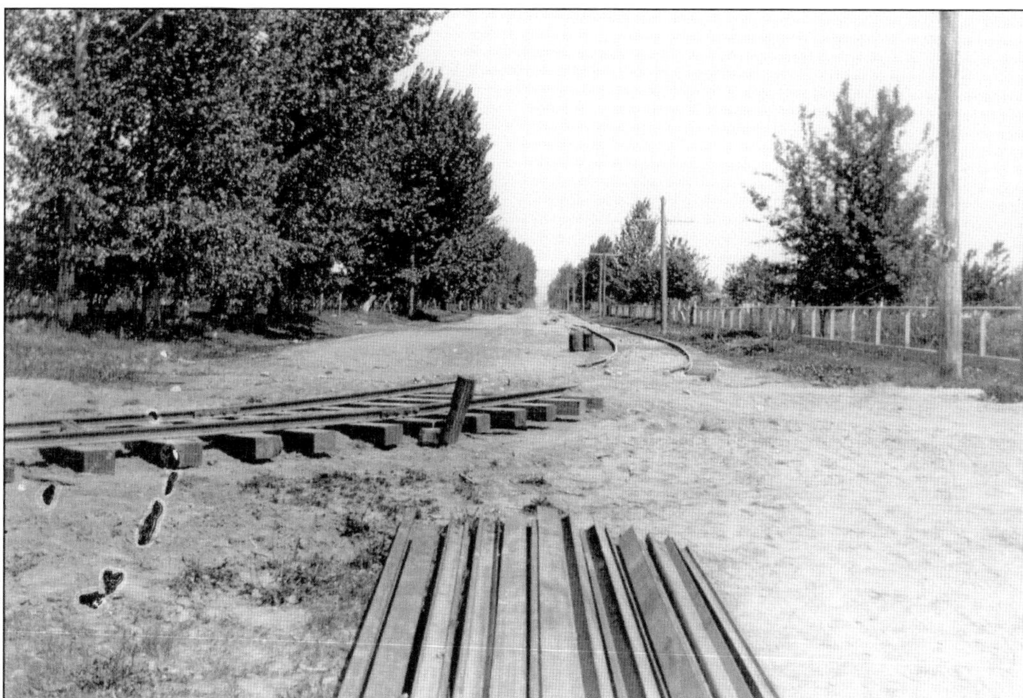
This c. 1906 photograph shows rail lines for the BVR under construction. That year, the company began to extend the line west from Boise to Meridian and Nampa. The connection was completed to Meridian in 1908, and to Nampa in 1909. The company ordered several tons of rails from the Lackawanna Steel Company of Buffalo, New York, for construction of the line. George Butler of Boise was awarded the contract for the wood ties.

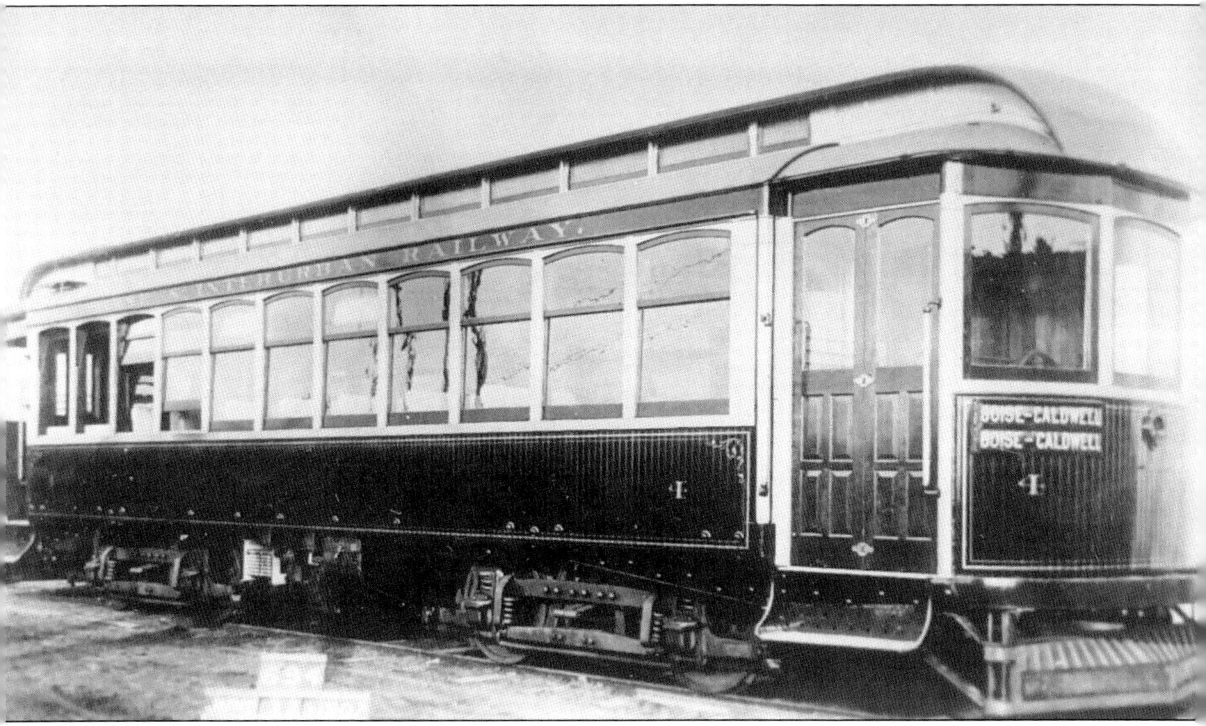

Both the BVRC and the B&I ordered cars from the American Car Company factory in St. Louis. According to a 1907 issue of *Electric Railway Review*, the Brill semi-convertible car shown here was one of the first cars to be operated to Caldwell on the completed B&I railway.

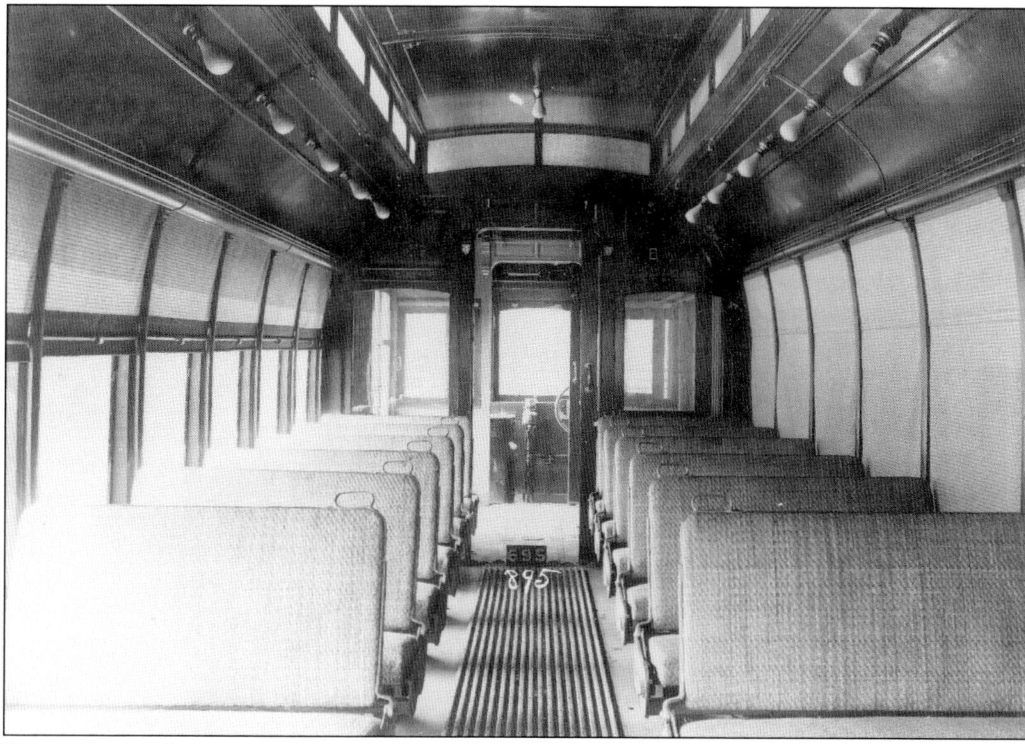

This photograph is an interior view of Car No. 23, manufactured by the American Car Company. The "walkover" seats are covered with rattan, the material most commonly used for that purpose. This car is equipped with window shades and passenger-compartment lights. Resistors regulated electricity for the compartment lights, vestibules, headlight bulbs, and conductor's bell.

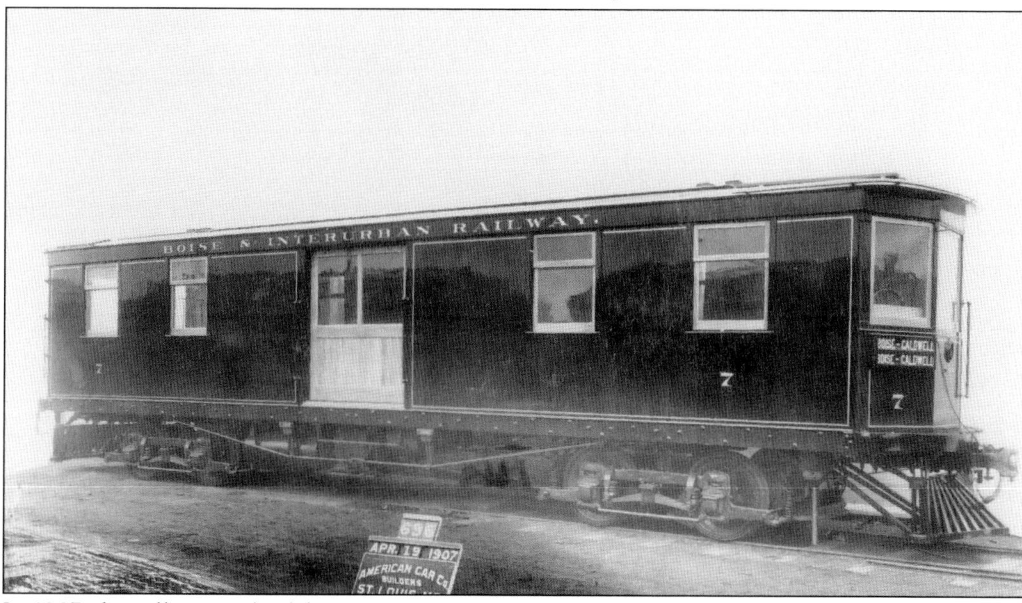

In 1907, the rolling stock of the B&I consisted of seven cars—four Brill semi-convertible cars, two cars with passenger and baggage compartments, and one express and light-freight car. Pictured here is B&I Car No. 7.

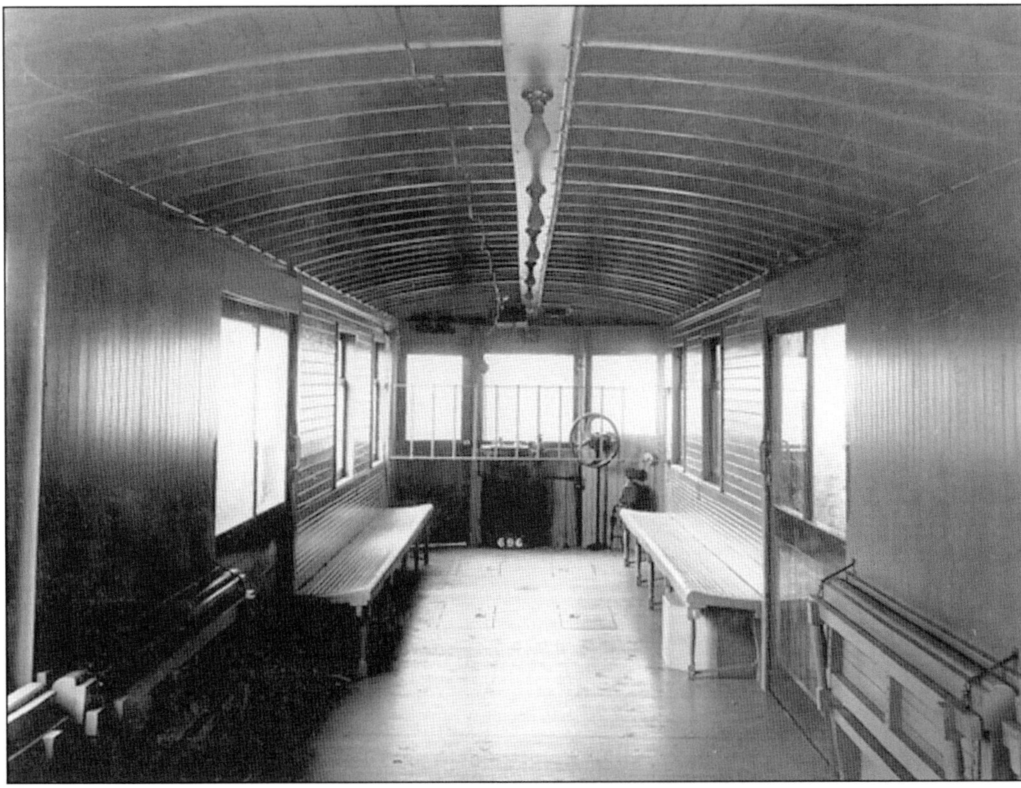

This is an interior view of B&I Car No. 7, a combination freight and passenger car, at the factory in St. Louis, Missouri. The car is equipped with hinged wood-slat seats, which could be folded up or down to allow additional space for baggage, freight, or passengers. The motorman stood in the vestibule to operate the car. The controller, which regulated the speed of the car, is visible at the center, and the air brake, which stopped the car, is to the right.

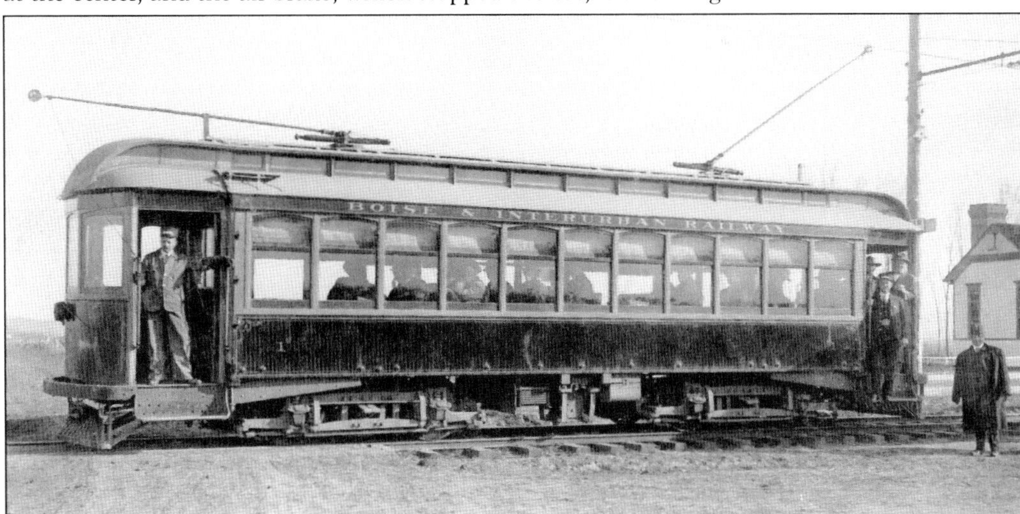

On August 8, 1907, the B&I line between Boise and Caldwell, which passed through Eagle, Star, and Middleton, opened for traffic. In this photograph, B&I Car No. 1 is loaded with passengers ready to leave Boise.

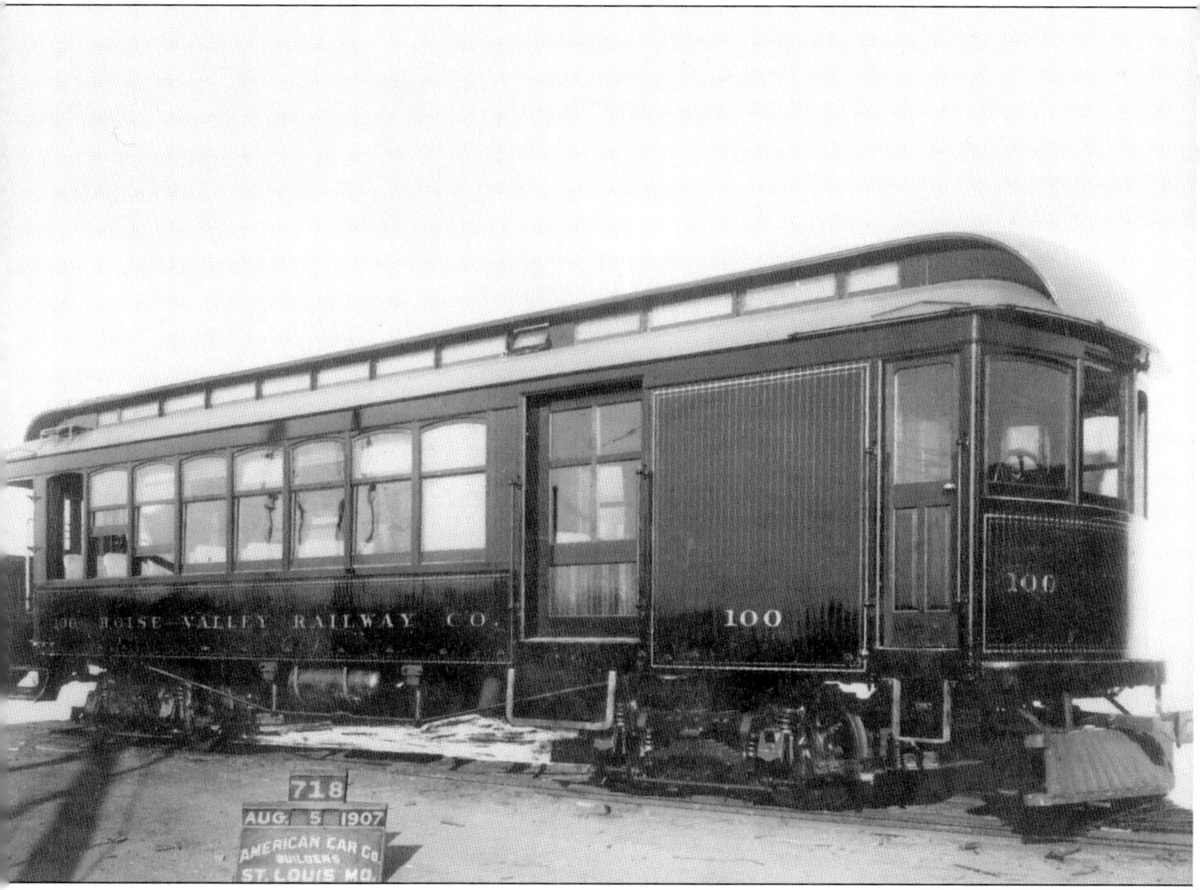

The combination cars used by the B&I had an unusual feature, as shown here on Car No. 100. The side door of the baggage compartment was adjacent to the door of the passenger end instead of the partition, which was the more usual method of construction.

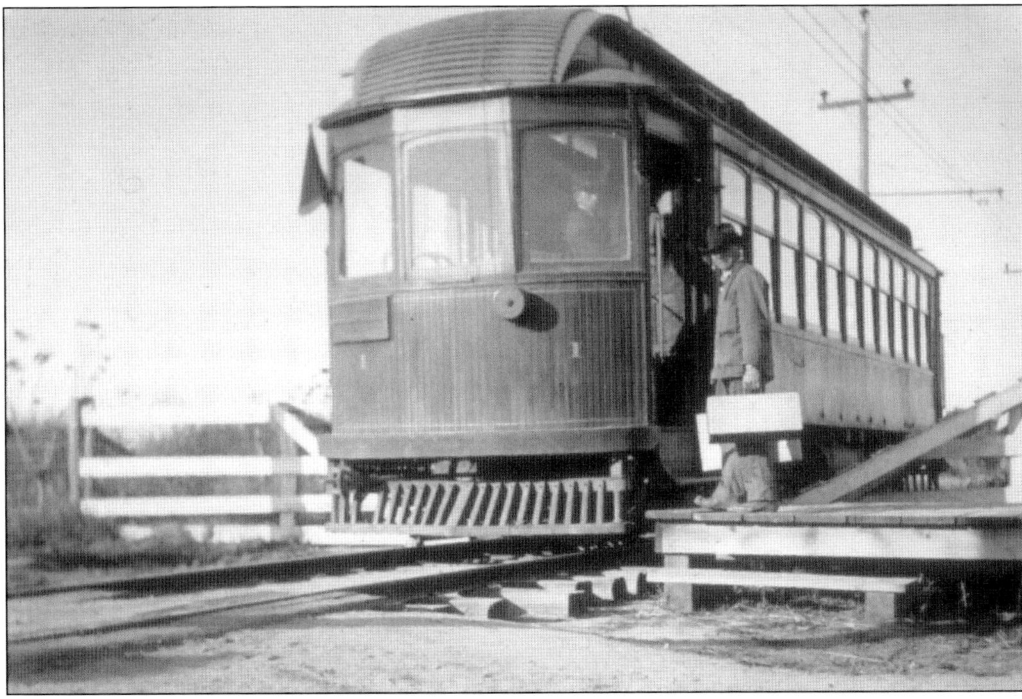

An unidentified man, bags in hand, prepares to board B&I Car No. 1. The car is stopped at Whiffen Station, the first stop west of Middleton on the Boise-to-Caldwell line. (Courtesy of the Meridian Historical Society, Jim and Anne Witherell Collection.)

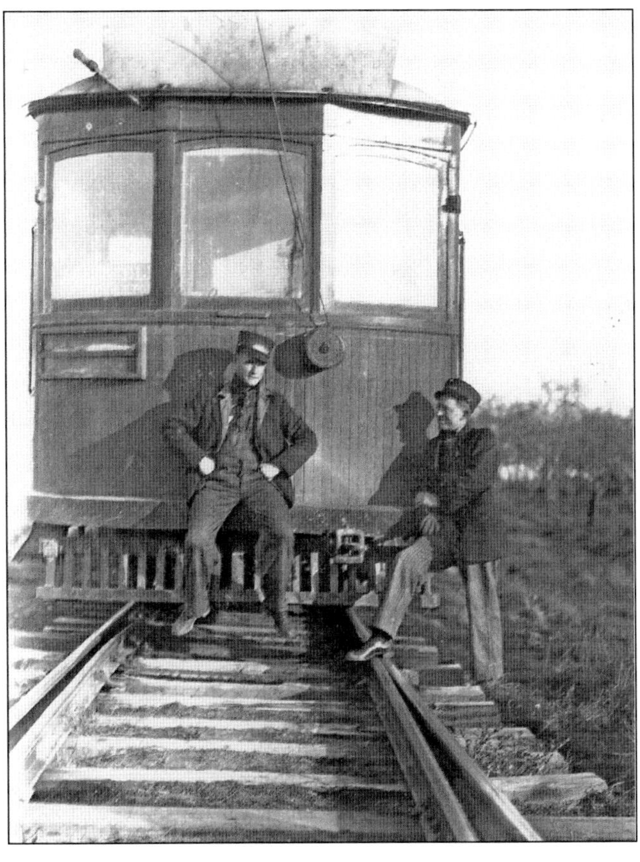

In this photograph, B&I conductor Russell Campbell (right) relaxes with an unidentified motorman between runs to Caldwell. The B&I used double-ended cars, which could operate in either direction. The line from the trolley pole is attached to the trolley retriever (the round object to the right of the unidentified man). The trolley retriever automatically drew the trolley pole to the roof when the wheel left the wire.

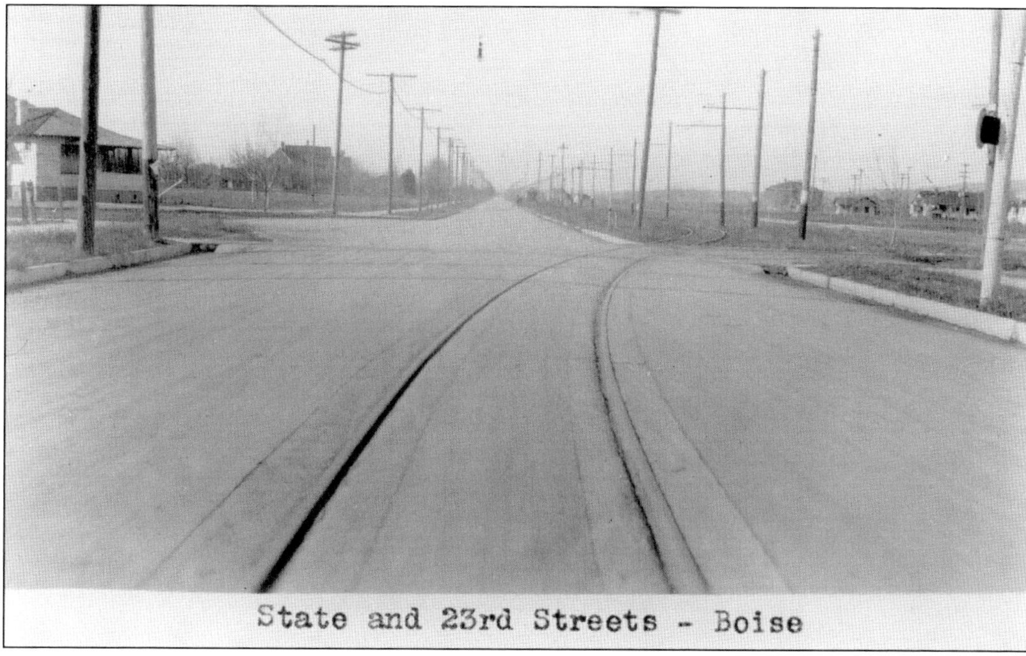

The main line of the B&I was 28.6 miles long, all located on privately fenced right-of-way, except where the road passed through town or city streets. The track was constructed of 60- and 72-pound rails, laid on standard ties and fully ballasted. Tracks in the lines through the city were seven-inch rails. This photograph shows the westbound B&I track at State and Twenty-third Streets in Boise.

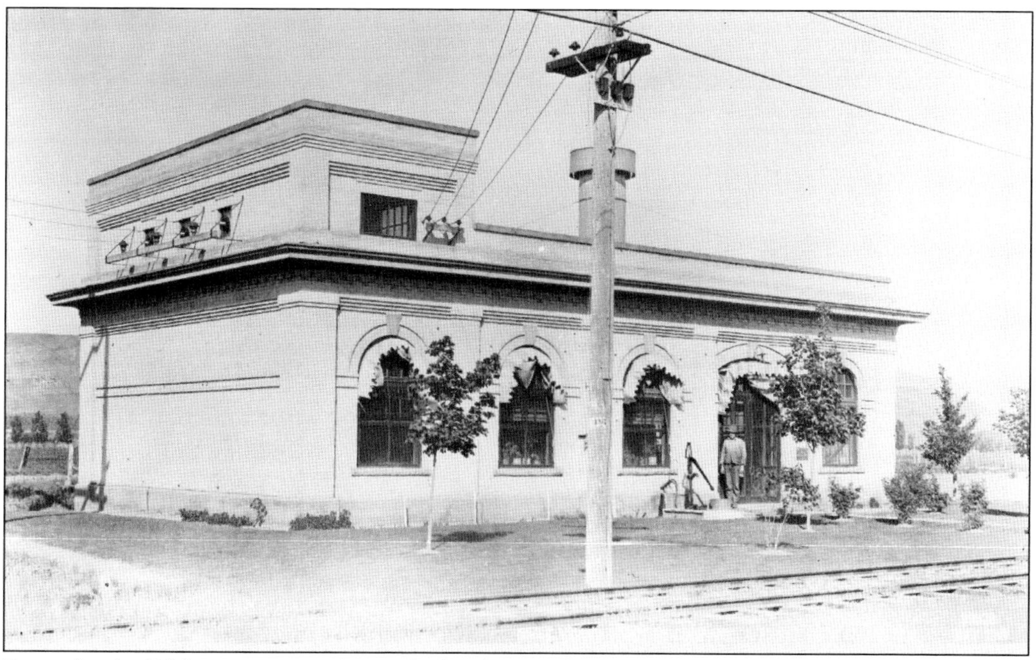

Power for the B&I system came from a hydroelectric plant on the Snake River at Swan Falls, about 40 miles southwest of Boise. B&I substations were located west of Boise at Pierce Park and at Middleton. In this photograph, an unidentified man stands outside the Pierce Park substation.

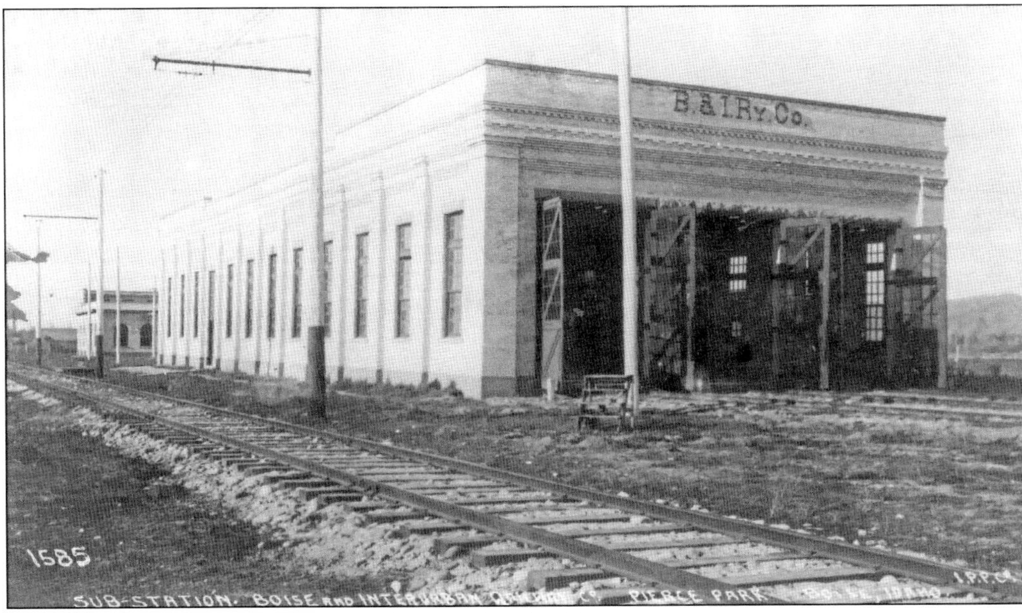

This photograph shows a carbarn and repair shop building located next to the substation at Pierce Park. The building was designed by the Boise architecture firm Tourtellotte & Hummel. It was demolished early in the 21st century.

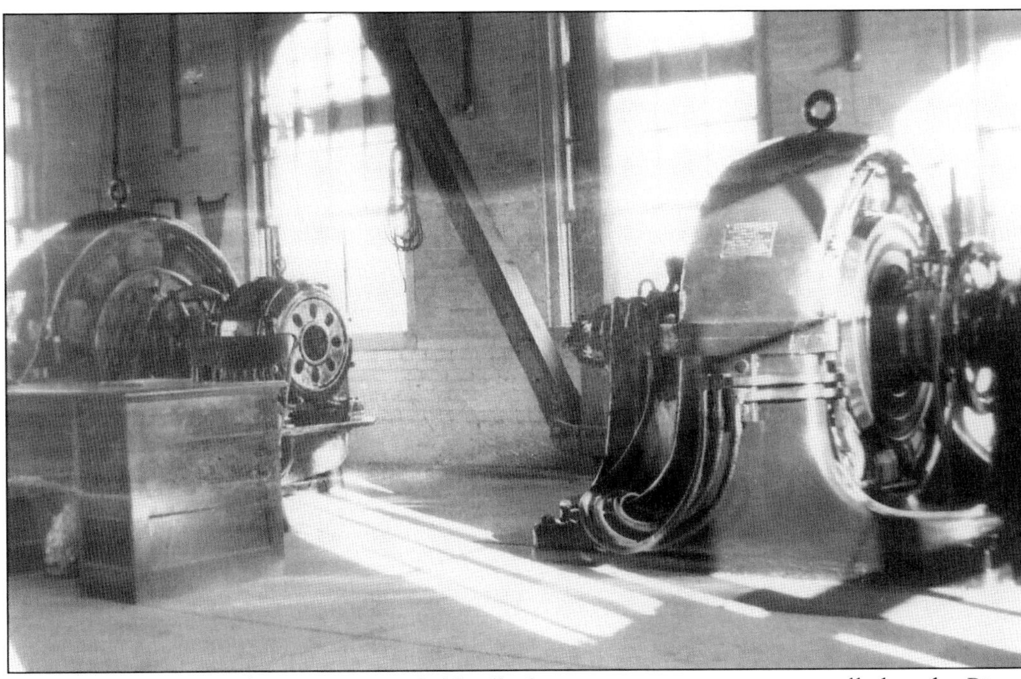

When the B&I started operations to Caldwell, the same equipment was installed at the Pierce Park and Middleton substations. This interior view of the Pierce Park substation shows some of the equipment, which included a 300-kilowatt, 600-volt, 60-cycle rotary converter; three transformers; switches; circuit breakers; and a four-panel switchboard.

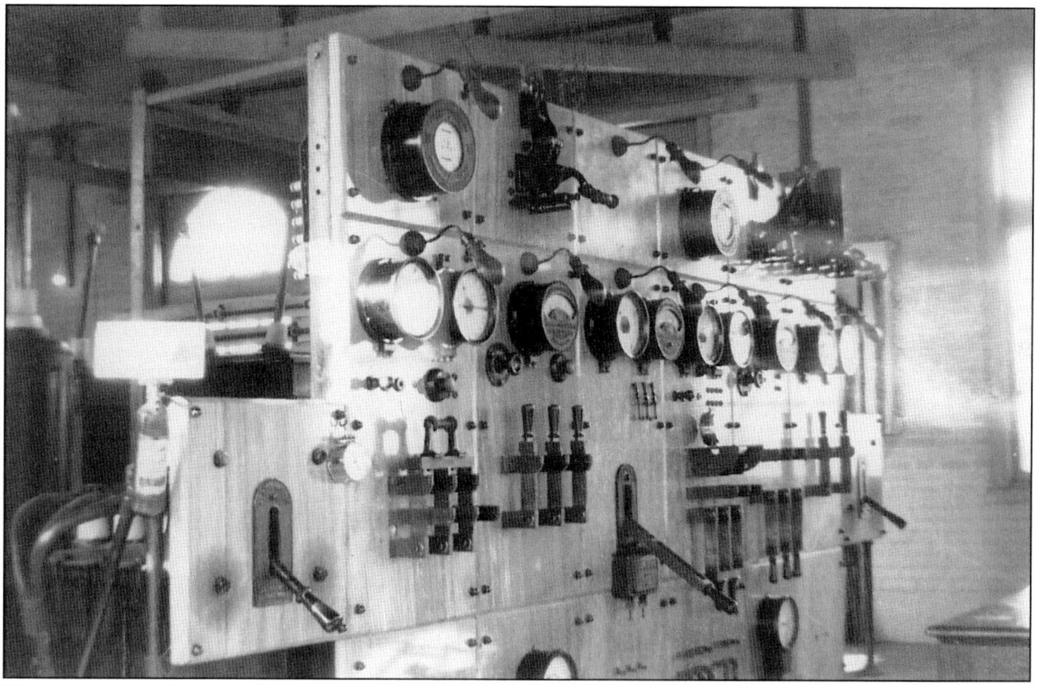

This photograph of an equipment panel was taken inside the Pierce Park substation.

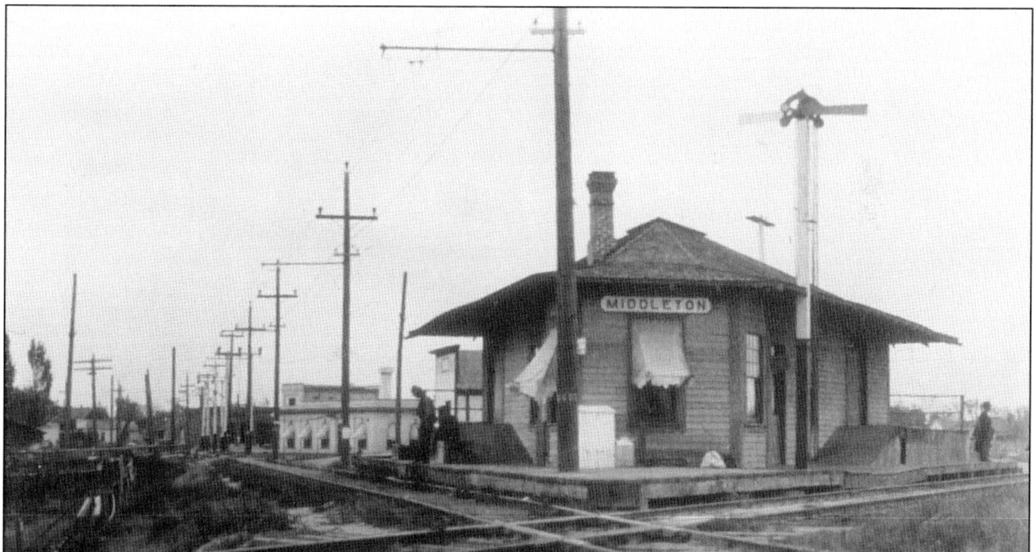

Union Station, the depot in Middleton, served both the Idaho Northern Railroad Company and the interurban. In 1900, William H. Dewey, a successful mining investor and Nampa real estate developer, organized the Idaho Northern to run north from Nampa through Middleton to Emmett and McCall. The railroad reached Middleton in 1902, and the station was constructed in 1907. The Middleton power substation can be seen in the background in this photograph.

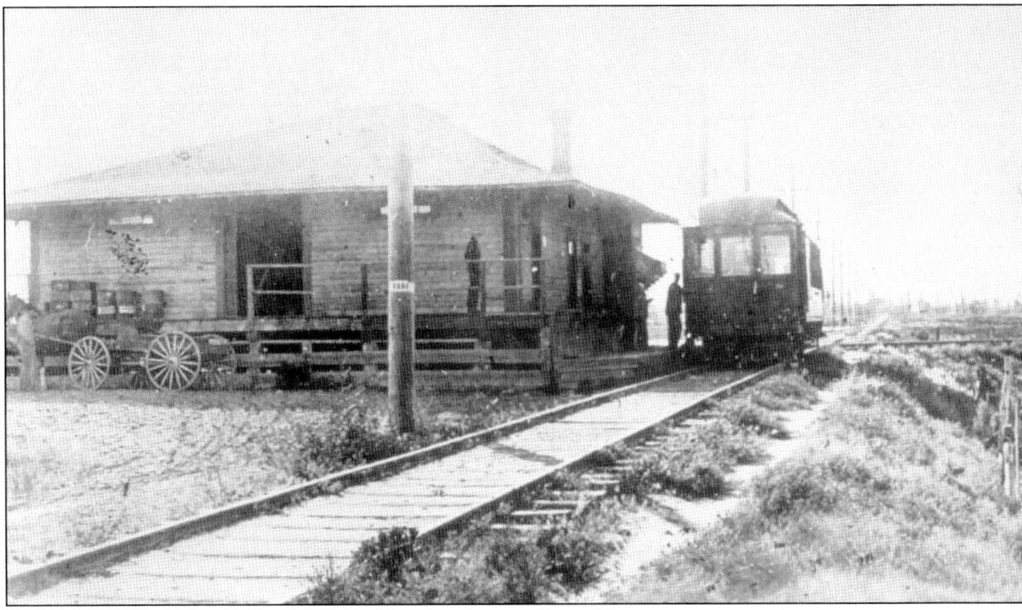

In this view, a B&I car is stopped at the Middleton depot, where freight can be seen stacked on the left side of the platform. Passengers are lined up on the platform, and the conductor is preparing to take tickets. The interurban car is headed east to Boise, as shown by the trolley pole attached to the front end.

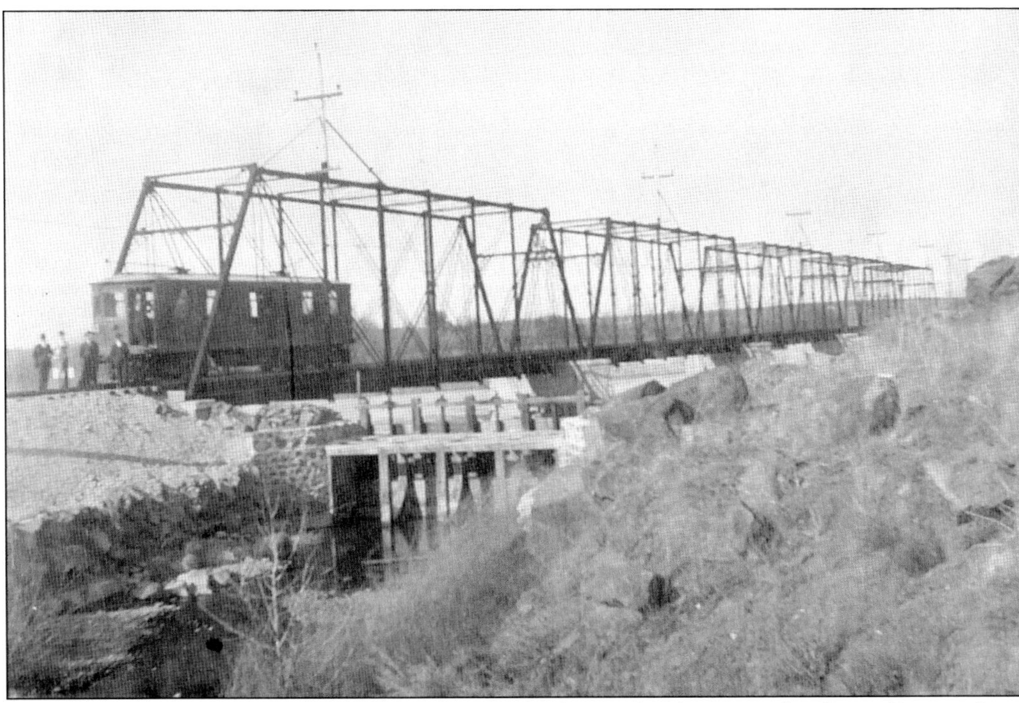

In this rare photograph, a B&I car crosses a steel truss bridge over the Boise River, above Caldwell. Note the stacked rock abutments. The bridge was completed in January 1907. Bad weather delayed work on other parts of the line, which reached Caldwell by the fall. (Courtesy of John Aguirre.)

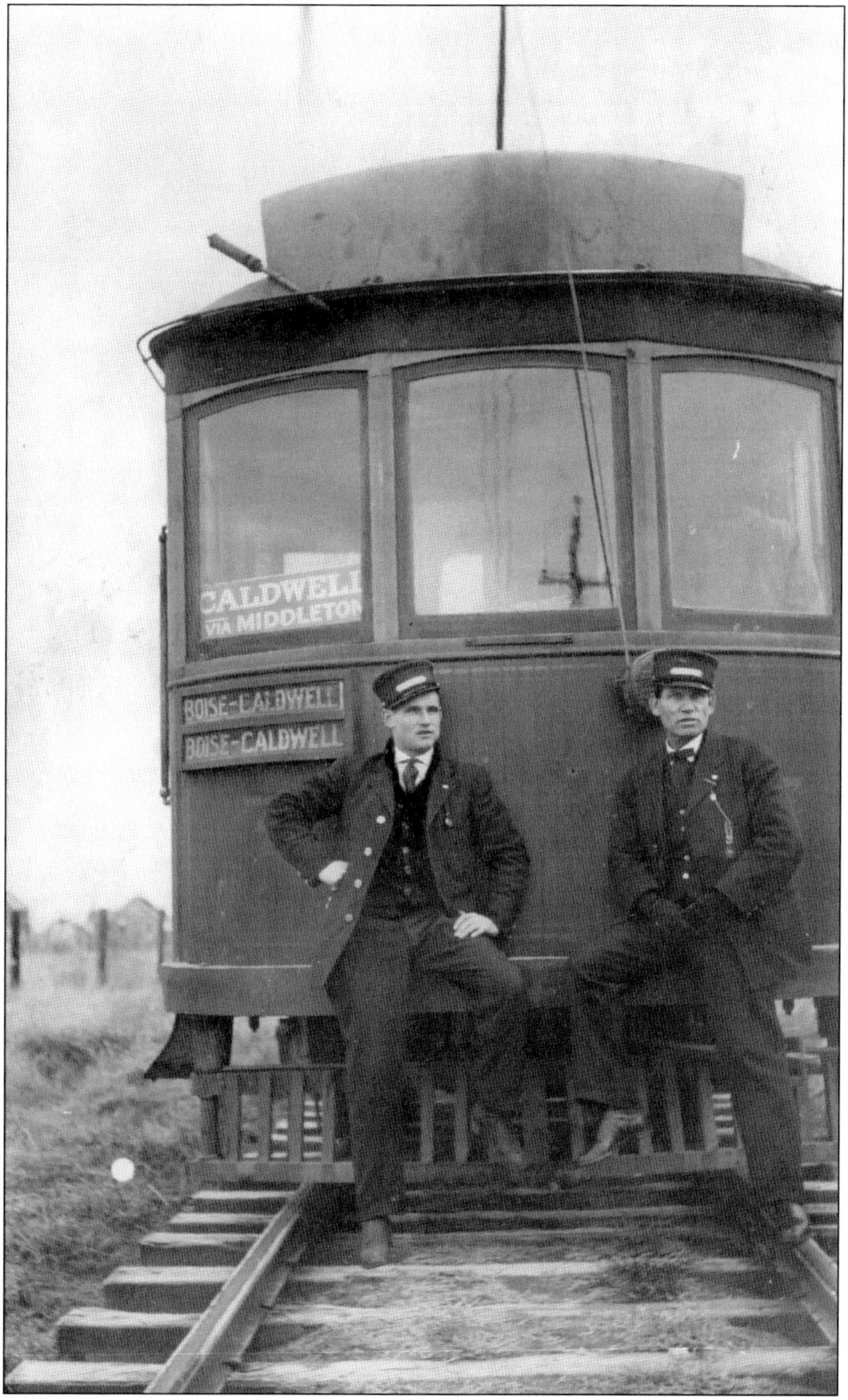

An unidentified motorman and conductor take a break on the B&I route. Most cars on the B&I were staffed by a motorman and a conductor/ticket taker. The motorman drove the car, and the conductor collected fares, managed baggage, and assisted passengers. In later, years the conductor/ticket taker was replaced by an automatic fare machine, leaving cars staffed by just a motorman. (Courtesy of John Aguirre.)

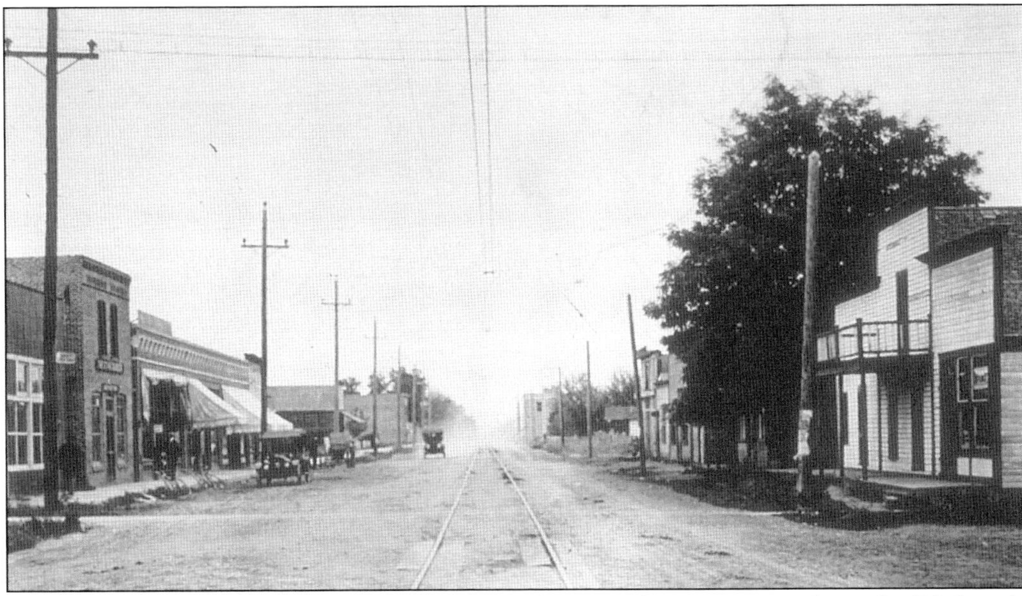

Star, Idaho, is a small farming town located 15 miles west of Boise. As seen here, the B&I tracks were laid down the center of the town's Main Street, allowing for horse and car traffic to pass on either side.

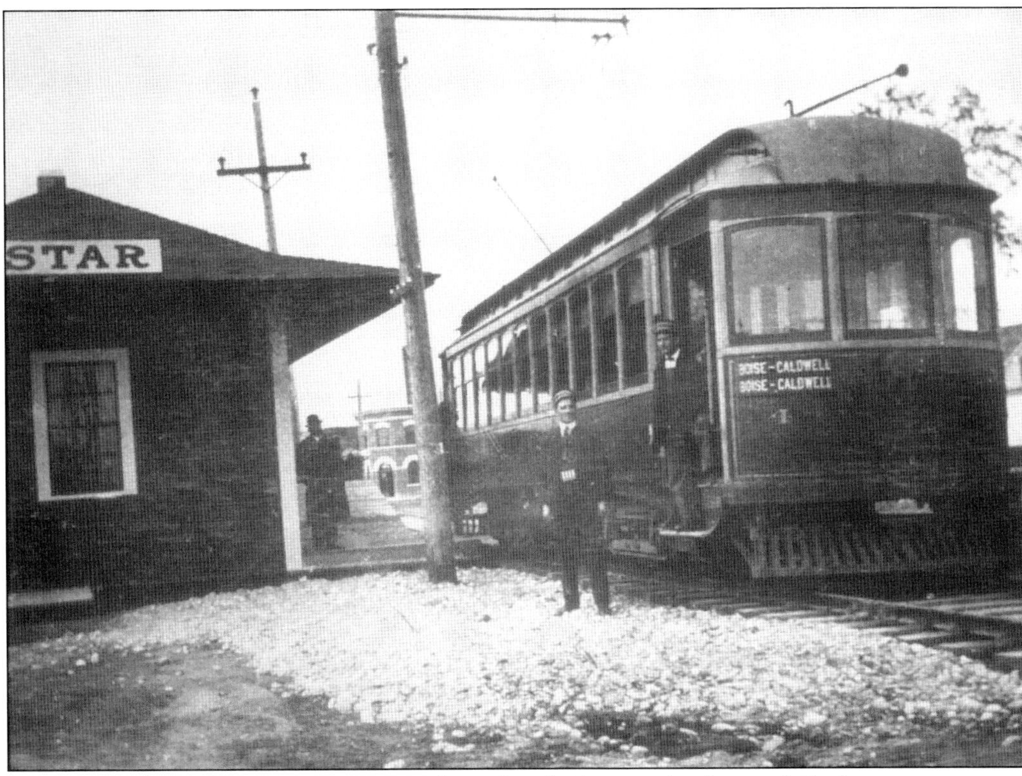

On a snowy day in Star, a passenger stands on the platform at the depot while the motorman and the conductor pose next to the car. The Star depot was moved from this location and remodeled into a coffee shop in the late 20th century.

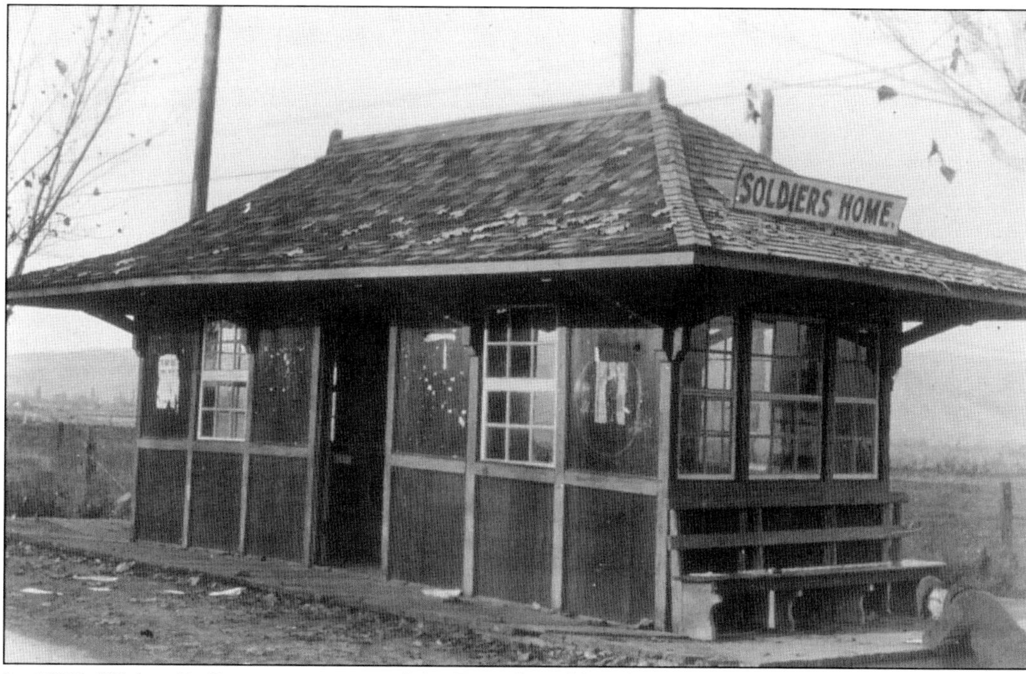

In 1906, Walter E. Pierce, manager of the B&I, hired local architect John Tourtellotte to design passenger shelters. This shelter was located west of Boise near the Soldiers' Home, a residence for Civil War veterans.

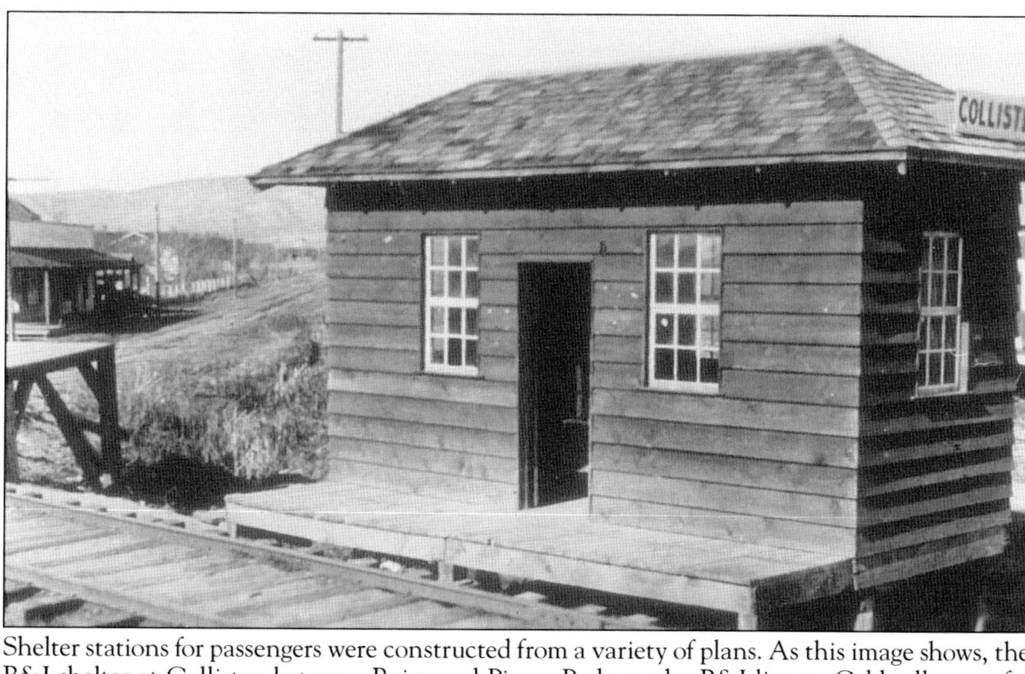
Shelter stations for passengers were constructed from a variety of plans. As this image shows, the B&I shelter at Collister, between Boise and Pierce Park on the B&I line to Caldwell, was of a different design than the shelter at Soldiers' Home.

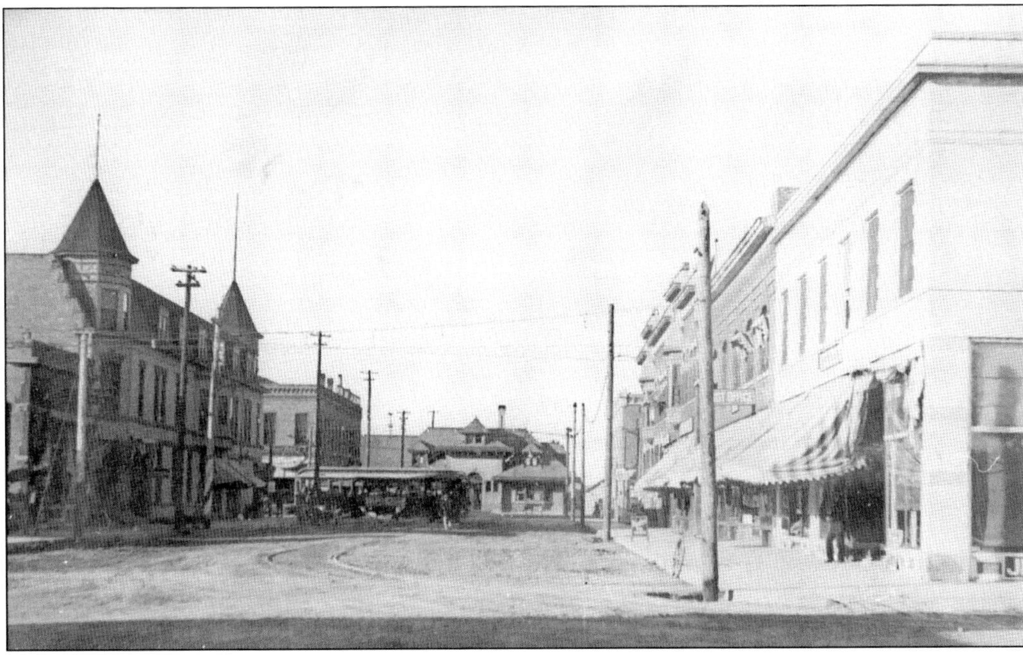

A B&I car passes the Oregon Short Line depot in Caldwell at the north end of Seventh Avenue. The white banner on the side of the car is an advertisement for Pierce Park, an amusement park in Boise that was developed by Walter E. Pierce as a streetcar destination. (Courtesy of John Aguirre.)

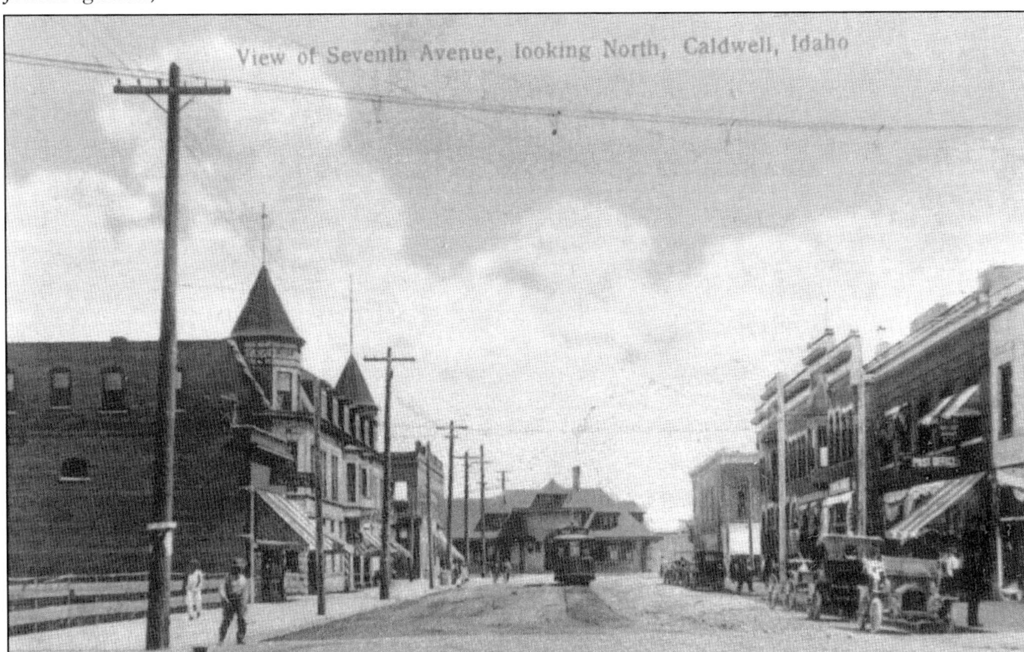

In this 1912 postcard view, the ITC interurban is headed down the center of Seventh Avenue in Caldwell. The Oregon Short Line Railroad depot is visible in the background, and the Saratoga Hotel can be seen on the left. (Courtesy of John Aguirre.)

Three

Streetcar Suburbs

The electric railway was instrumental in the development of neighborhoods and small communities in the Treasure Valley. Residential growth in Boise was tied directly to the lines that extended from downtown to new developments on the edges of the town. In Boise, real estate developer Walter E. Pierce and his partners Lindley Cox and John Haines developed neighborhoods in the north and east ends of town. They advertised special streetcar rates and encouraged residents to take Sunday rides on the streetcar to visit the subdivisions so they could experience the convenient and timely commute from the downtown core to the new neighborhoods.

Harlan P. Ustick, a BVRC investor, platted the community of Ustick two miles west of downtown Boise, promoting five- and ten-acre plots in conjunction with the expansion of the electric railway line to the area. In April 1906, the company ran special excursion cars to Ustick, where potential buyers were served light refreshments and given tours of the new development.

In 1905, the BVRC extended its line to serve South Boise, an incorporated village on the south side of the river, whose residents had waited several years for streetcar service. A bridge built over the Boise River in 1892 was designed to be wide enough to accommodate a streetcar. The track initially went approximately one and a half miles to Garfield School, but was later extended another mile to Ivywild, a small neighborhood of one- and five-acre lots platted along the base of the Ridenbaugh Canal.

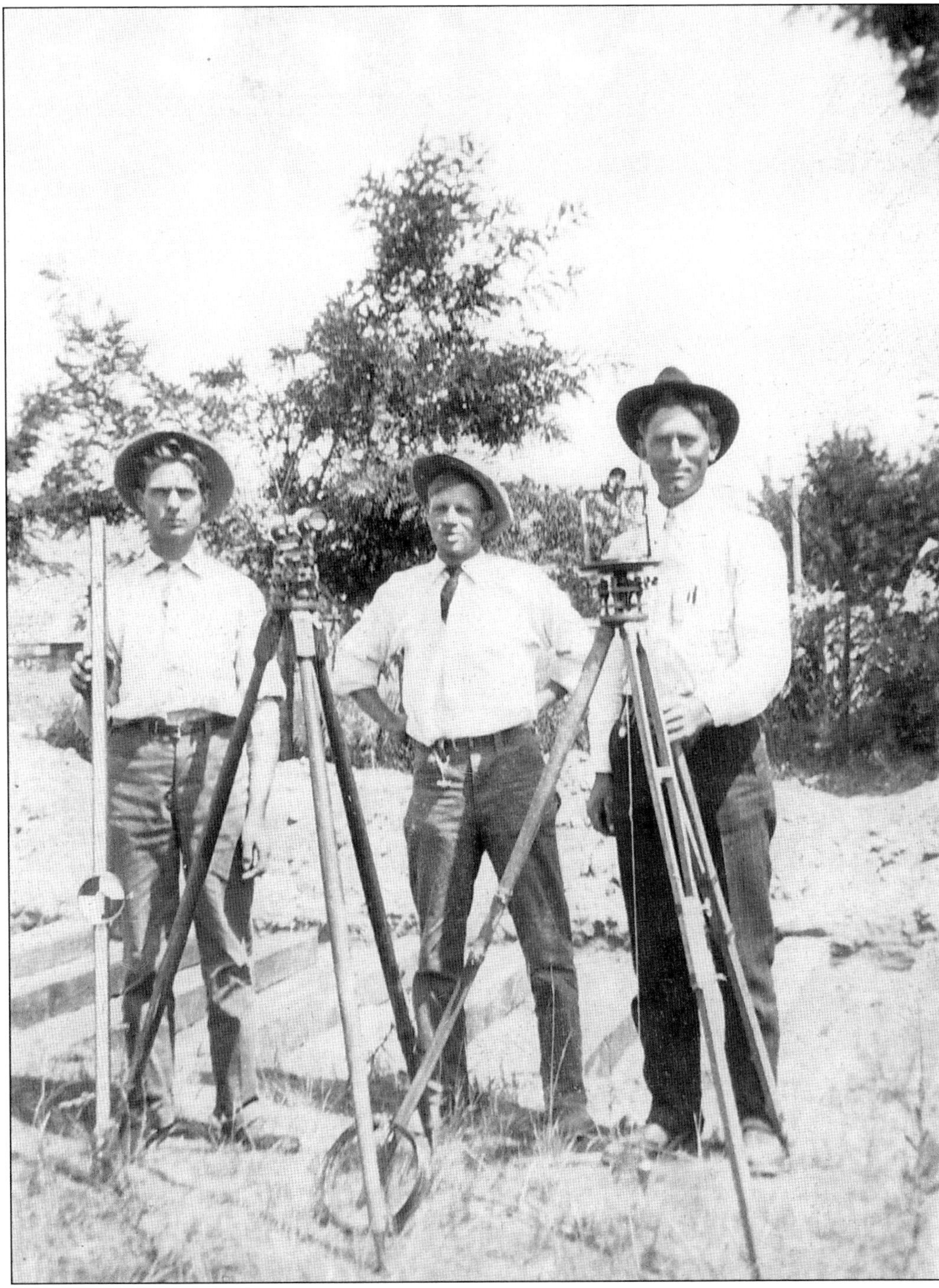

Ed Brown (left), J.F. McBirney (right), and an unidentified coworker are shown working on a survey of the B&I line that extended to Eighteenth Street (now Nineteenth Street) in Boise's North End. After the B&I interurban line was completed to Caldwell, the company concentrated on building a city line. Two companies, the B&I and the BVRC, provided city streetcar service to Boise residents.

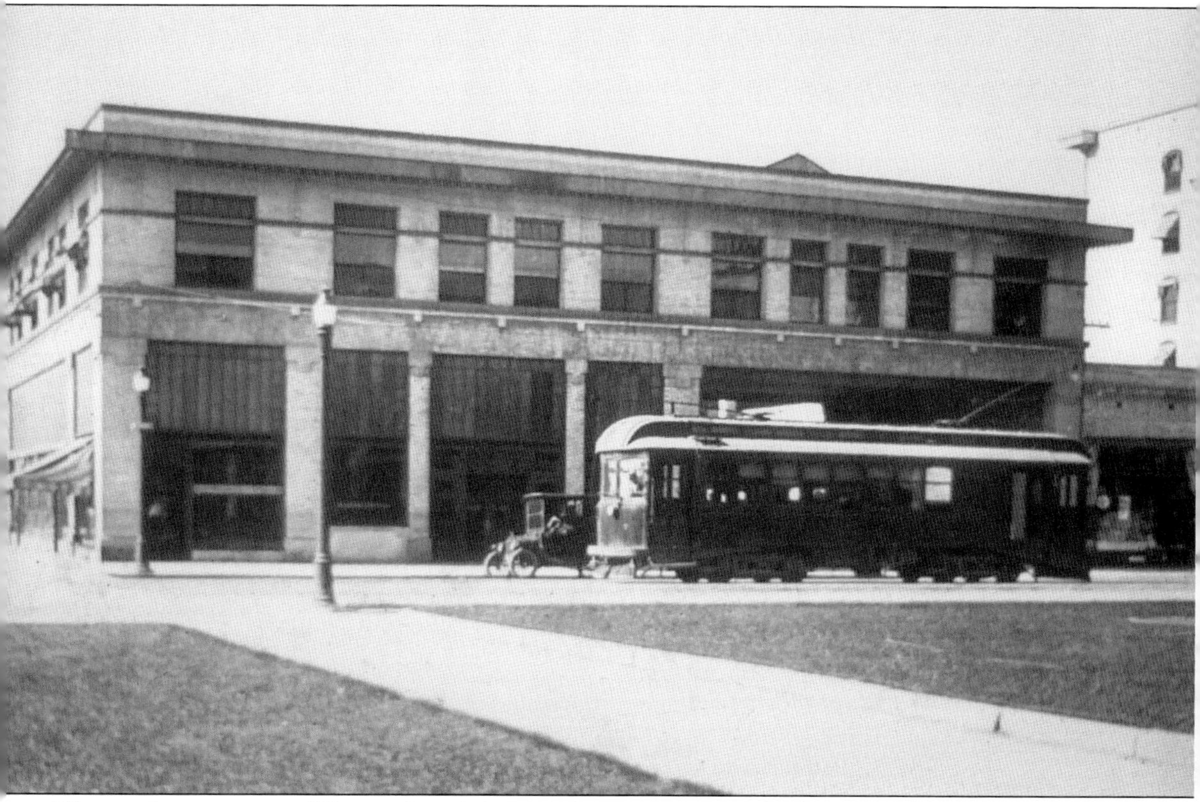

The southwest corner of Bannock and Seventh Streets was once the location of the B&I's main passenger station, a two-story building designed by architects Tourtellotte & Hummel. At street level were a large waiting room, a newsstand, a coatroom, and a smoking room for the gentlemen. Company offices, including a room reserved for the conductors, were located on the second floor. A parking garage and bank now stand at the location where passengers once waited to board the interurban to travel to all parts of the Treasure Valley.

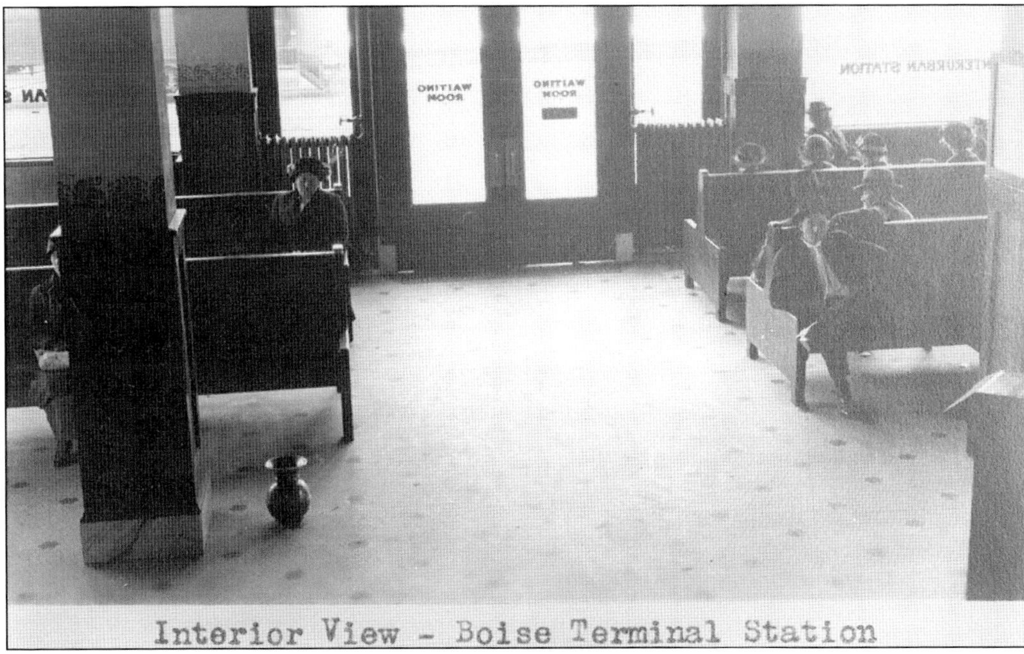

These passengers are waiting for interurban cars inside the B&I's main passenger station. A streetcar is visible through the windows on the left side of the photograph. The station provided a large, airy waiting room, furnished with oak benches. Although the depot was built in 1910 for the B&I, eventually interurban and streetcar service for all of the Boise-based companies originated here.

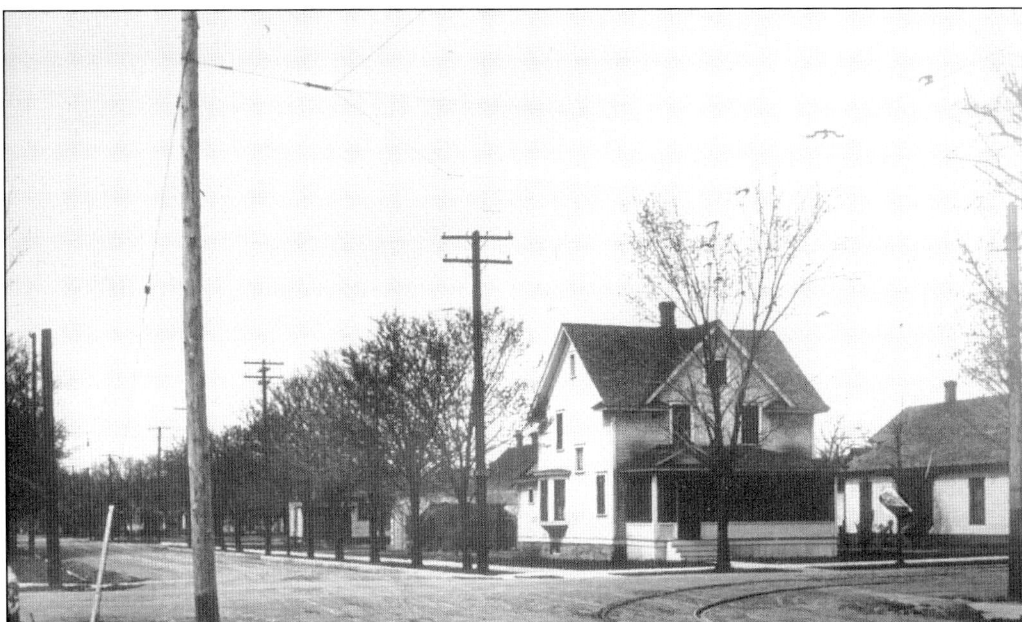

Neighborhoods north of downtown Boise were served by a belt line that ran north from the B&I depot on Bannock and Seventh Streets to the residential district. This photograph shows the curve at Fifteenth and Brumback Streets. Cars ran on the line from 6:30 a.m. until midnight.

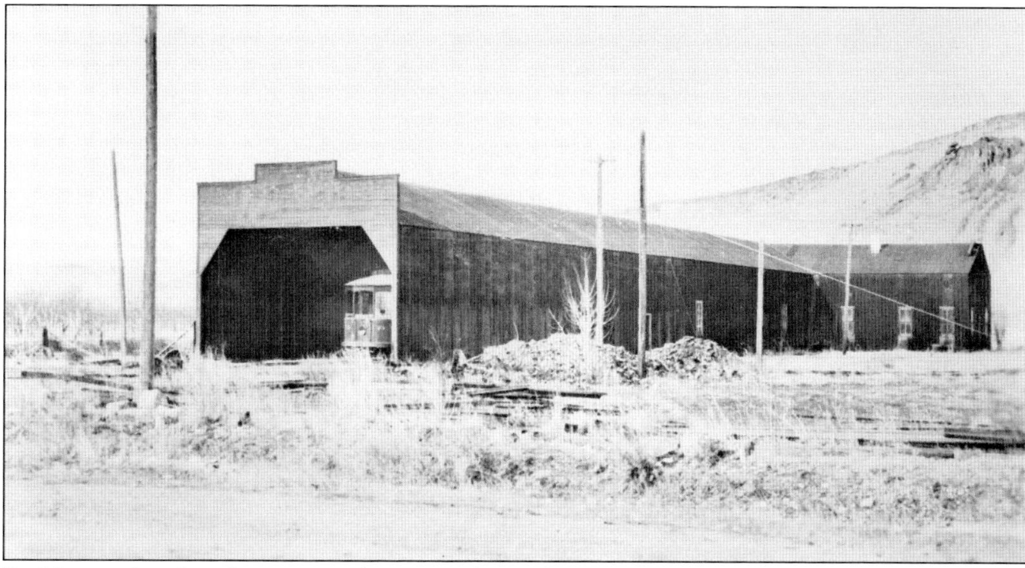

Buildings related to the street railway were located in several neighborhoods throughout Boise, Nampa, and Caldwell. Pictured here, around 1910, is a carbarn located on the north side of Warm Springs Avenue, near the entrance to the Idaho State Penitentiary. The building was later destroyed by fire.

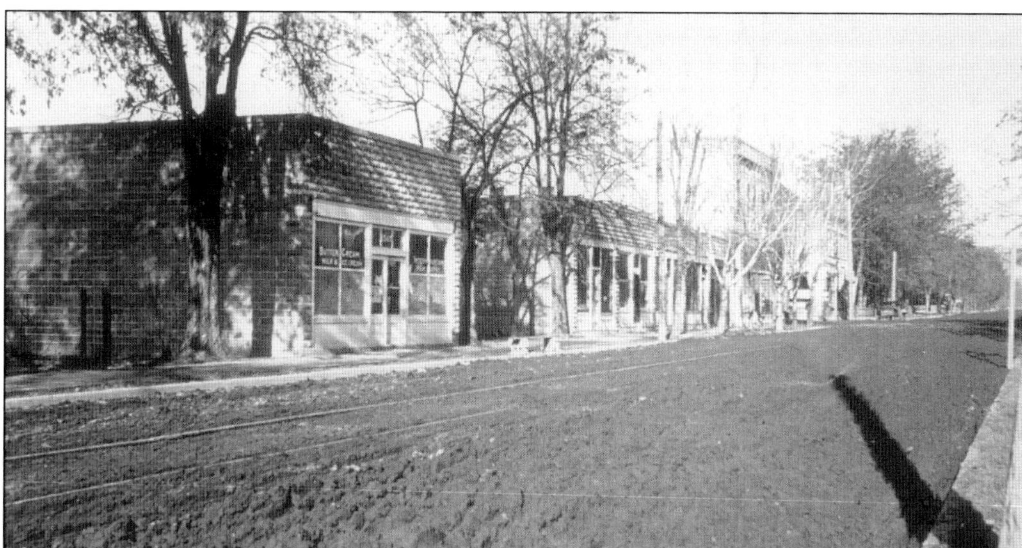

Streetcars travelled down Thirteenth Street to Hyde Park, a neighborhood with a small commercial district. The electric street railway made travel to downtown Boise fast and convenient, and many Boise neighborhoods were platted in anticipation of streetcar service. Streetcar suburbs were developed not only in Boise, but also in hundreds of towns throughout the United States.

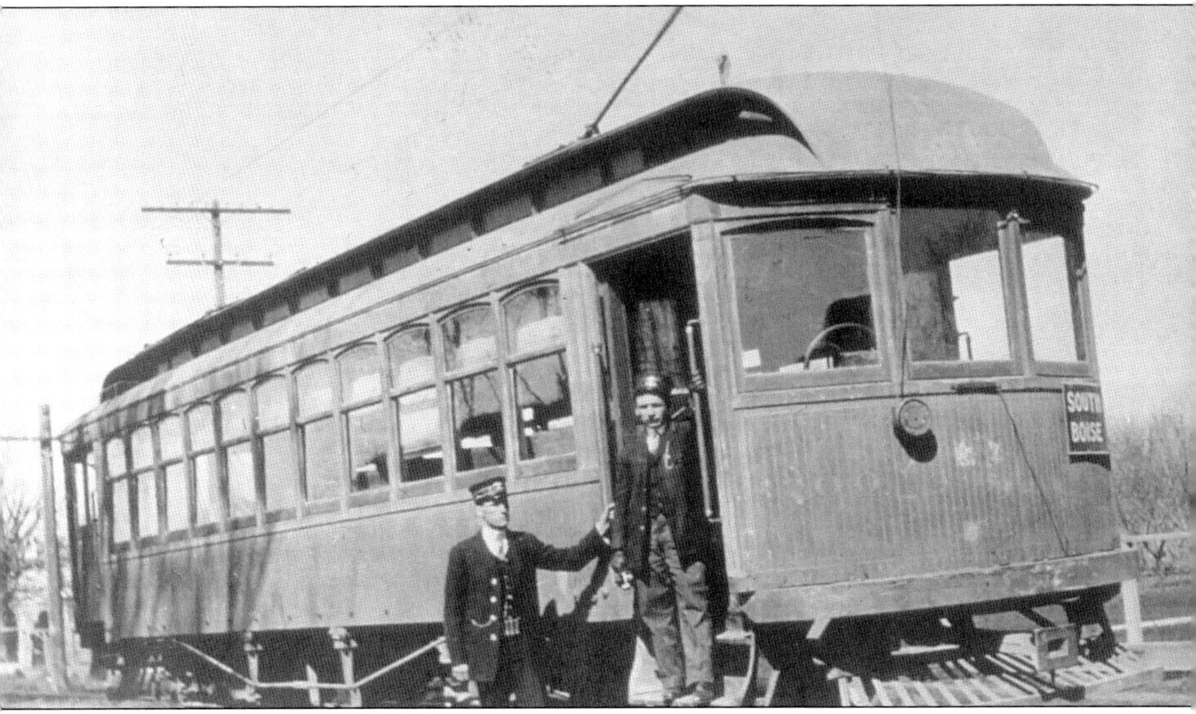

The South Boise car has just stopped at the end of the line on Broadway Avenue. No circular turnaround was located here. The seats would be flipped to face the opposite direction, and the conductor and the motorman would move from one end of the car to the other and proceed north on Broadway Avenue, back to downtown Boise.

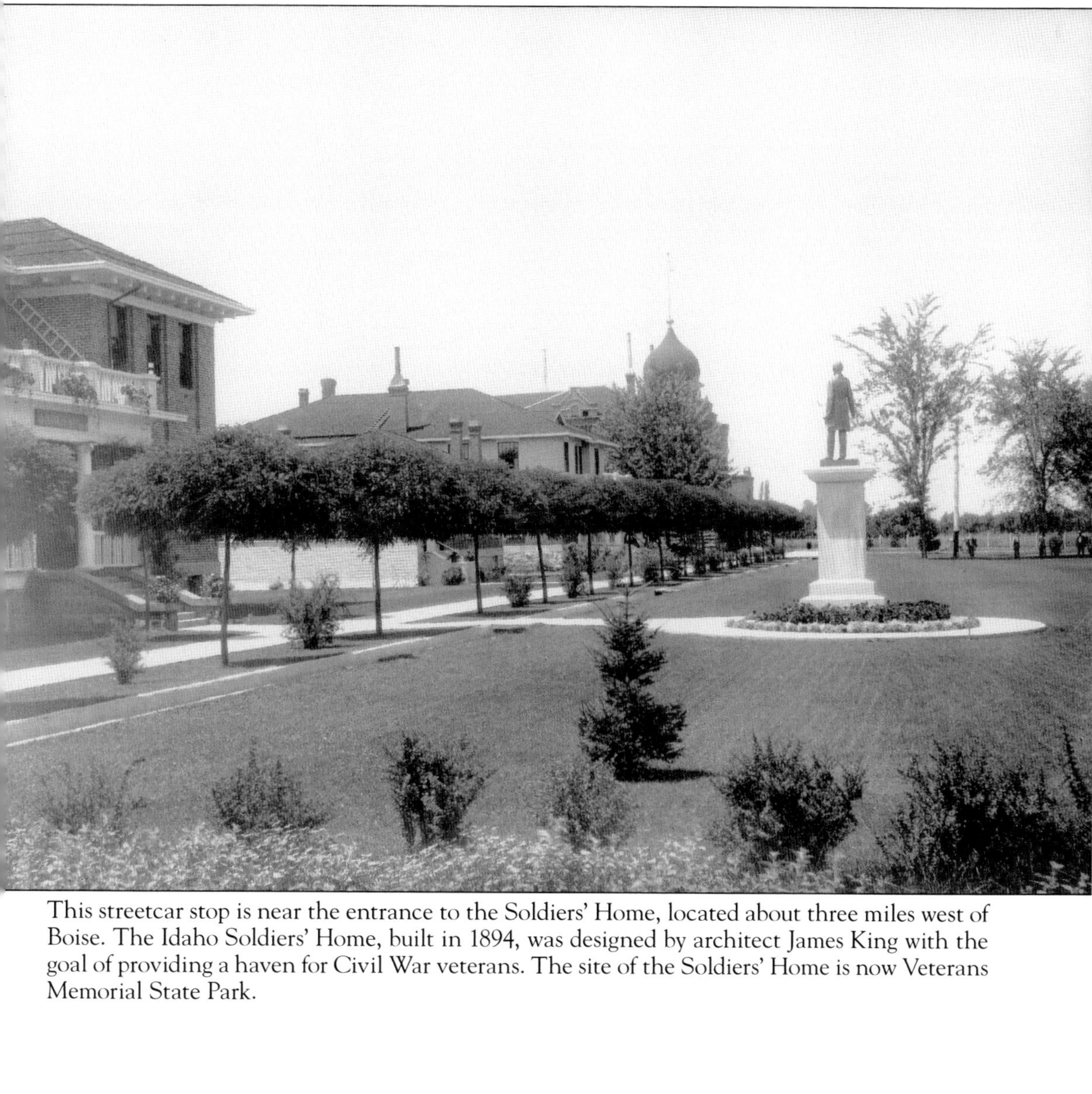

This streetcar stop is near the entrance to the Soldiers' Home, located about three miles west of Boise. The Idaho Soldiers' Home, built in 1894, was designed by architect James King with the goal of providing a haven for Civil War veterans. The site of the Soldiers' Home is now Veterans Memorial State Park.

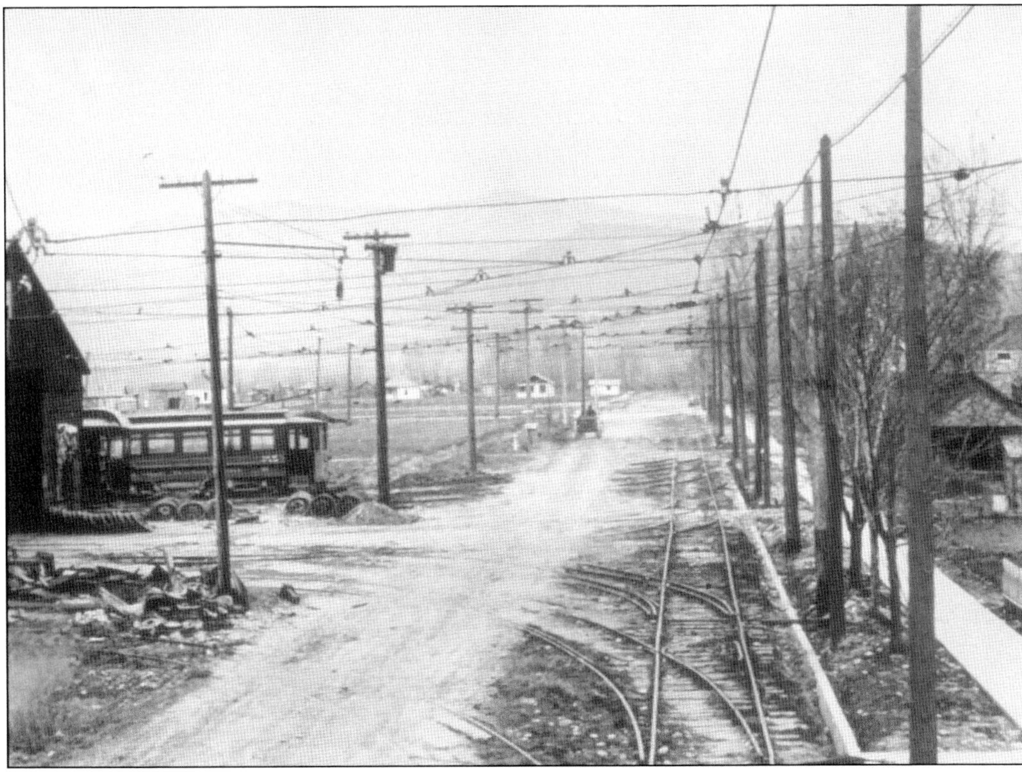

The South Boise carbarn was located in Boise on Rossi Street, west of Broadway Avenue. This photograph was taken around 1910, when the carbarn was a busy site on the BVRC. This eastward view shows cars waiting for maintenance. Table Rock, a local landmark, can be seen in the background.

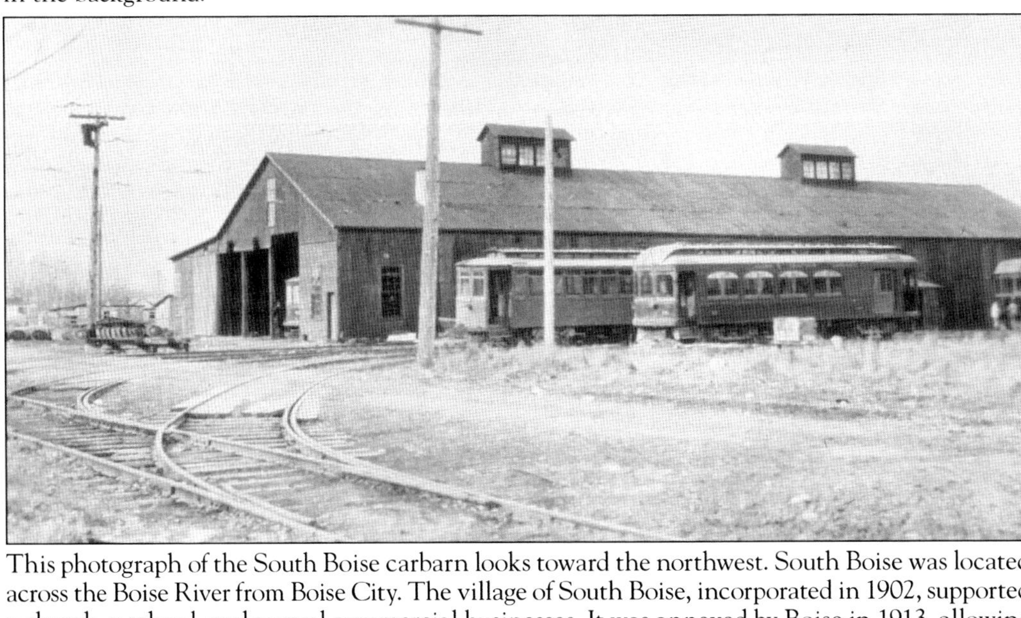

This photograph of the South Boise carbarn looks toward the northwest. South Boise was located across the Boise River from Boise City. The village of South Boise, incorporated in 1902, supported a church, a school, and several commercial businesses. It was annexed by Boise in 1913, allowing its residents access to sewer, electricity, fire protection, and other municipal services.

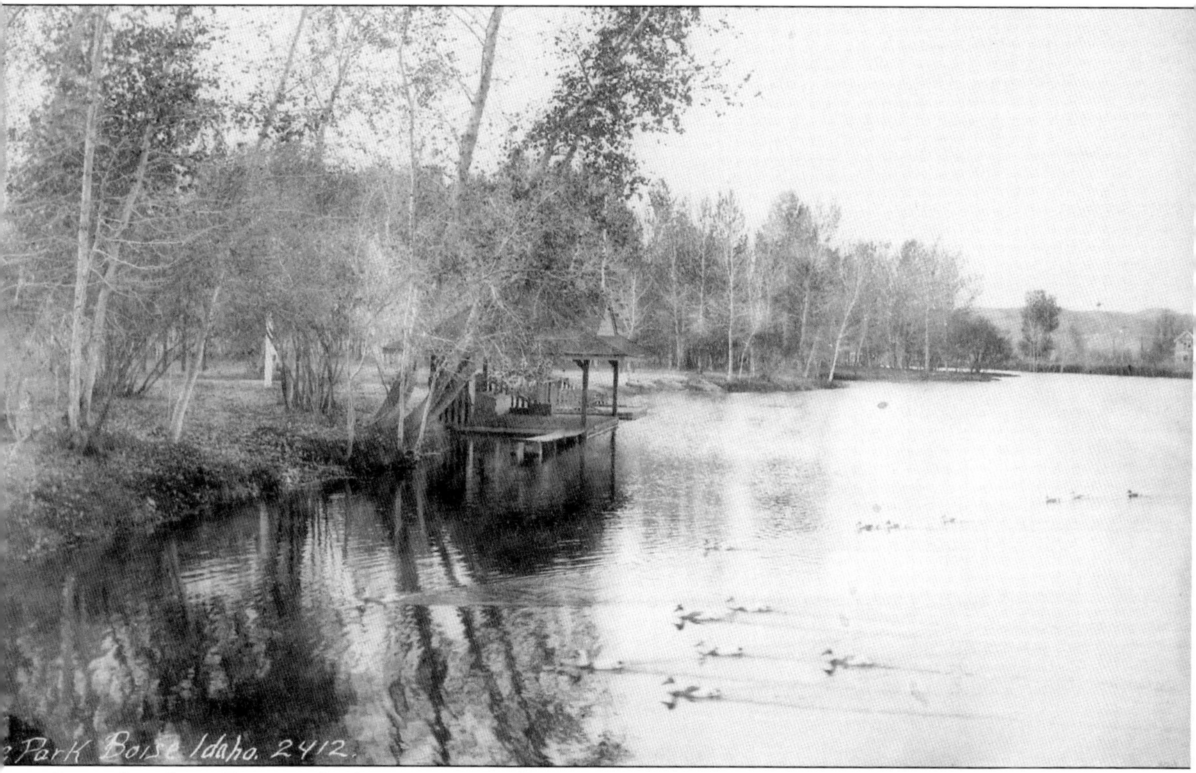

Several parks in Boise and other Treasure Valley towns were developed by the streetcar companies. Walter E. Pierce developed Pierce Park about four miles west of downtown Boise. This postcard shows the boat pavilion on the south side of Lake Elmore, the park's man-made lake.

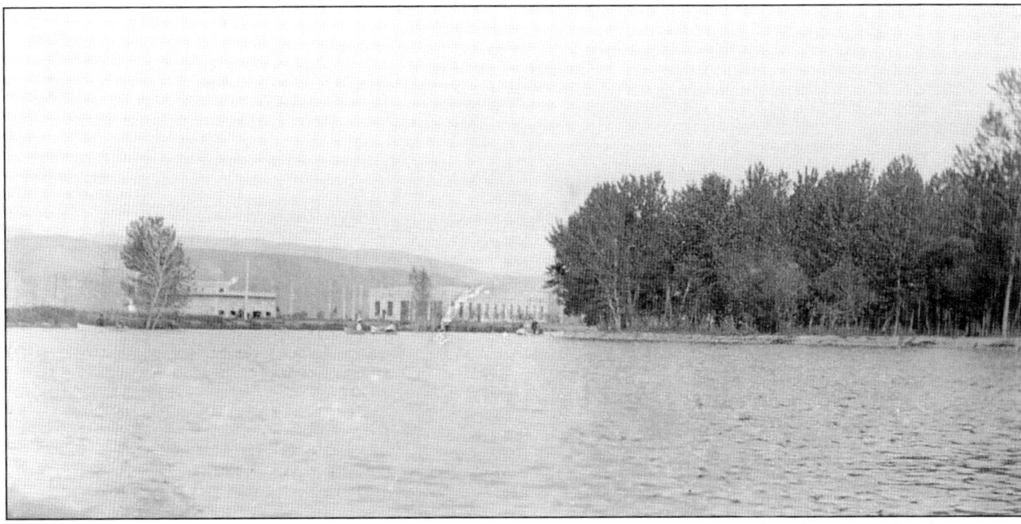

Pierce Park opened in August 1907. In this view, boaters are seen on Lake Elmore, which was one of the improvements made in 1908. The powerhouse and carbarns are in the background.

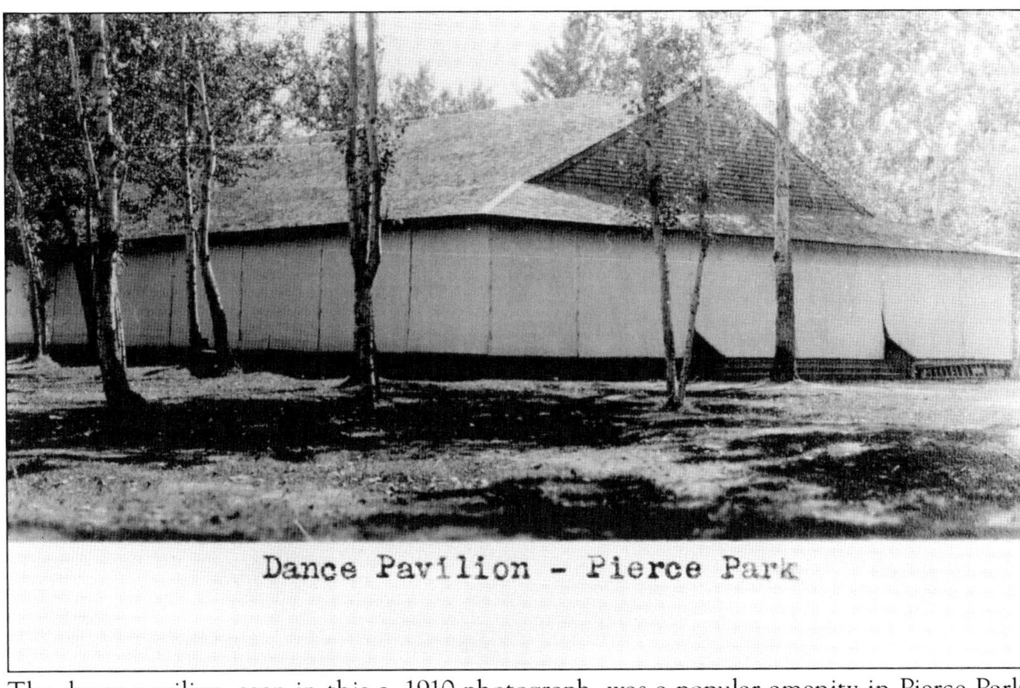

The dance pavilion, seen in this c. 1910 photograph, was a popular amenity in Pierce Park. The B&I contracted with the Columbia Band, a local Boise group, to provide entertainment at the park. The company sponsored many special musical events to entice residents to ride the interurban line to visit the park.

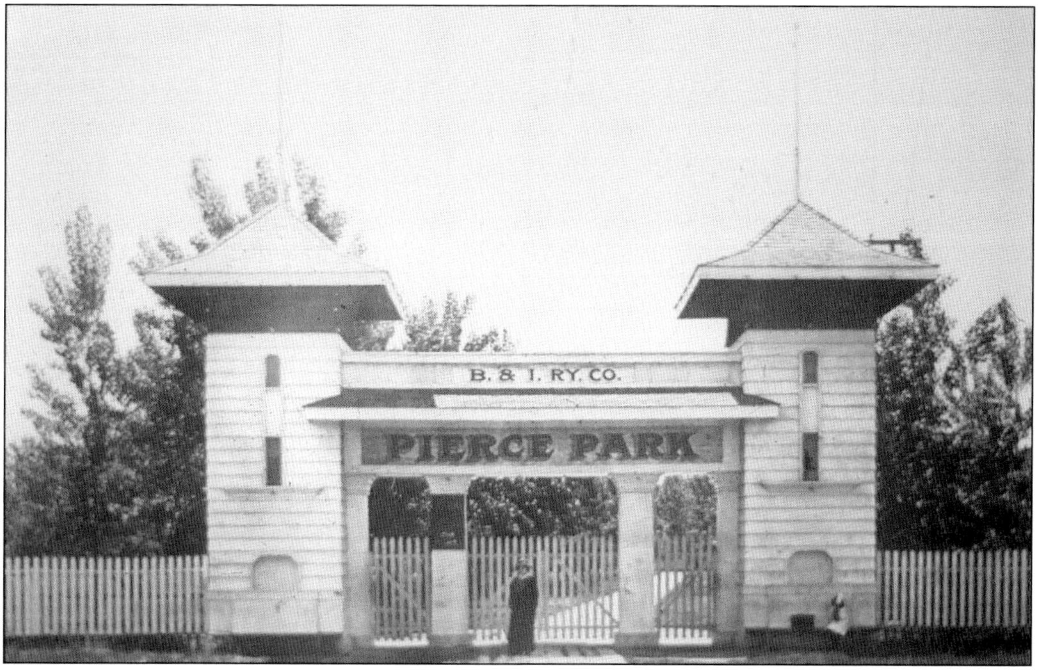

An elaborate gate was built at the entrance to Pierce Park. The B&I encouraged the use of the park for community celebrations, such as Labor Day and Memorial Day.

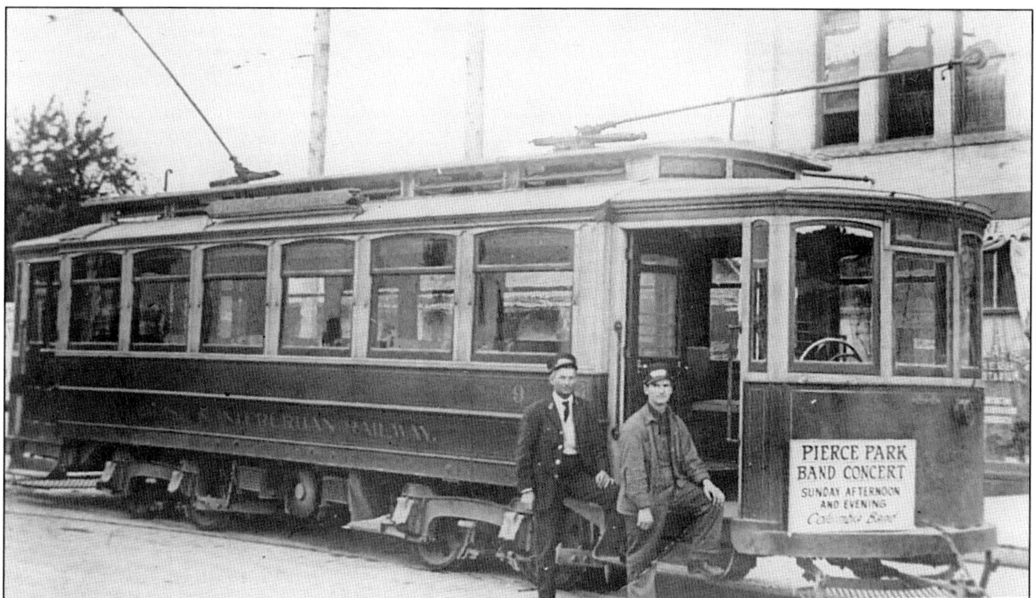

An unidentified motorman and conductor pose with B&I Car No. 4 in downtown Boise. The B&I often provided special excursion rates for programs at Pierce Park. The advertisement on the car promotes a concert by the Columbia Band, a local band that entertained at parades, dances, and ball games. (Courtesy of John Aguirre.)

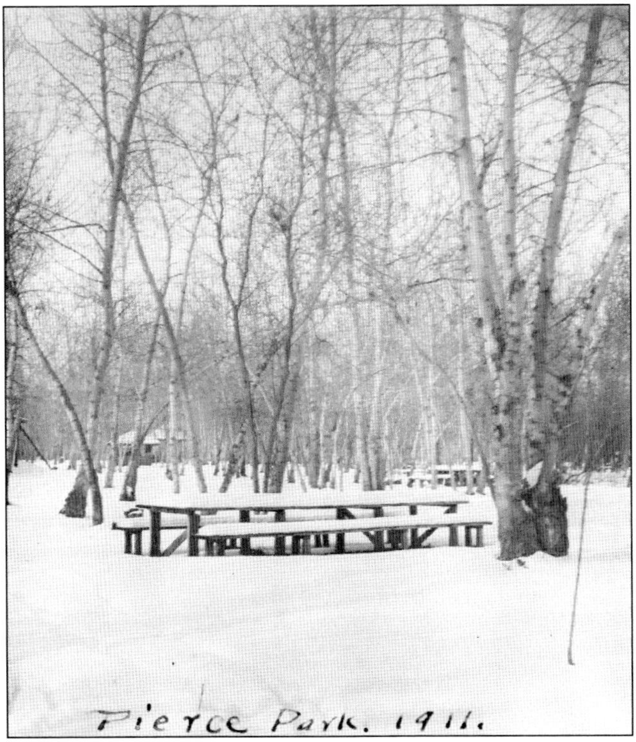

During the summer months, Pierce Park was crowded and busy. This 1911 photograph shows the contrast during the winter.

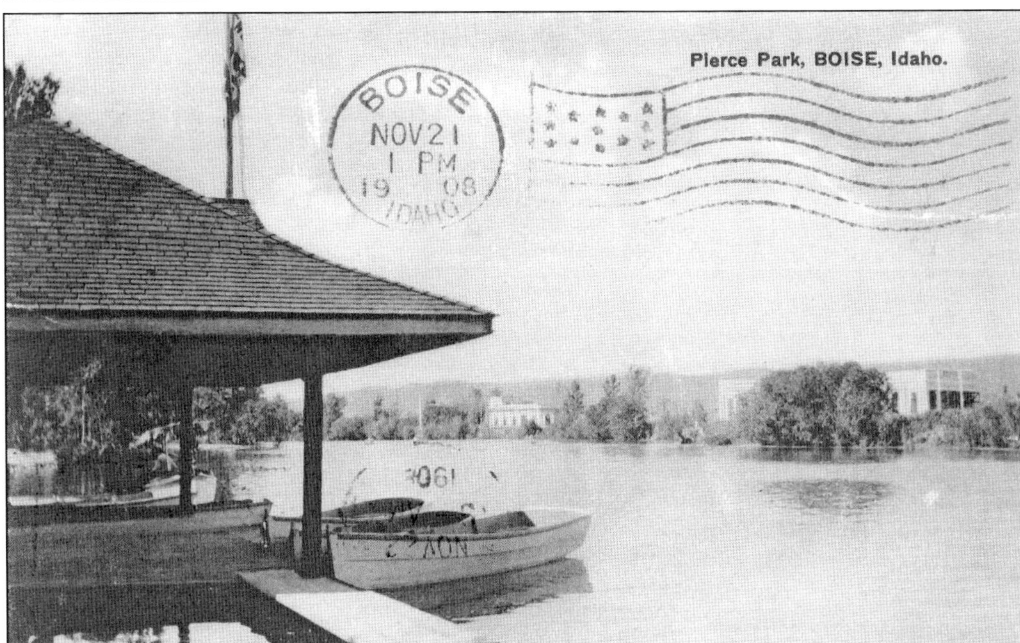

This postcard view of Pierce Park shows the boathouse and Lake Elmore on the south side of State Street, opposite the carbarns and powerhouse, which were located on the north side of the street. The artificial lake, excavated in March 1908, was a half mile long. The lake's four-foot depth accommodated both man-powered and electric-powered boats in the summer. In the winter, the lake was a popular with ice-skaters.

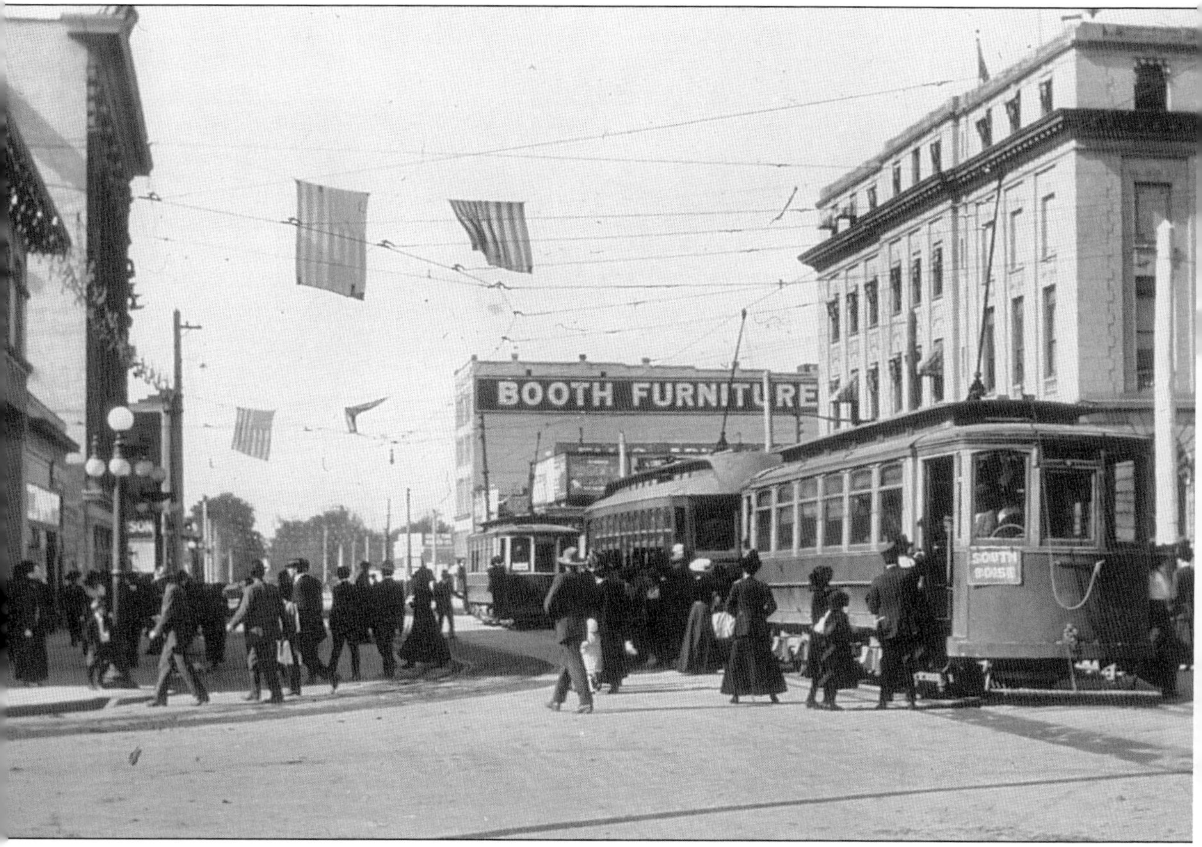

At the turn of the 20th century, downtown Boise bustled with pedestrians, shoppers, and streetcar commuters. This view shows the intersection of Bannock and Seventh Streets on a busy day. The cars of the BVRC and the B&I are lined up, ready to take passengers to the surrounding neighborhoods.

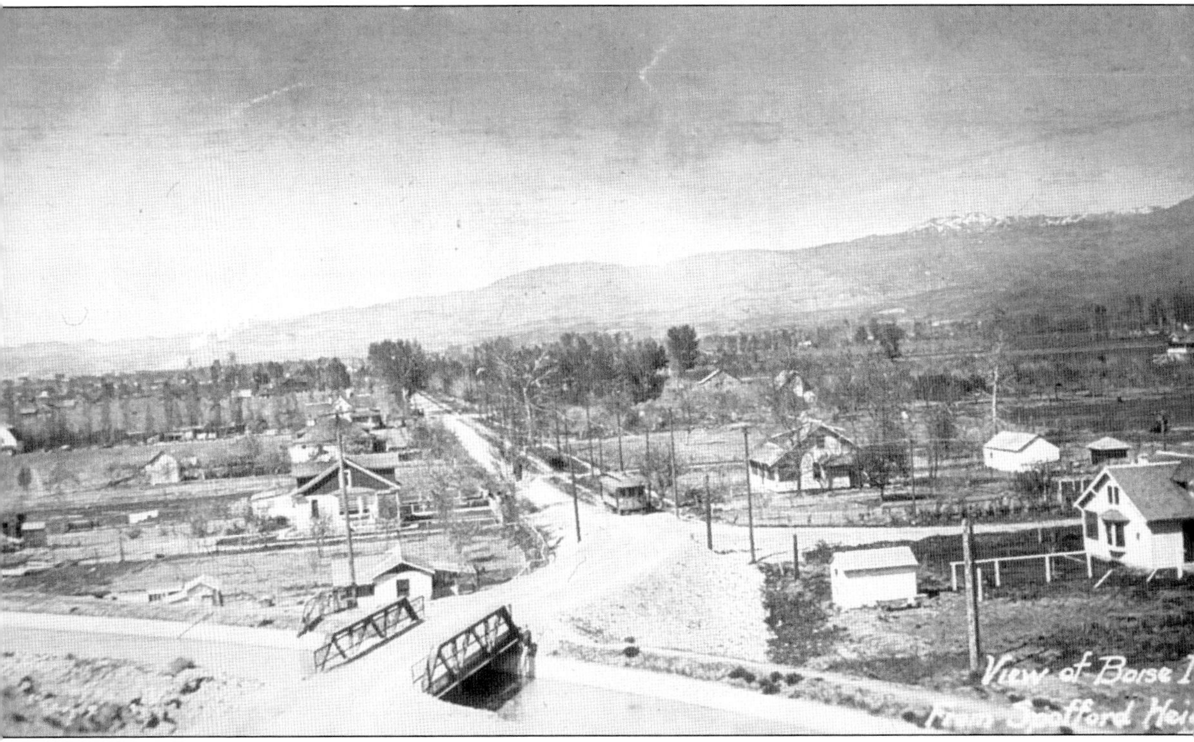

The BVRC line ran south from downtown Boise across the Boise River to South Boise. In this view, a BVRC car is stopped at the end of the line near the Ivywild addition, a subdivision on the south end of Broadway Avenue.

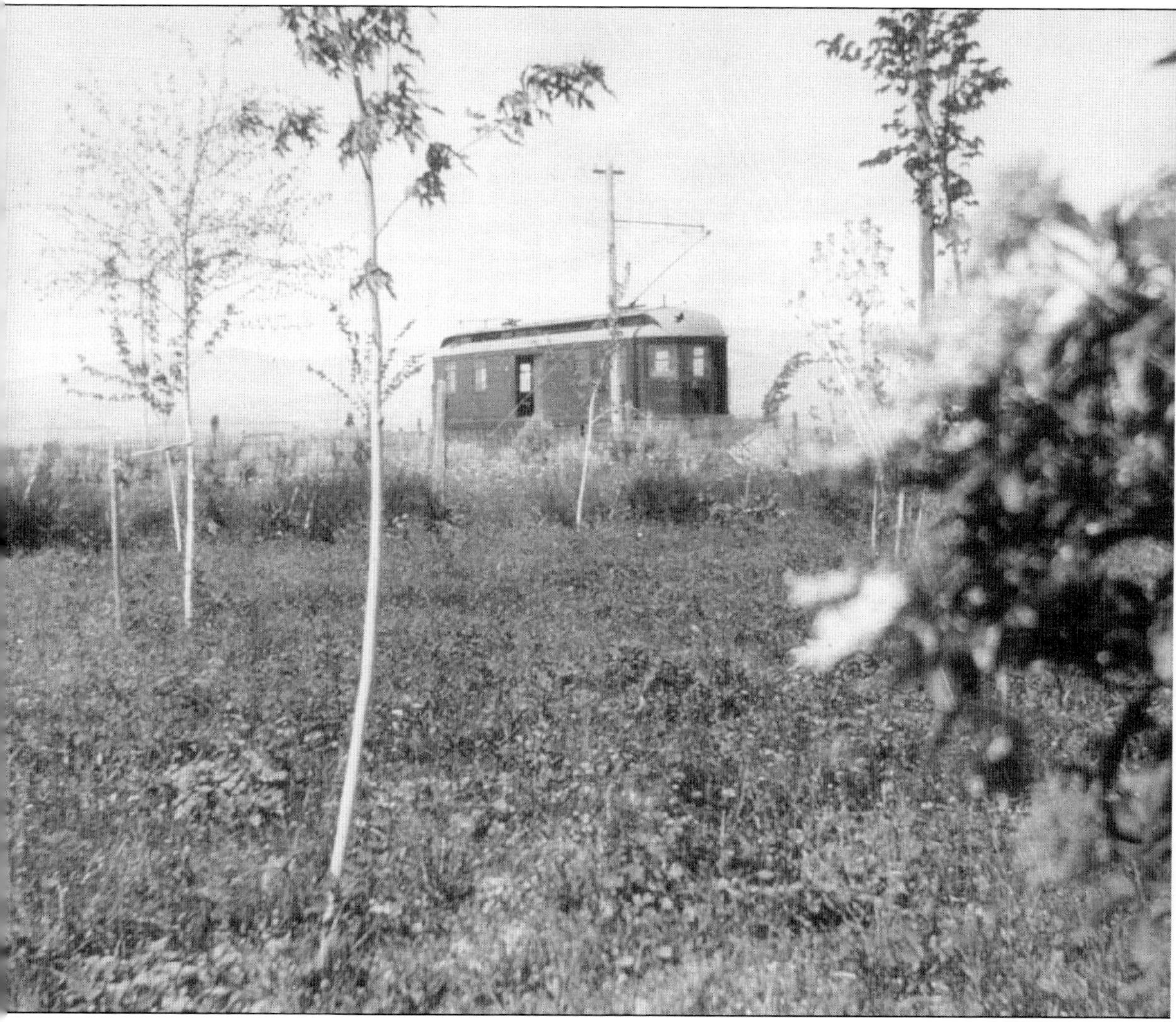

Between 1910 and 1920, the streetcar companies continued to extend the rail lines to new neighborhoods. This photograph shows a BVRC car on the Morris Hill route. This neighborhood, located on the bench area south of downtown Boise, developed from farmland and orchards.

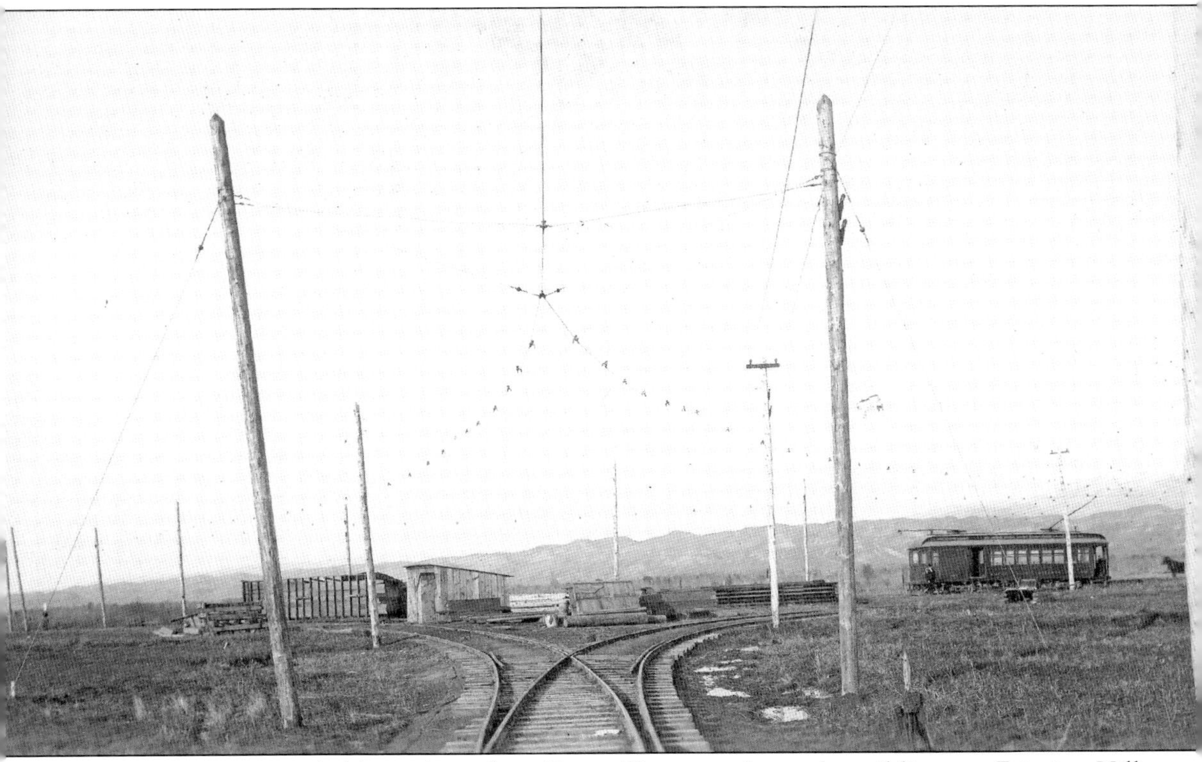

The BVRC extended lines throughout Boise. This view shows the rail lines on Fairview Hill, west of downtown Boise. The car in the photograph is eastbound to Boise.

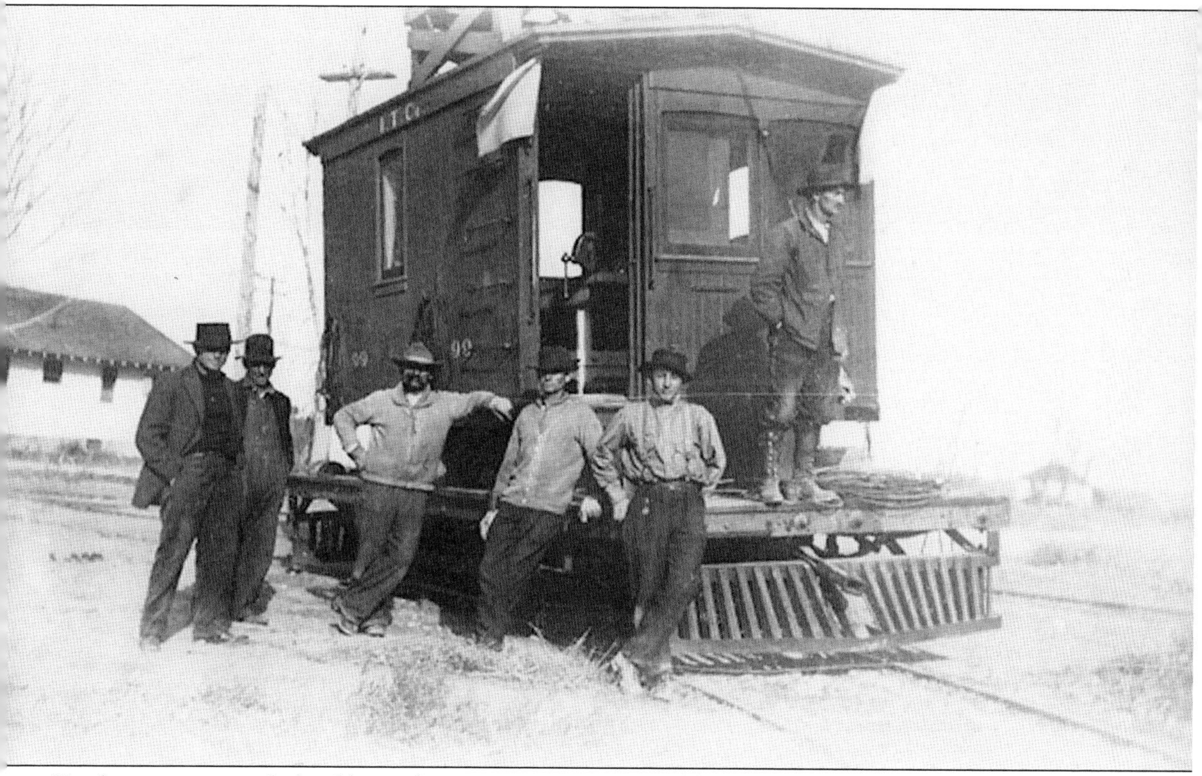

Track maintenance helped keep the streetcars running safely and efficiently. This track crew is posing with ITC Work Engine No. 99 on the Ustick road line.

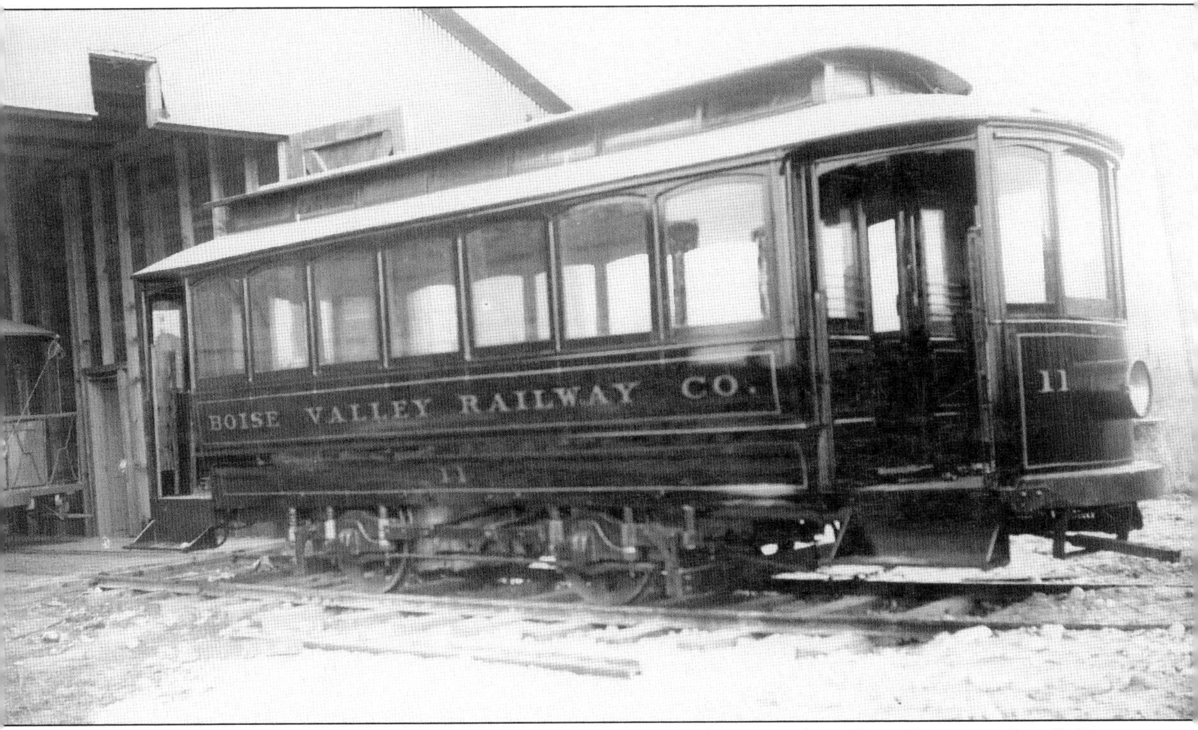

BVRC operated three streetcar lines between 1906 and 1910: a line from Boise to South Boise, a line southwest from Boise to the fairgrounds and Morris Hill cemetery, and a line from Boise westward to Ustick and Onweiler. Here, Car No. 11 is stopped at the South Boise carbarn.

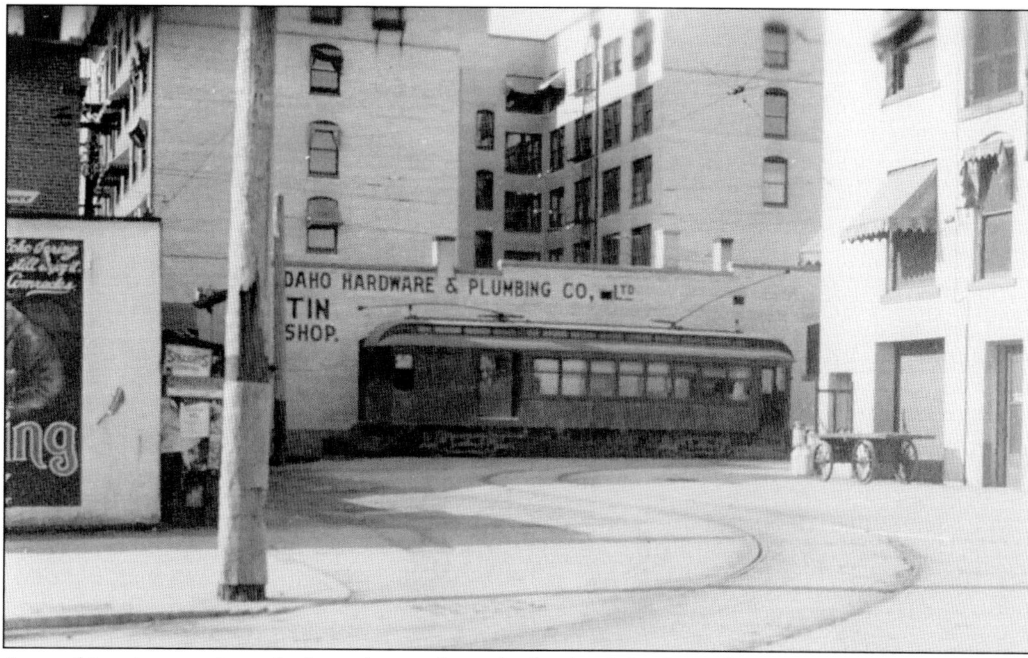

A combination car is parked on the track at the back of the B&I depot. Milk cans are stacked, ready for pickup or loading. The depot faced Bannock Street, with an open area at the back of the building. The cars left Bannock Street on the tracks that can be seen in the photograph, circled the building, and emerged on Seventh Street.

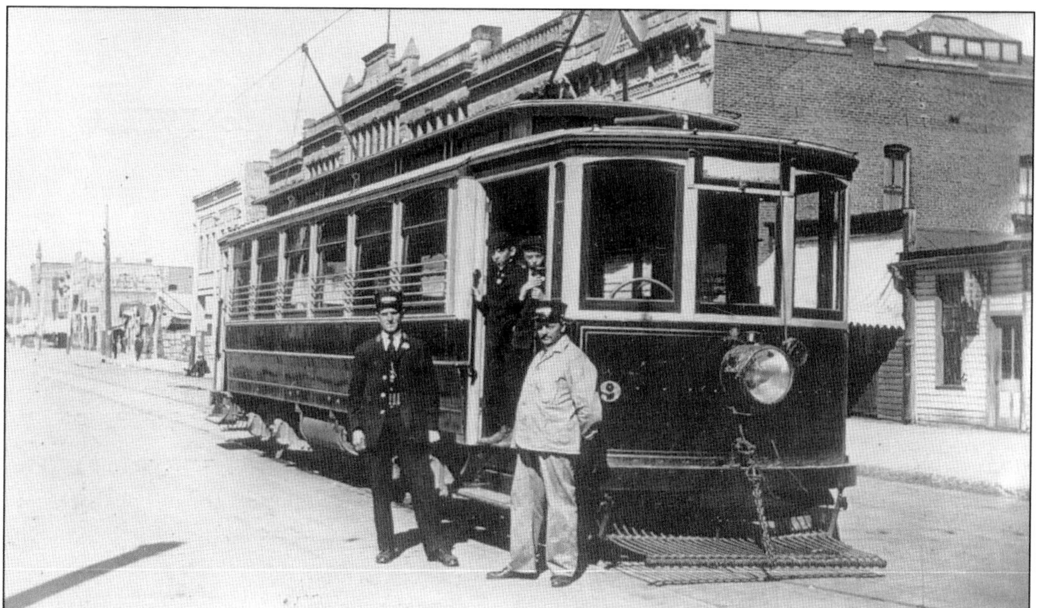

This c. 1908 photograph shows B&I City Car No. 9 stopped on Idaho Street. Motorman Henry Baker (right) and an unidentified conductor pose for the camera as two young boys peer out from the streetcar. The sandstone-and-brick facade of the Union Block can be seen in the background. Designed by Boise architect John E. Tourtellotte, the Union Block was constructed in 1902. (Courtesy of John Aguirre.)

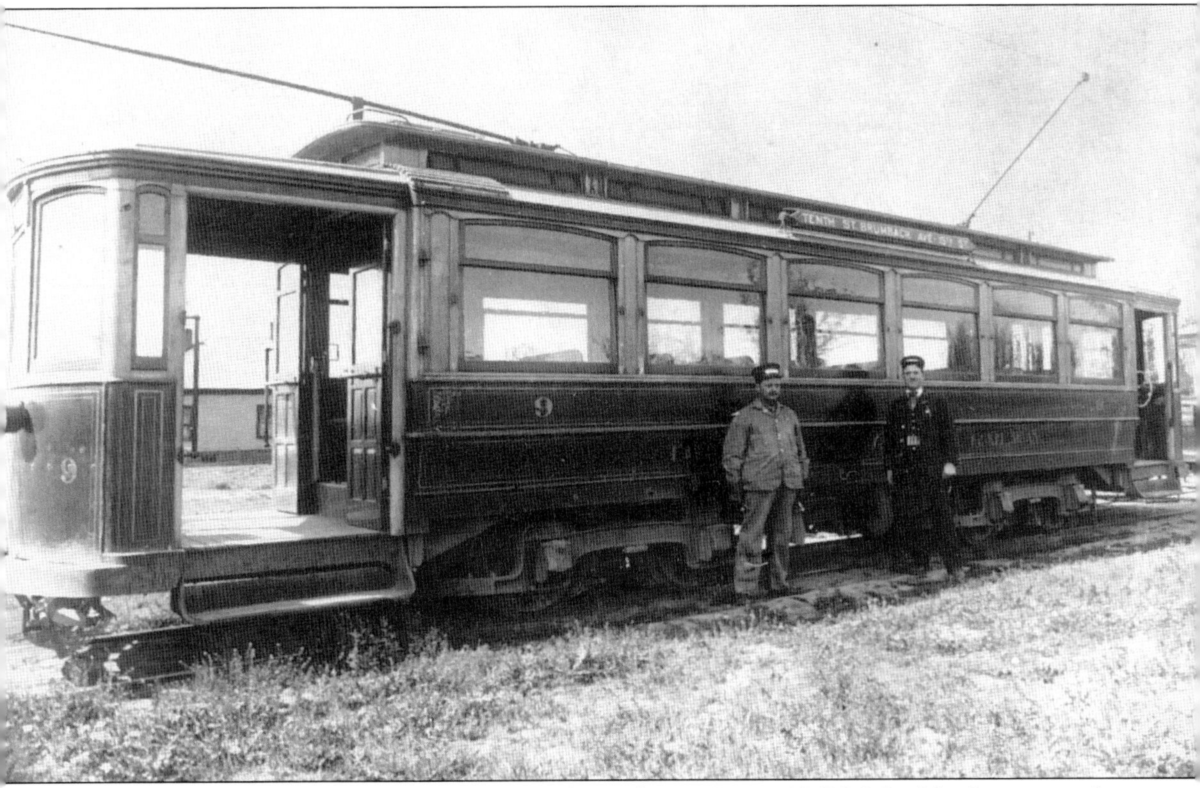

The B&I built a city loop line, known as the "Belt Line," in 1907. B&I Car No. 9 was one of two cars used on the line, which ran north on Tenth and Fifteenth Streets to Dewey Street in Boise's North End, then returned downtown via Eighteenth Street. Here, conductor Curtis W. Martindale and motorman Henry B. Baker pose at the Dewey Street switch. (Courtesy of John Aguirre.)

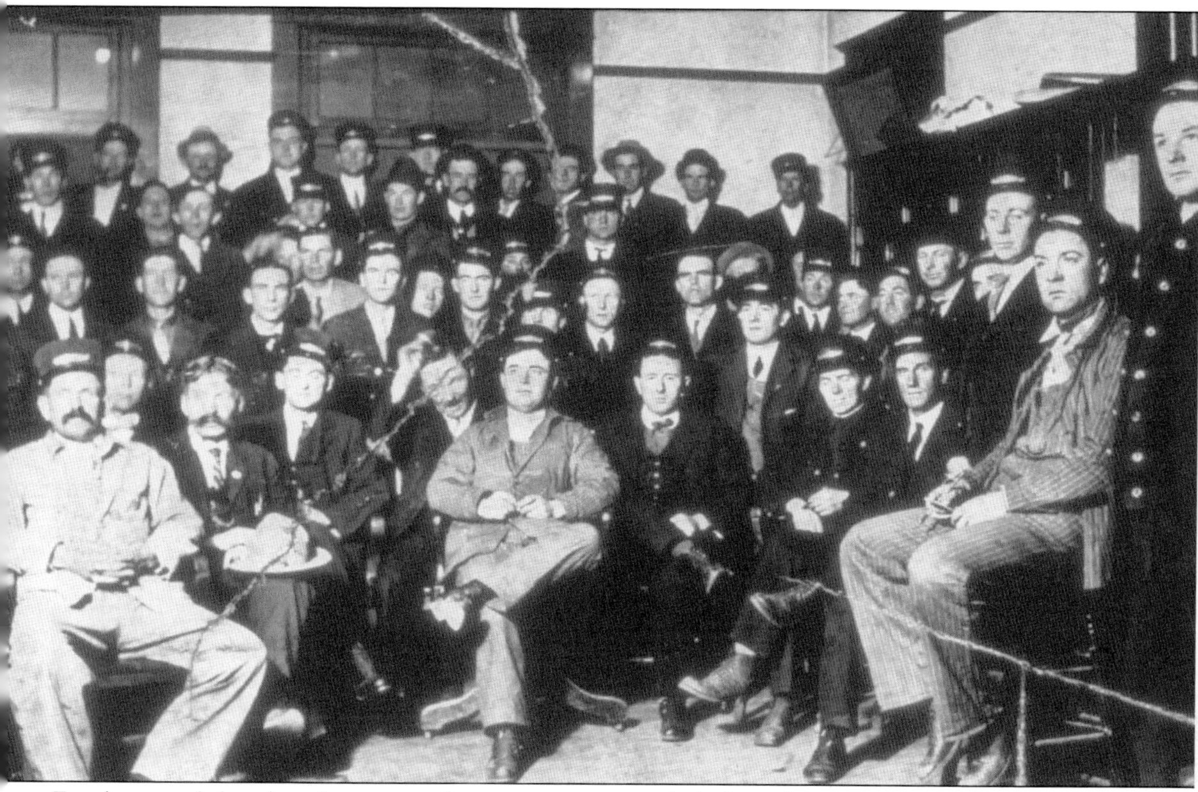

Employees of the electric street railway companies included conductors, motormen, station agents, and mechanics. In this photograph, a group of unidentified employees have gathered for a meeting, possibly at the B&I depot.

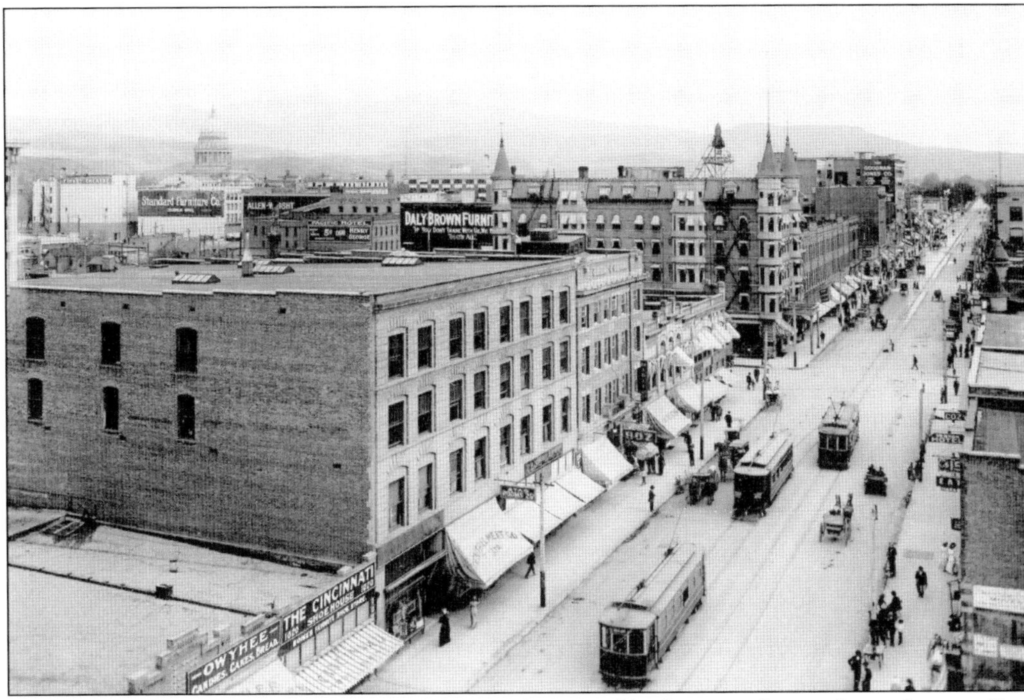

This photograph, a view from the roof of the Owyhee Hotel looking northeast, shows three trolleys on Main Street—two headed west and one headed east. The double tracks can be seen in the center of the photograph. The Idanha Hotel, with its three turrets, is in the background.

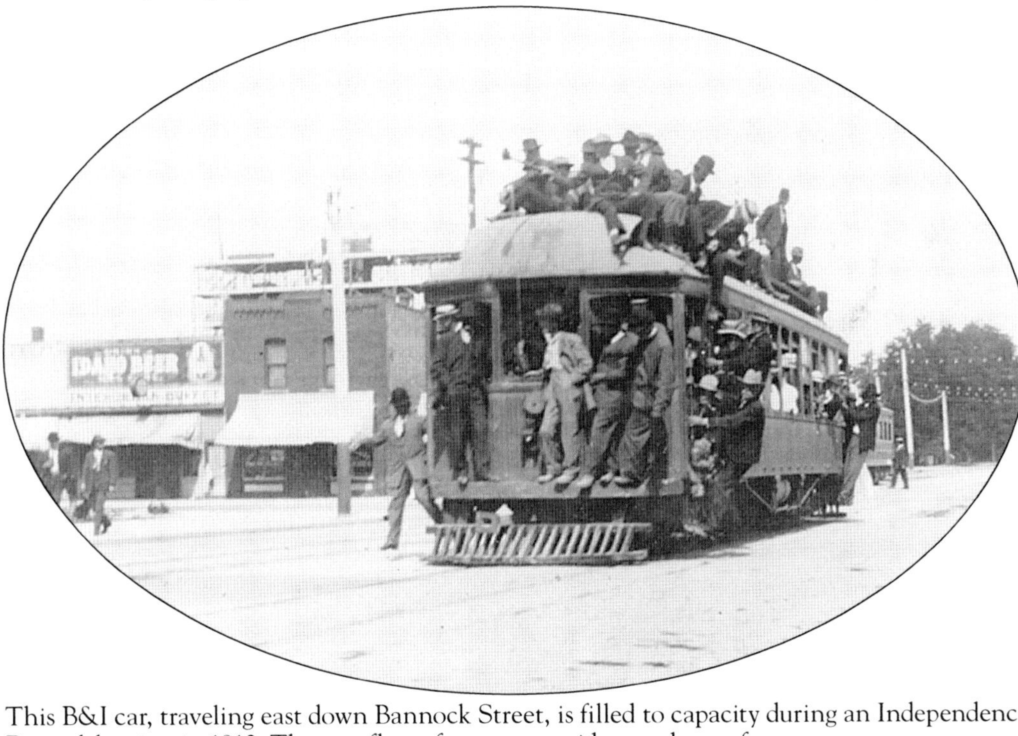

This B&I car, traveling east down Bannock Street, is filled to capacity during an Independence Day celebration in 1910. The overflow of passengers rides on the roof.

Four

"Looping the Loop"

By 1909, the B&I line extended from Boise to Caldwell, a distance of approximately 25 miles. The route travelled west from Boise, stopping at Collister, Eagle, and Star before continuing on to Middleton. At Middleton, the route turned south, crossed the Boise River, and ended at the Caldwell depot at Third Avenue and Main Street. The Caldwell Interurban Company (CIC) route used the same track and travelled southwest from Caldwell to the College of Idaho and then west to Deer Flat Reservoir (now known as Lake Lowell, after James T. Lowell, an important supporter of irrigation projects.)

Meanwhile, cars on the BVRC line left Boise and travelled west to Ustick and then to Onweiler Station, one and a half miles south of Meridian. Construction on a route to Nampa began in 1906. Progress was slow as the BVRC had difficulty obtaining investors, partly because of a national financial panic in 1908. Finally, in 1909, Nampa resident Robert Noble invested in the BVRC, and the line to Nampa was completed in October 1910.

The interurban companies went through several changes. The interurban loop, which linked communities in Ada and Canyon Counties, was completed in 1912. Brothers James S. and W.S. Kuhn, Pittsburgh capitalists, combined the BVCR and the B&I with power-generating facilities they owned at Swan Falls, Salmon Falls, and Shoshone Falls, creating the Idaho Traction Company (ITC). In 1913, the ITC became part of the Idaho Railway Light & Power Company, one of the predecessors of the Idaho Power Company.

The line was improved with heavier rails and new cars and was redirected to go directly to Meridian and then south to Nampa, a route that eliminated dangerous curves. New depots were constructed at Meridian, Caldwell, and Nampa, and the ITC featured special events to boost ridership, encouraging folks to "loop the Loop" on Sunday afternoons.

In 1915, the ITC became the Boise Valley Traction Company (BVTC). The BVTC was formed to operate the electric traction properties acquired from Idaho Railway Light & Power Company.

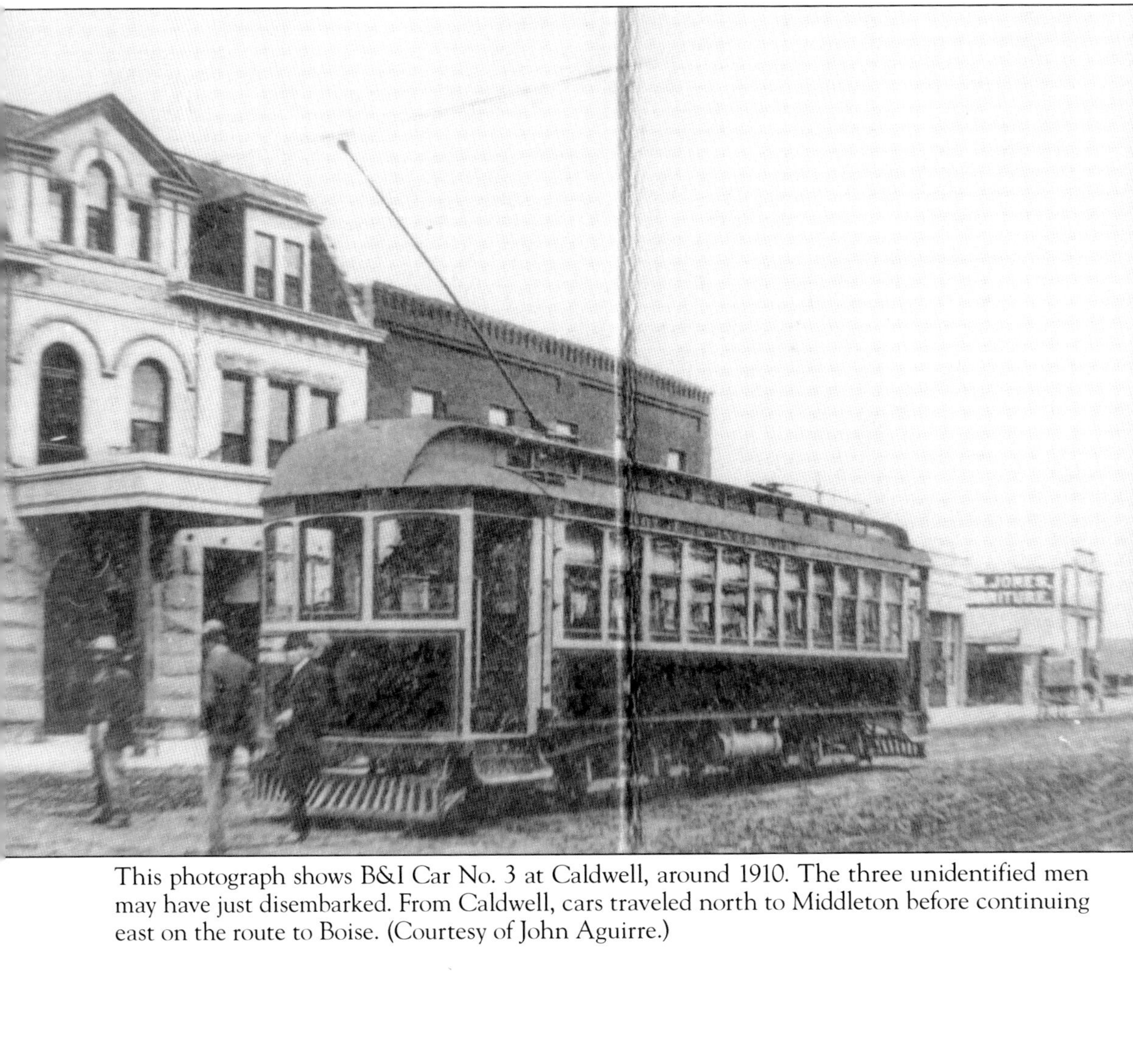

This photograph shows B&I Car No. 3 at Caldwell, around 1910. The three unidentified men may have just disembarked. From Caldwell, cars traveled north to Middleton before continuing east on the route to Boise. (Courtesy of John Aguirre.)

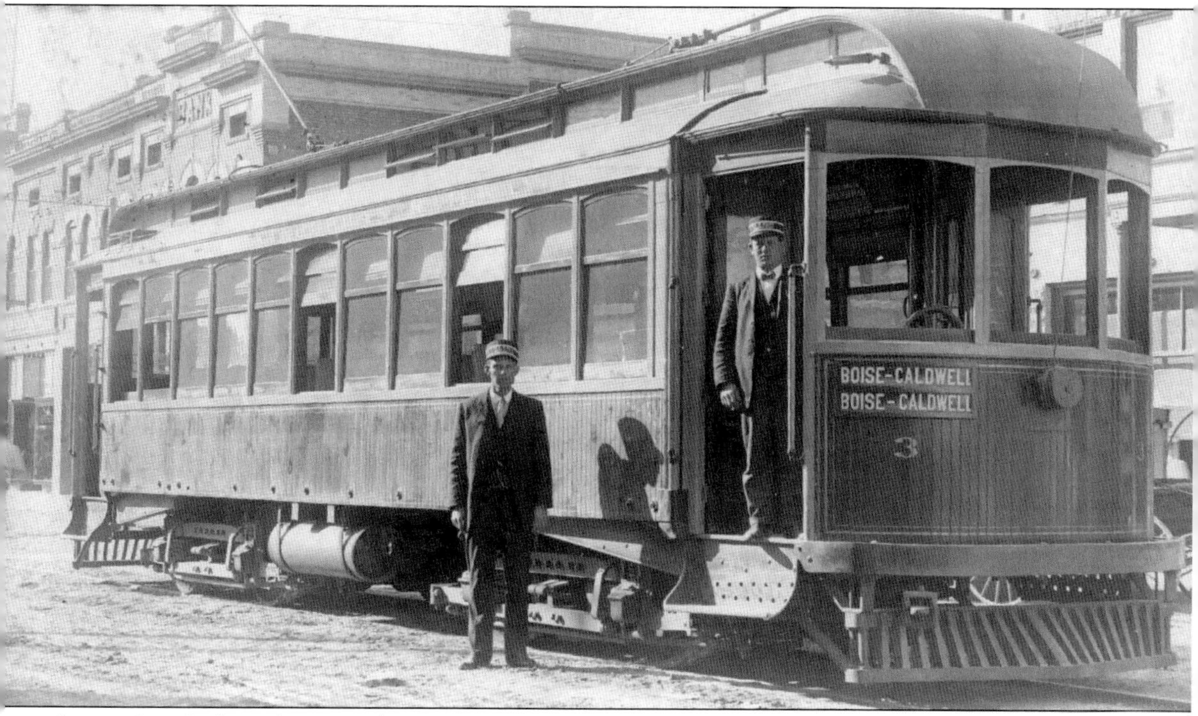

An unidentified conductor and motorman pose with B&I Car No. 3 in downtown Caldwell. The Steunenberg Block, one of a number of downtown buildings built in Caldwell between 1905 and 1906, is visible in the background. During the boom years, Caldwell acquired electric power, a flour mill, a grand hotel, county fairgrounds, and the interurban line. (Courtesy of John Aguirre.)

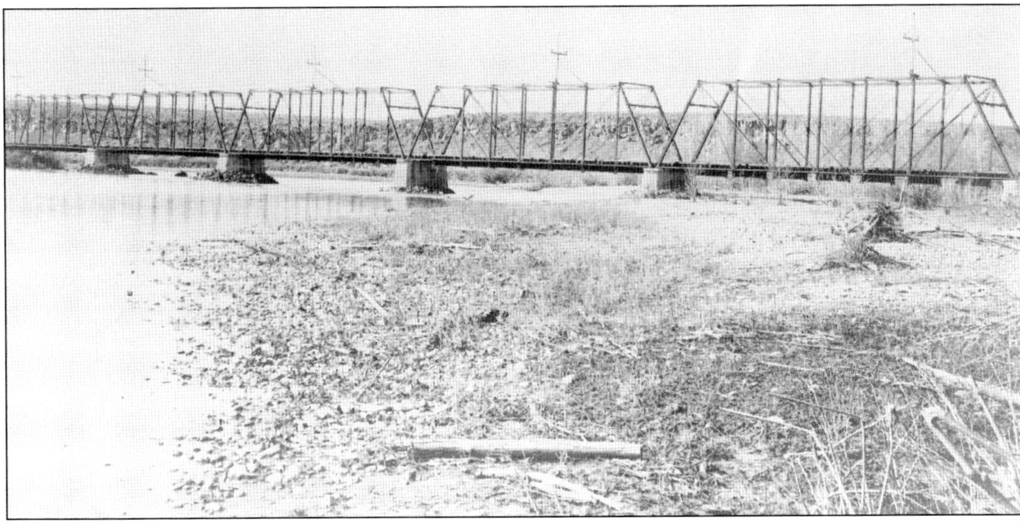

Interurban cars crossed the Boise River on this five-span Whipple truss bridge. The bridge, built by Caldwell construction contractor J.H. Forbes, was completed in 1907 for the B&I.

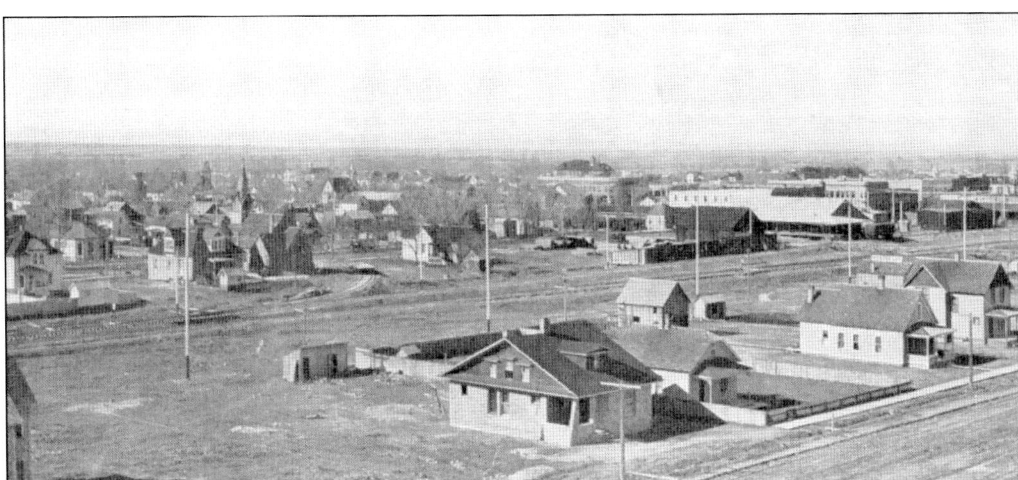

This c. 1907 postcard shows a view of Caldwell before interurban service was inaugurated. Caldwell would have two interurban lines. In 1906, the B&I built an electric line in the town, and the Caldwell Interurban Railway Company was organized by local businessman Walter R. Sebree and other investors. The Caldwell company operated a seven-mile line from Caldwell to Deer Flat Reservoir (now Lake Lowell). (Courtesy of John Aguirre.)

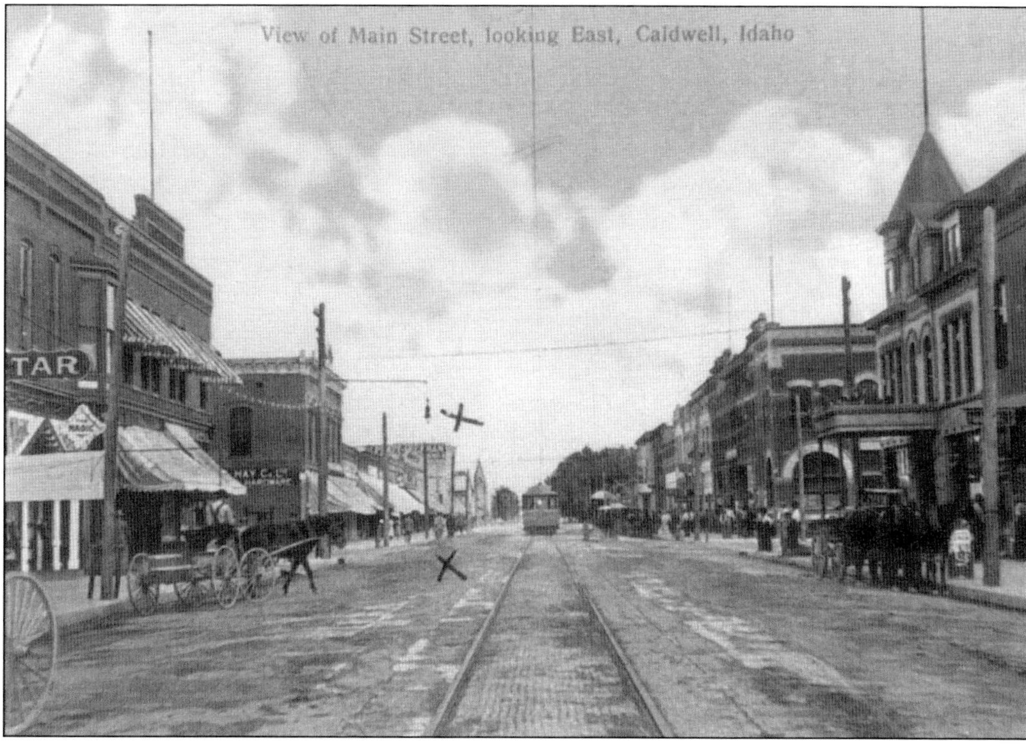

In this photograph, a B&I car heads west to the commercial district on Caldwell's Main Street. The turret on the right is a feature of the Saratoga Hotel, built by Howard Sebree, president of the First National Bank. The Saratoga was a Caldwell landmark until it was destroyed by fire in 1990. (Courtesy of John Aguirre.)

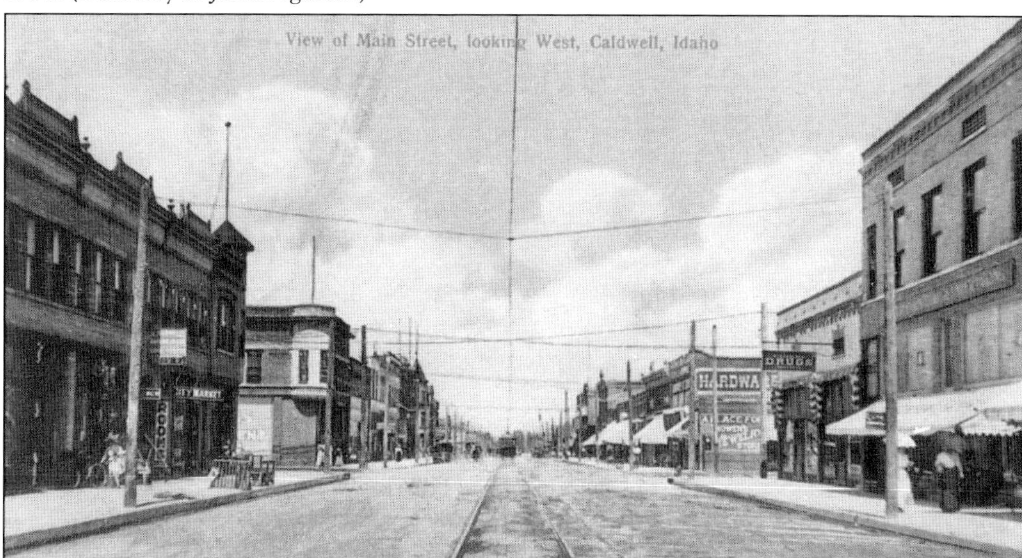

A view of downtown Caldwell's Main Street shows the business district with the streets still unpaved. The system of wires that provided power for the electric street railway can be clearly seen in this view. The trolley wires are suspended overhead, strung between the poles that line the sidewalks. (Courtesy of John Aguirre.)

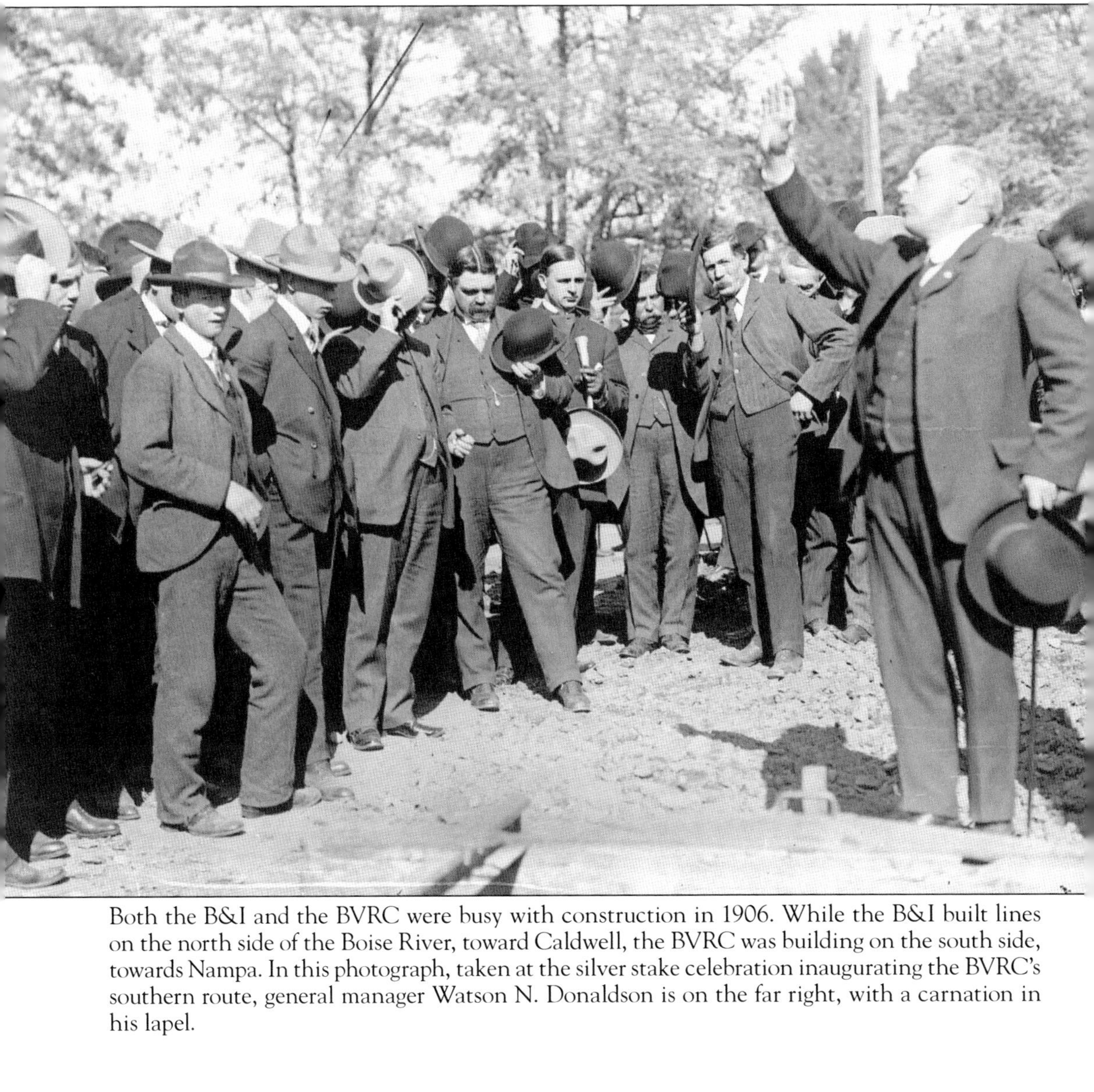

Both the B&I and the BVRC were busy with construction in 1906. While the B&I built lines on the north side of the Boise River, toward Caldwell, the BVRC was building on the south side, towards Nampa. In this photograph, taken at the silver stake celebration inaugurating the BVRC's southern route, general manager Watson N. Donaldson is on the far right, with a carnation in his lapel.

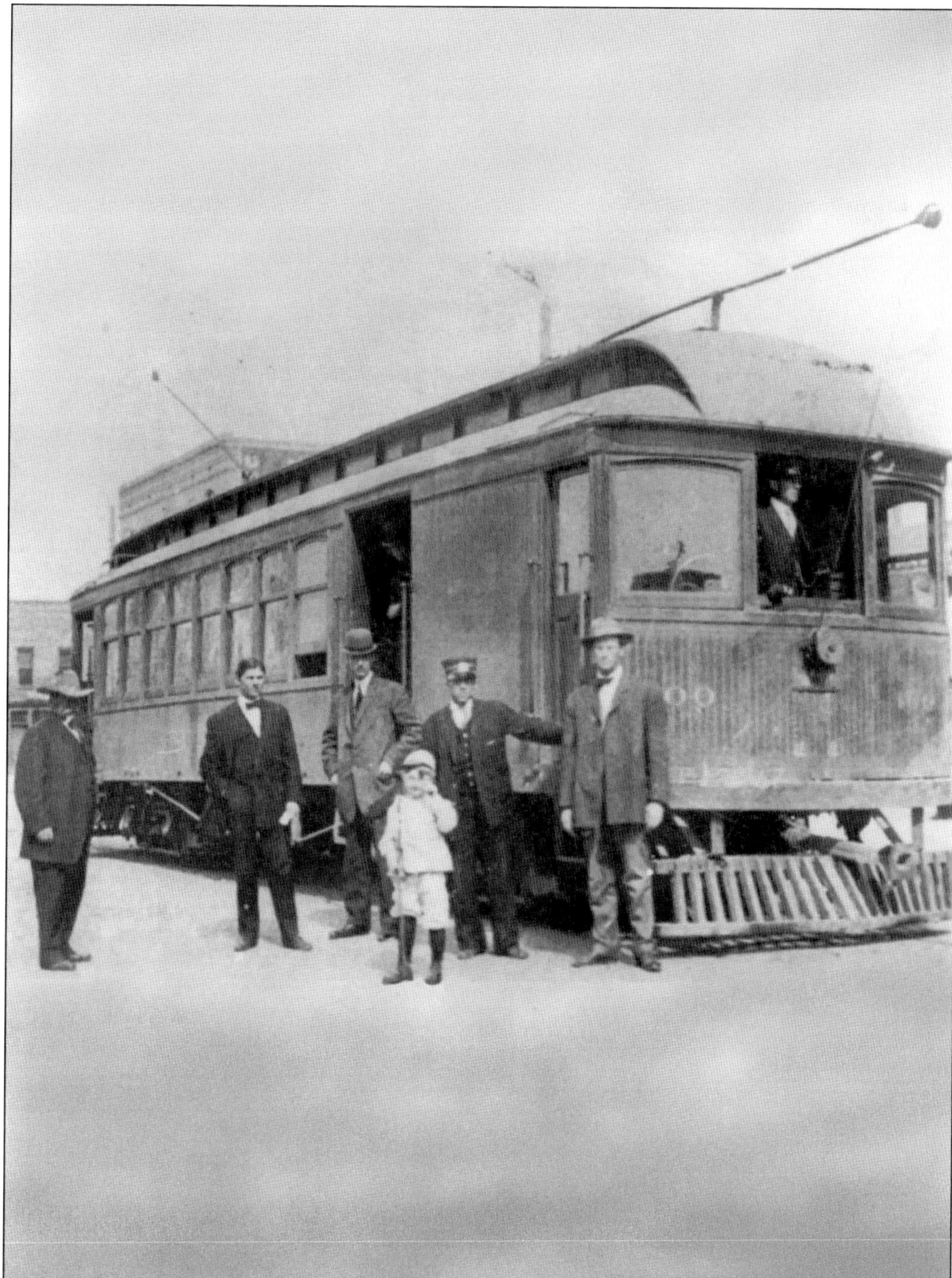

It would take three years for the BVRC to complete the route to Nampa. On October 12, 1909, Car No. 100 sped into Nampa on First Street. Pictured here are, from left to right, Robert Noble (builder of the line), V.T. Elver (Nampa ticket agent), Frank Estabrook Sr., an unidentified young boy, an unidentified conductor, A.W. McNeil, and an unidentified motorman. (Courtesy of the Canyon County Historical Society.)

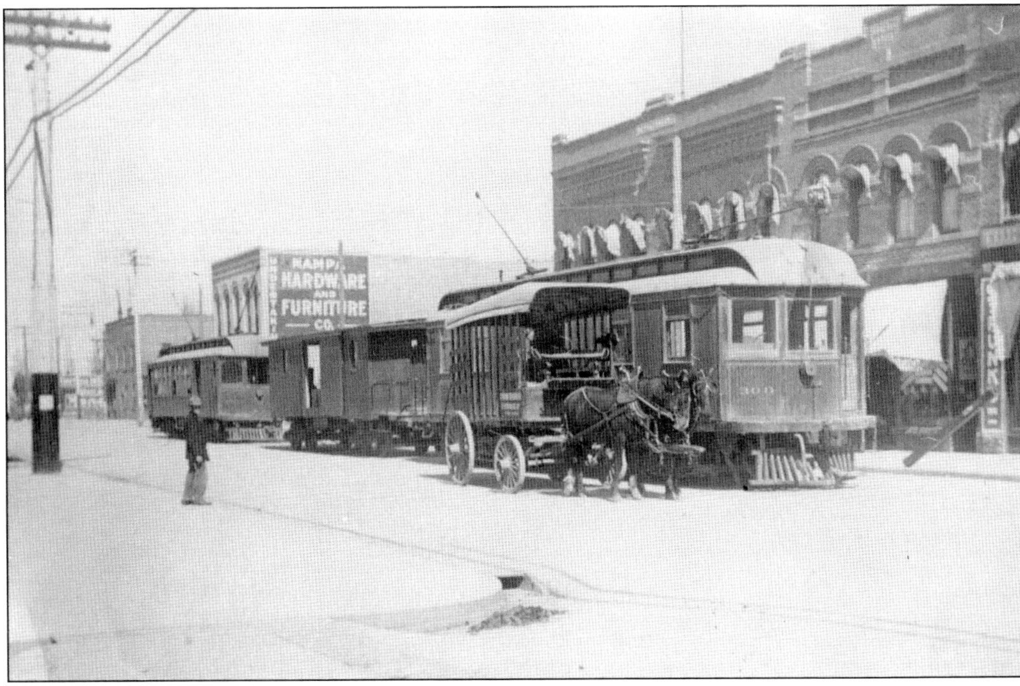

Two BVRC passenger cars and a freight car are stopped on Nampa's Main Street. For passengers, the trip between Nampa and Boise took one hour and ten minutes. Local farmers used the freight service to ship produce between towns—particularly sugar beets, which became a leading industry for Nampa and the surrounding area. (Courtesy of John Aguirre.)

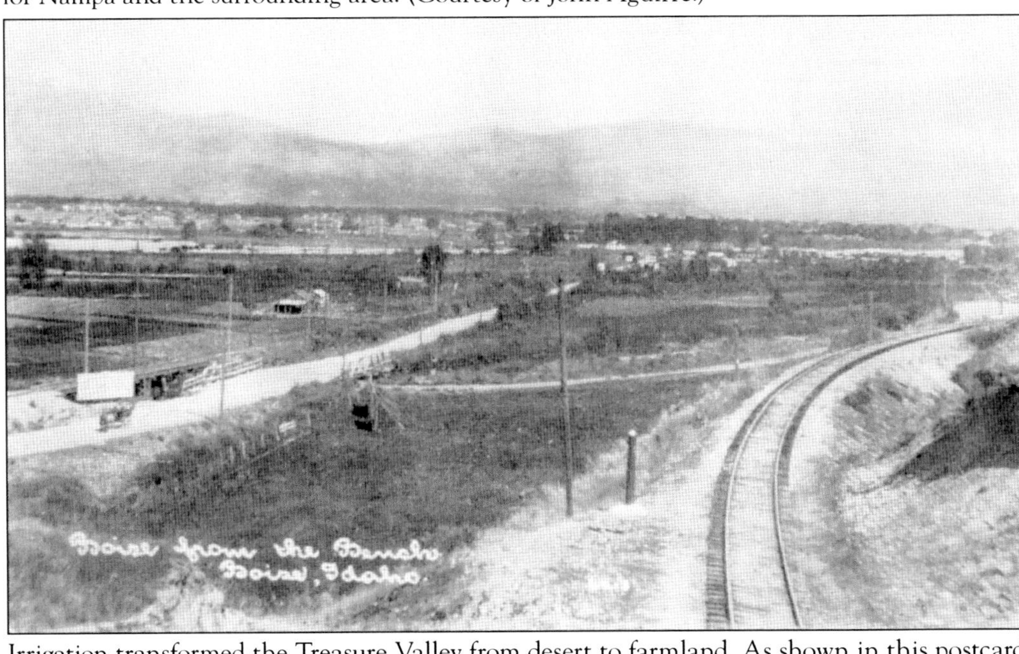

Irrigation transformed the Treasure Valley from desert to farmland. As shown in this postcard, the interurban routes followed many of the canals. The curve of the track follows the curve of the Settlers Canal west from Boise, which can be seen in the background. (Courtesy of John Aguirre.)

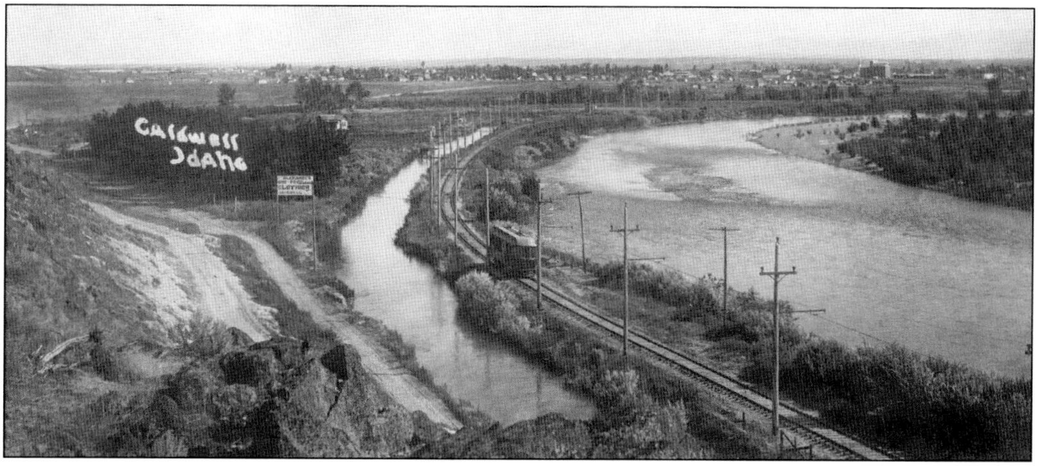

This B&I car is headed south into Caldwell. The track passes the Boise River on the right and Riverside Canal on the left. (Courtesy of the College of Idaho.)

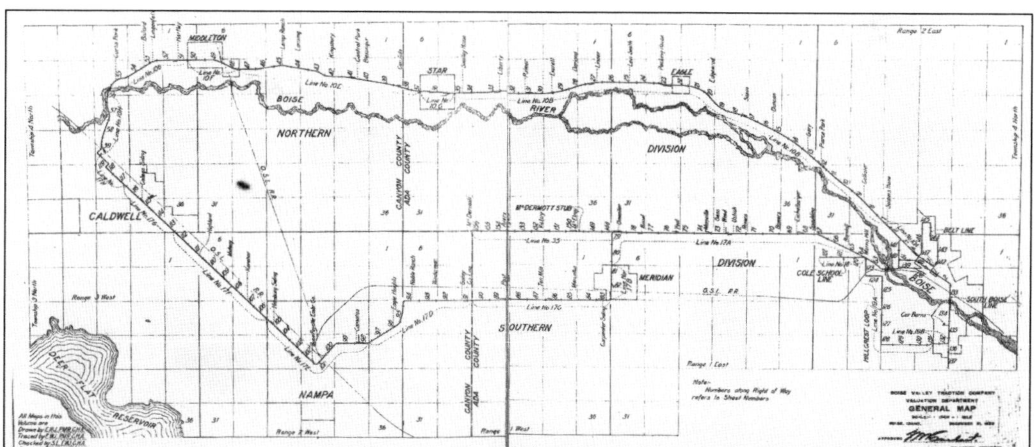

Although an interurban route connecting Nampa and Caldwell was discussed for years by the various electric railway companies, it was not completed until 1912. This 1920 route map shows the complete loop and the various stops and stations along the way.

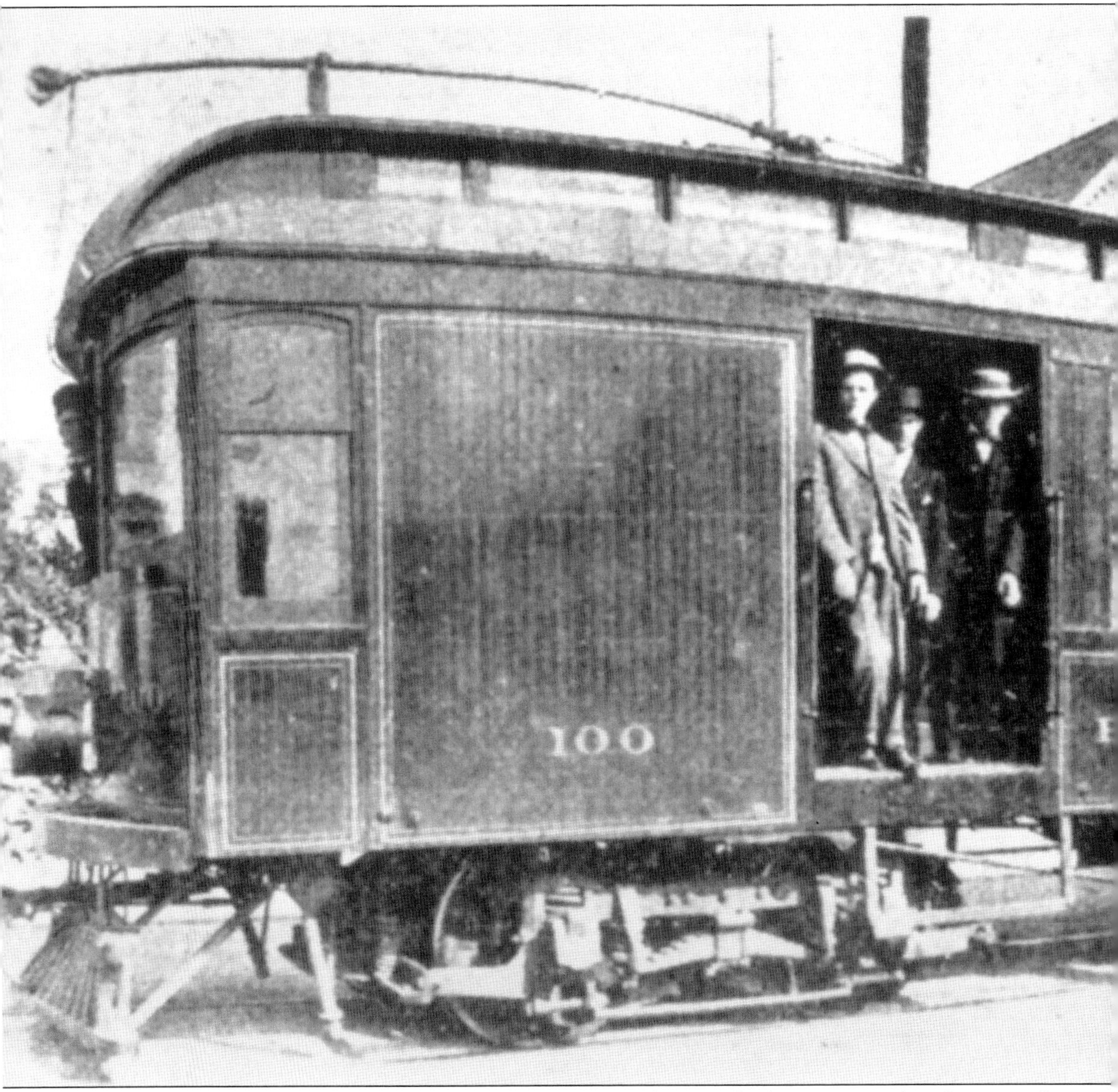

A lively group of passengers fills BVRC Cars 100 and 300, which are stopped in Boise at the west corner of Eighth and Bannock Streets, in front of the BVRC depot. The Federal Building,

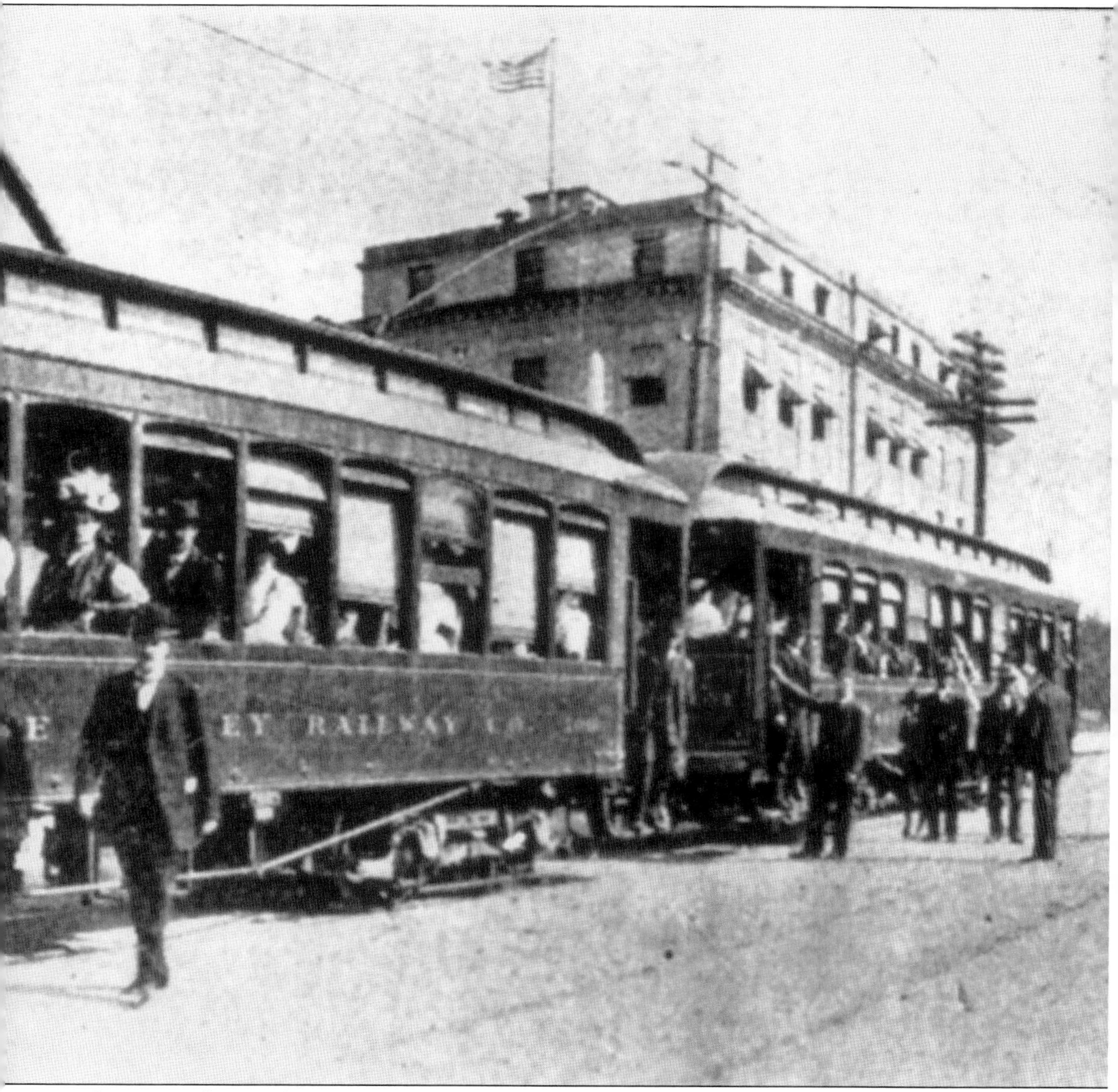

now known as the Borah Station Post Office, is shown in the background on the right.

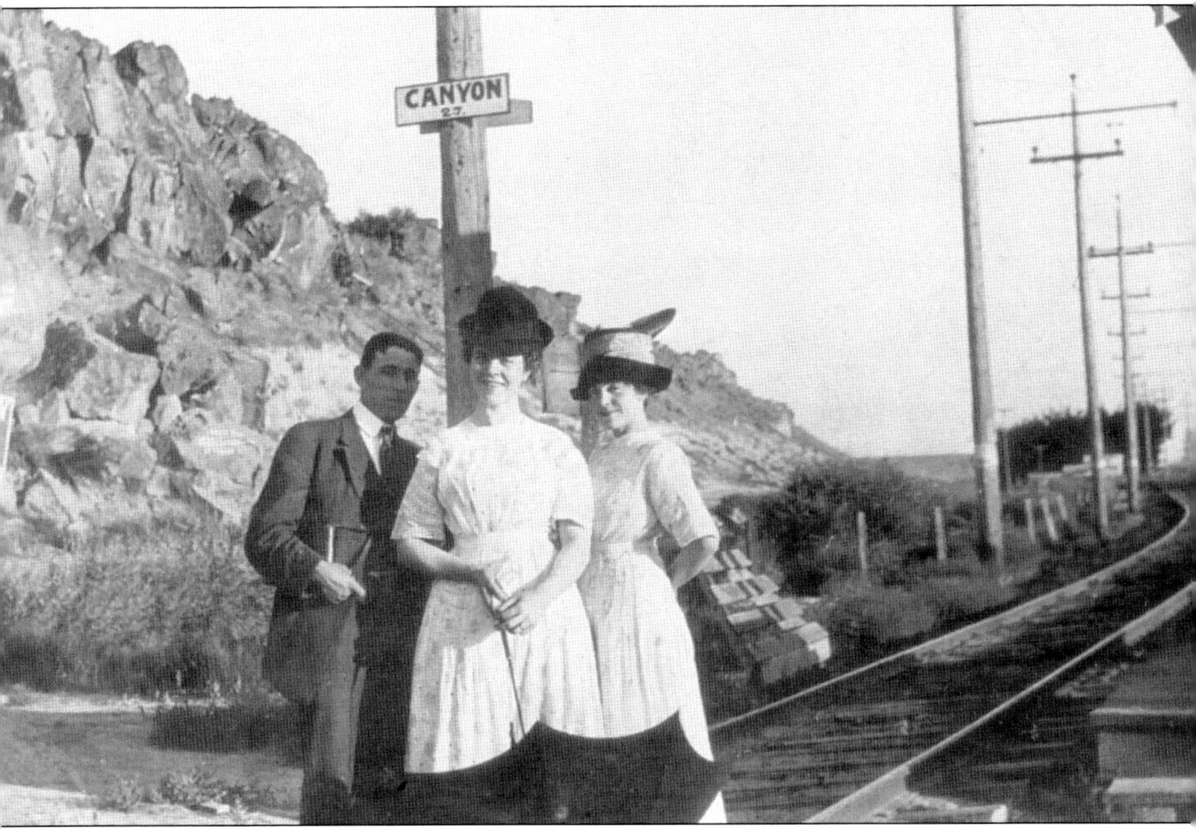

This c. 1910 photograph shows three unidentified people waiting for the interurban at the Canyon stop, located approximately one and a half miles north of Caldwell.

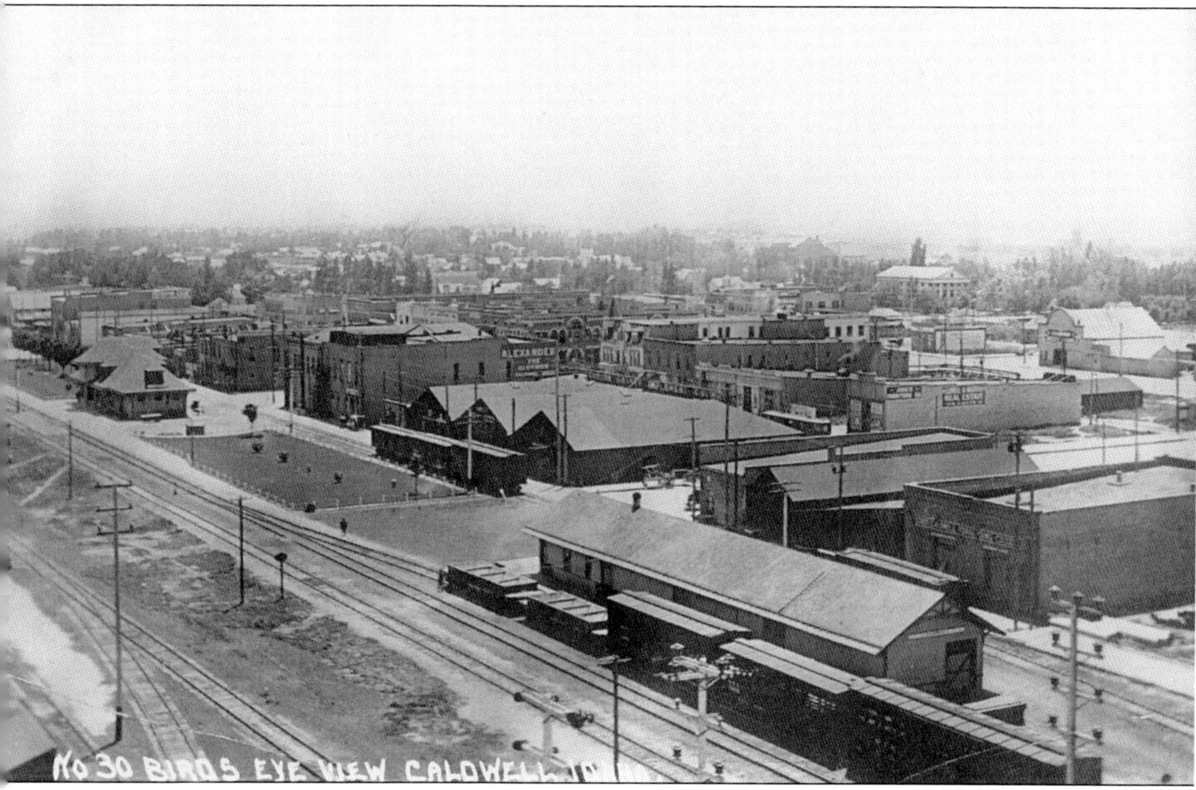

The railroad and the interurban street railway were vital to the growth and development of Caldwell. The Oregon Short Line Railroad depot is visible on the left side of this image. An interurban car can be seen on Main Street, passing in front of the Jones Furniture Company building. (Courtesy of John Aguirre.)

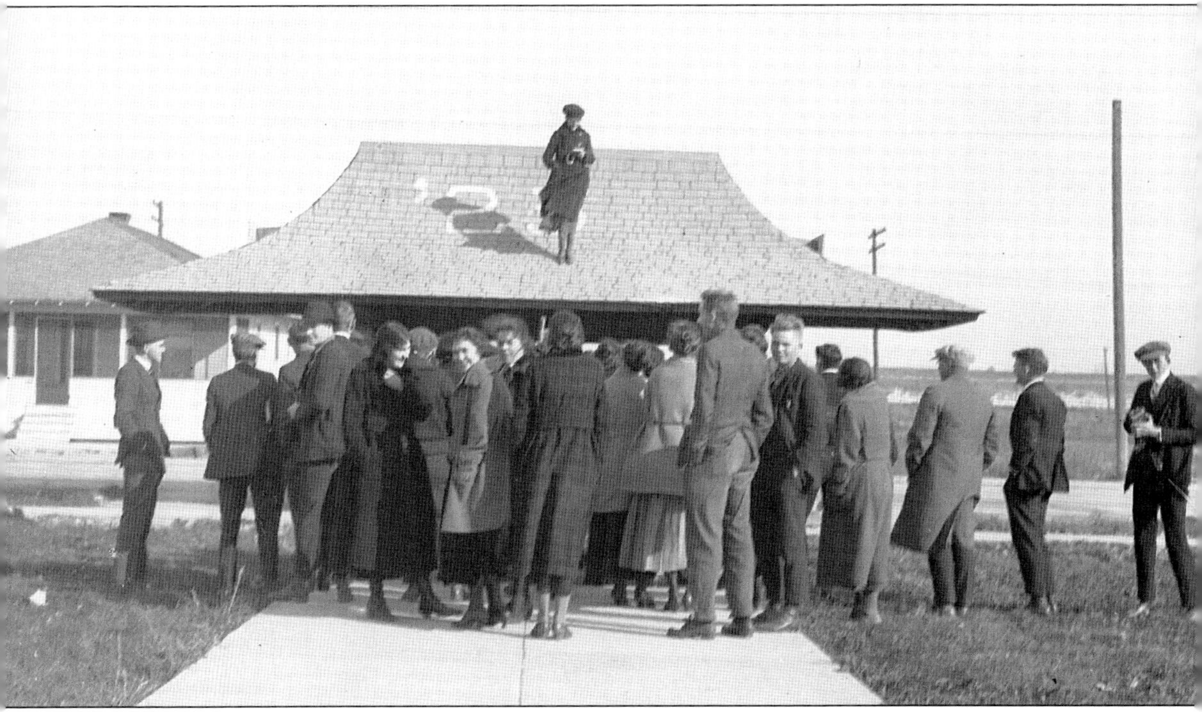

The Idaho Traction Company (ITC) constructed a passenger waiting station at the College of Idaho campus in 1912. The structure, affectionately called "the Hat" because of its resemblance to the fashionable merry widow hat, became a symbol for the college. Lucy Miller is pictured standing on the roof of the Hat in 1923. (Courtesy of the College of Idaho.)

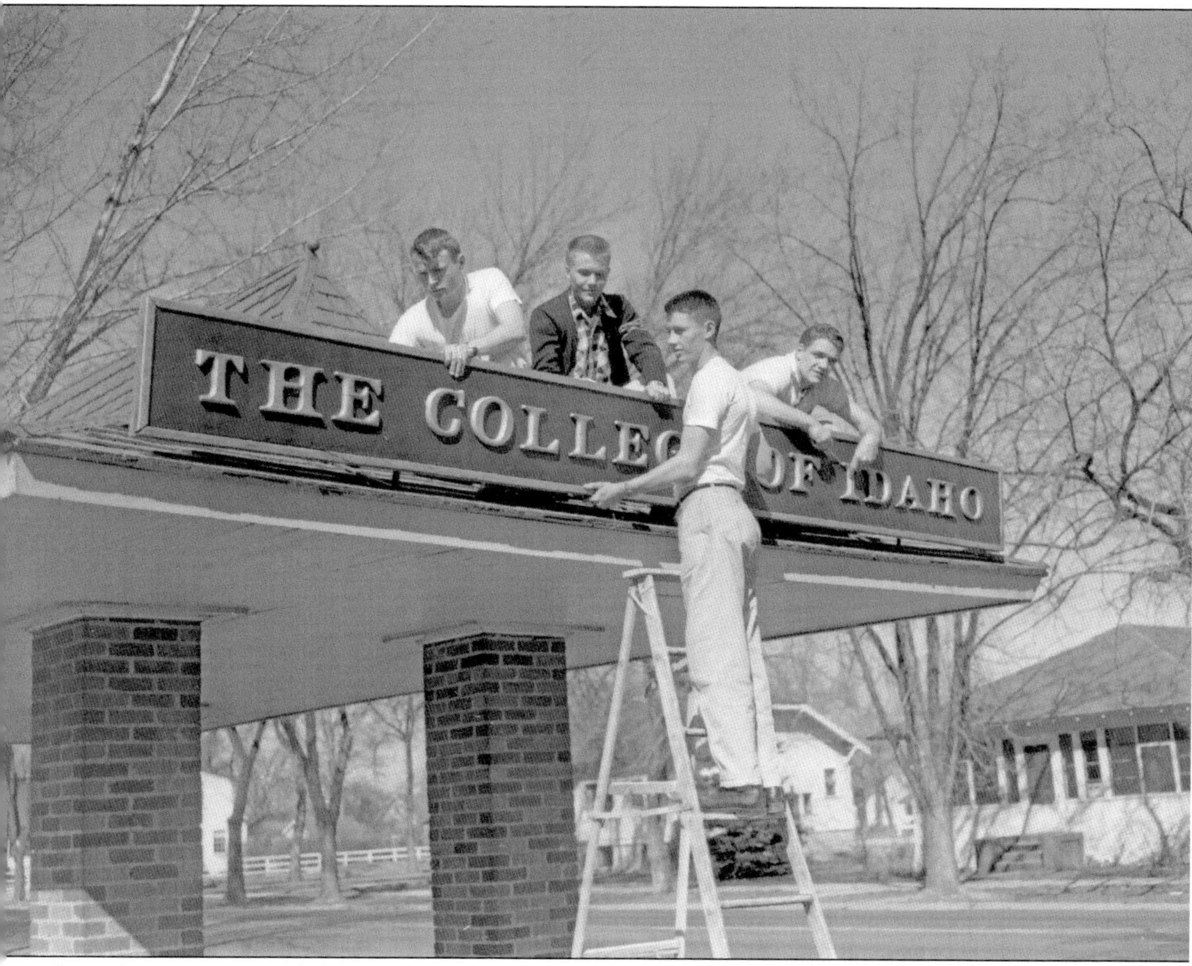

Over the years, many changes were made to the Hat. Originally constructed as a wood-enclosed building, its walls were removed and replaced with wood pillars clad with lapped siding. In 1926, College of Idaho students replaced the wood pillars with brick masonry, but kept the original roof in place. After it was struck by a bus and damaged, the Hat was moved from its original location on Cleveland Boulevard closer to campus. The rebuilt structure became the entrance to the campus. Here, unidentified students are shown placing a sign on the roof around 1950. (Courtesy of the College of Idaho.)

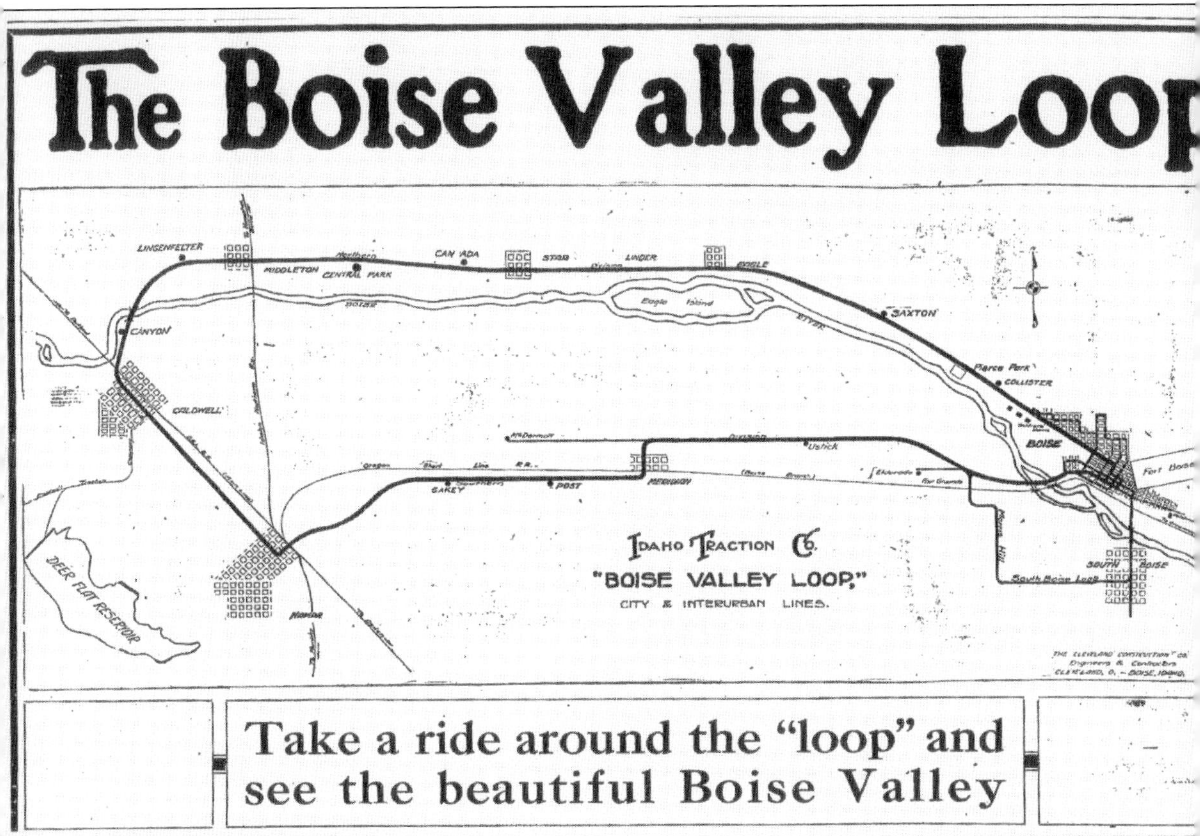

A 1912 advertisement shows the route of the interurban loop through the Treasure Valley. Sunday excursions on the loop to Pierce Park and Lake Lowell were advertised weekly in local newspapers. Round-trip excursion fares were $1.25 and included admission to the parks for boating, fishing, and attending baseball games and concerts.

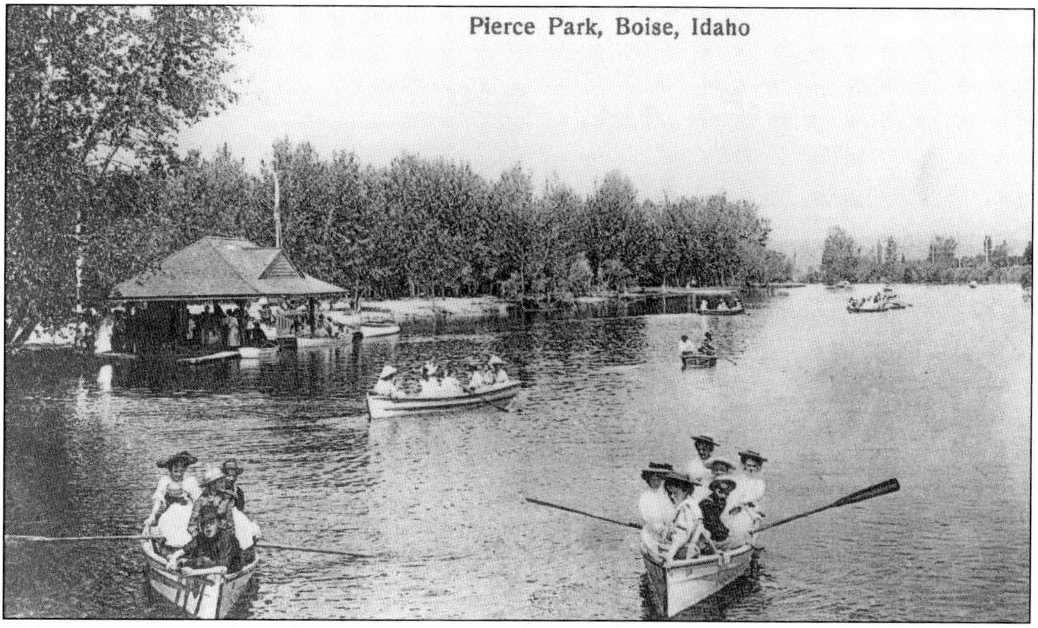

This postcard view shows boaters at Pierce Park, outside Boise. Pierce Park was not the only park on the loop; Walter Sebree and other Caldwell businessmen developed a park at Deer Flat Reservoir, which was also a popular destination. Area residents referred to the reservoir as "Lake Lowell" for many years before the name was officially adopted in 1948.

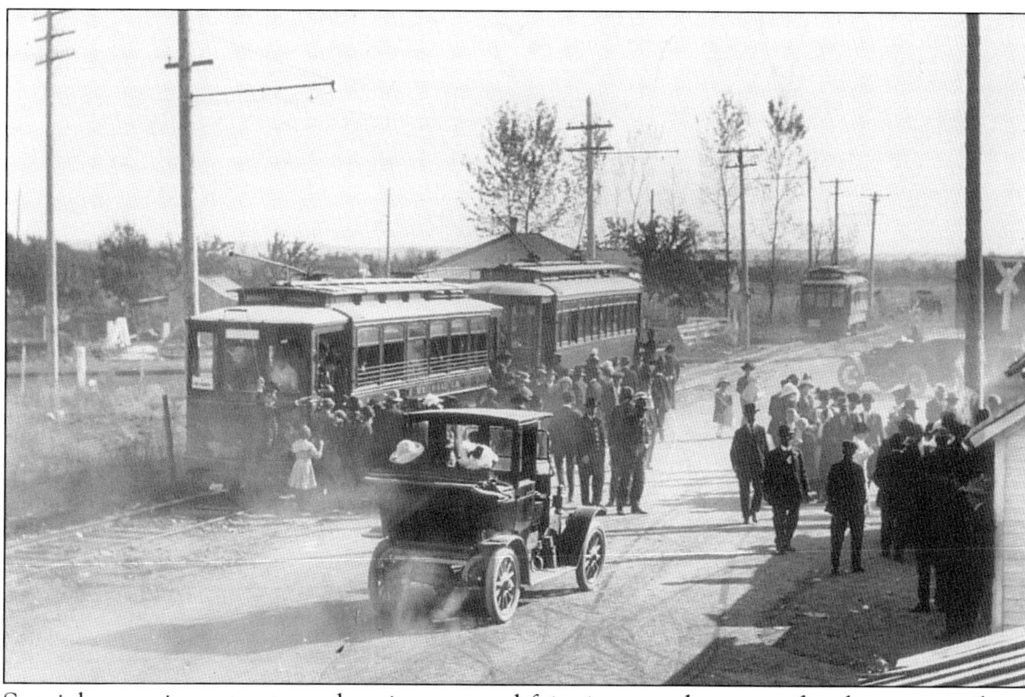

Special excursion rates to parks, circuses, and fairs increased revenue for the street railway companies. In 1915, the Ada County Fairgrounds were located at Orchard and Fairview Streets. This photograph shows a crowd of eager fairgoers disembarking.

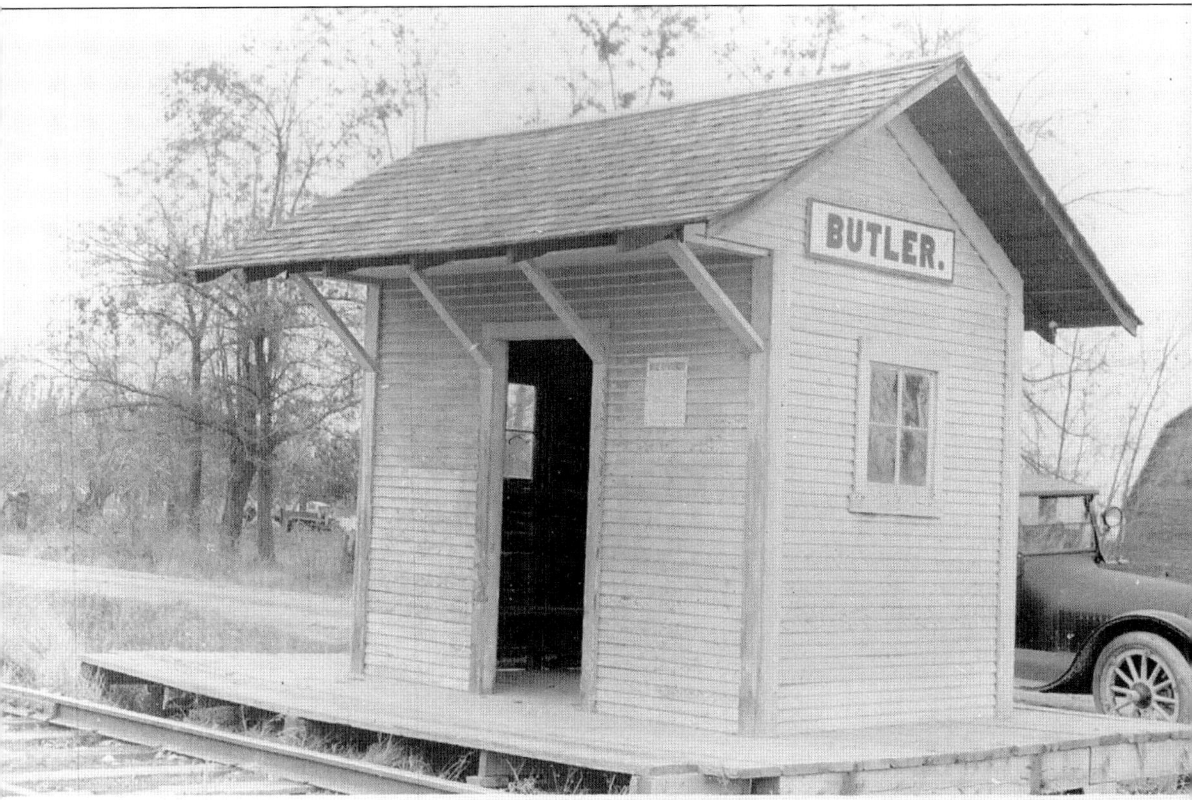

SHELTER STATION AT BUTLER 175

ITC contracted with the Cleveland (Ohio) Construction Company for construction of rail lines, bridges, and shelter stations. This station was located on the Southern Division of the loop, approximately seven miles from Boise.

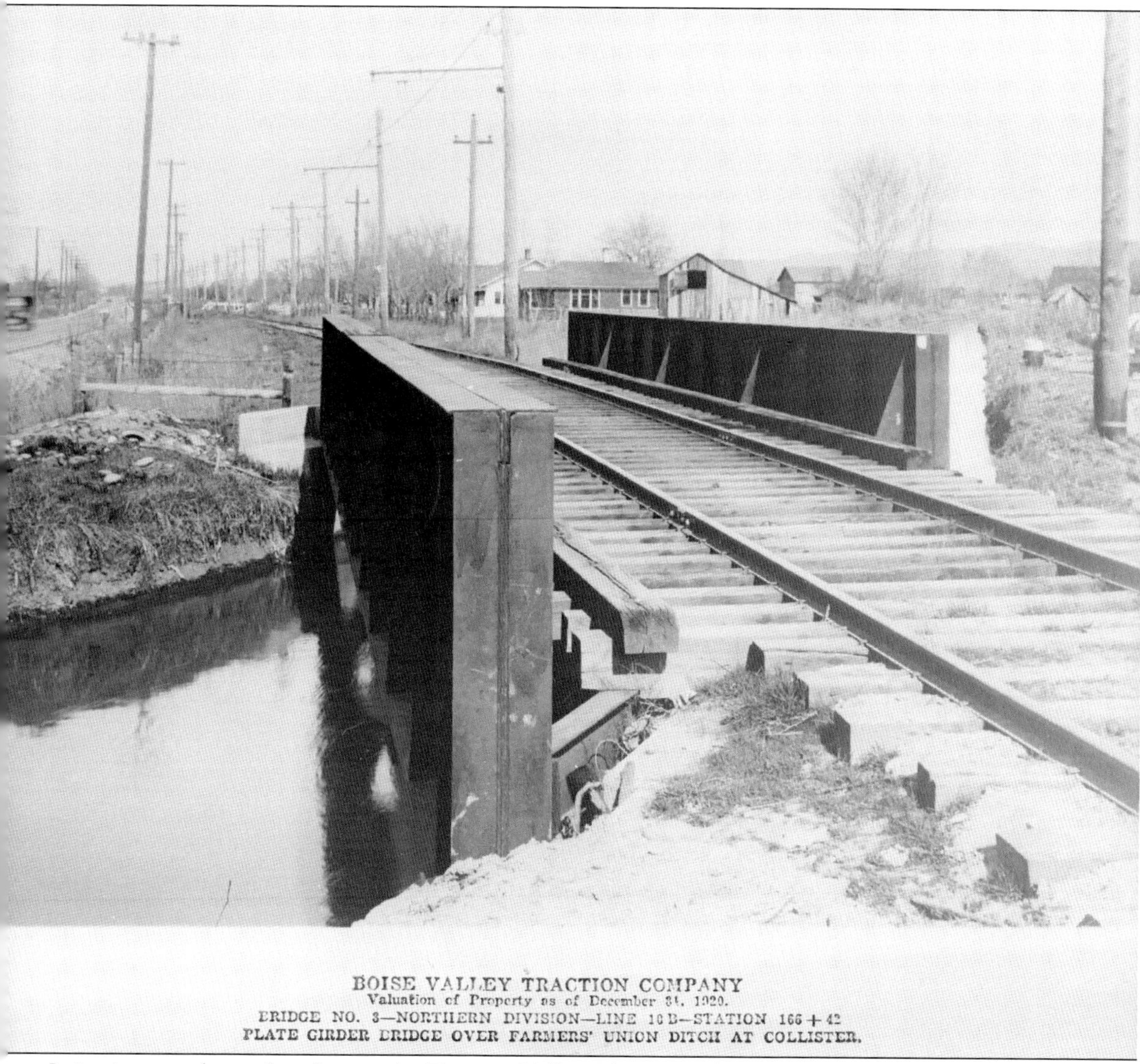

Irrigation canals are abundant in the Treasure Valley. This 1920 photograph shows a girder bridge over the Farmers' Union Ditch at Collister on the northern route.

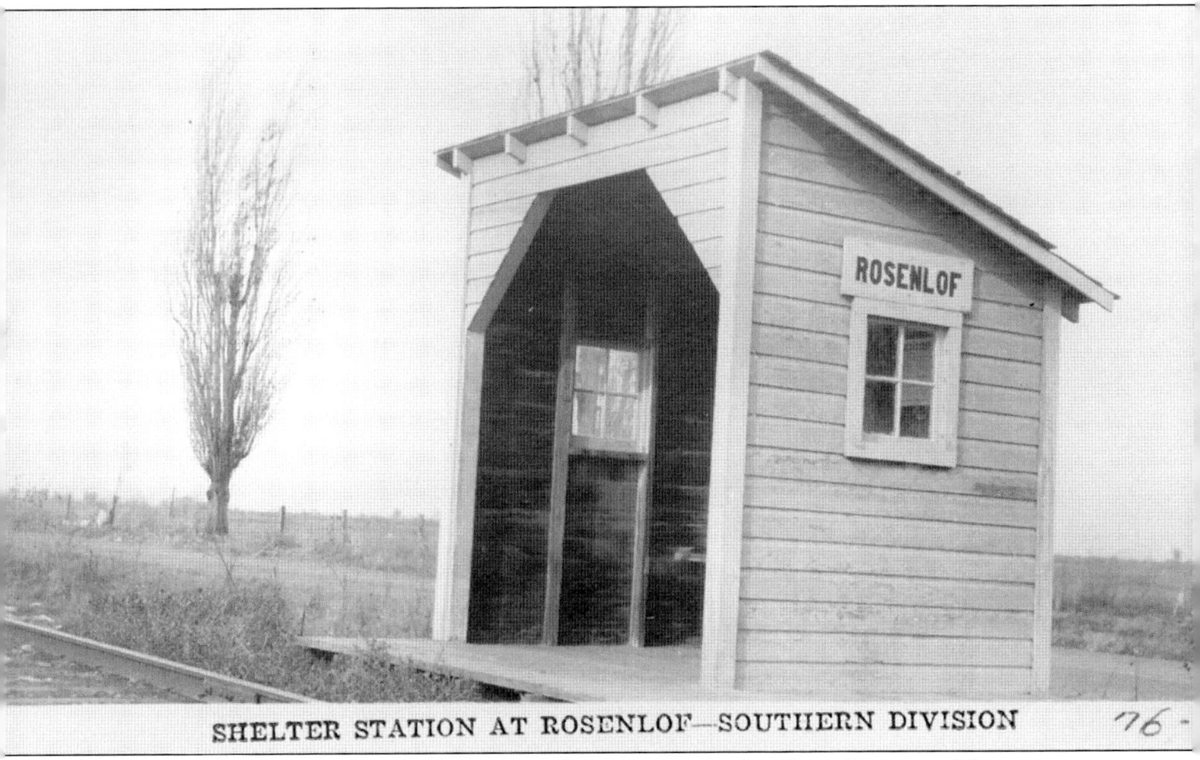

The shelter station at Rosenlof was east of Nampa, on the Southern Division. The stations were often named for the farmers whose land bordered the right-of-way for the line. Frank and Olive Rosenlof raised sheep and other livestock near the station, which bore their name.

Five

Serving the Treasure Valley

The streetcar and the interurban were a boon to town residents, farmers, and fruit growers. Most of the revenue came from passengers who paid to travel the 44-mile route between towns. Freight business also made up a significant percentage of revenue. Farmers and fruit growers were able to ship their sugar beets and fruit to connections with the Oregon Short Line, a subsidiary of the Union Pacific, at Caldwell, Nampa, and Middleton. When the line was rebuilt in 1912 with a connection from Boise to Nampa through Meridian, most of the old line was abandoned. The exception was a four-mile spur westward, from Onweiler to McDermott, which the company kept in service until 1922 under a lease agreement whereby local residents agreed to bear the losses.

The intricate relationship between the street railway companies and power companies is evident in the transfer of ownership between 1912 and 1918. As mentioned in the previous chapter, in 1912, the BVRC and the B&I were combined and jointly operated by the ITC. In 1915, the properties were transferred to a new company, the Boise Valley Traction Company, owned by the Idaho Power Company and a subsidiary (through a complicated pyramid of holding companies) of Electric Bond & Share.

The system remained profitable until 1920. World War I helped spur the freight and passenger service, but by 1924, the electric railway was feeling the effects of the increased use of trucks and automobiles. The streetcar company encouraged passengers to "Use the Street Car for Business – Your Automobile for Pleasure." But the lure of individual automobile ownership and improving public roads was too strong, and the electric railway companies in the Treasure Valley lost passengers in a nationwide trend. Revenues continued to decline, and, in 1925, bondholders started the long process of foreclosure. The system was finally abandoned in 1928.

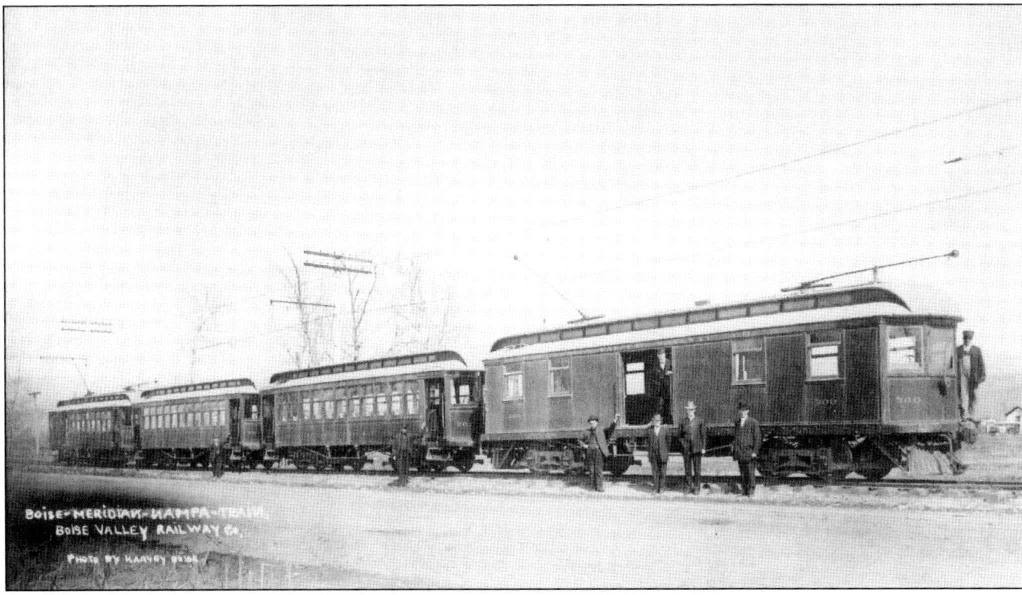

The BVRC was the first company to provide interurban service to Meridian, a farming community west of Boise, in July 1908. The line came from Onweiler Station at Ustick and Meridian Roads and was completed to Nampa the next year. Passenger and freight cars moved between Treasure Valley sites until May 1928. This photograph, taken around 1909, shows BVRC Car No. 300, a freight car, in front. Three passenger cars are lined up behind.

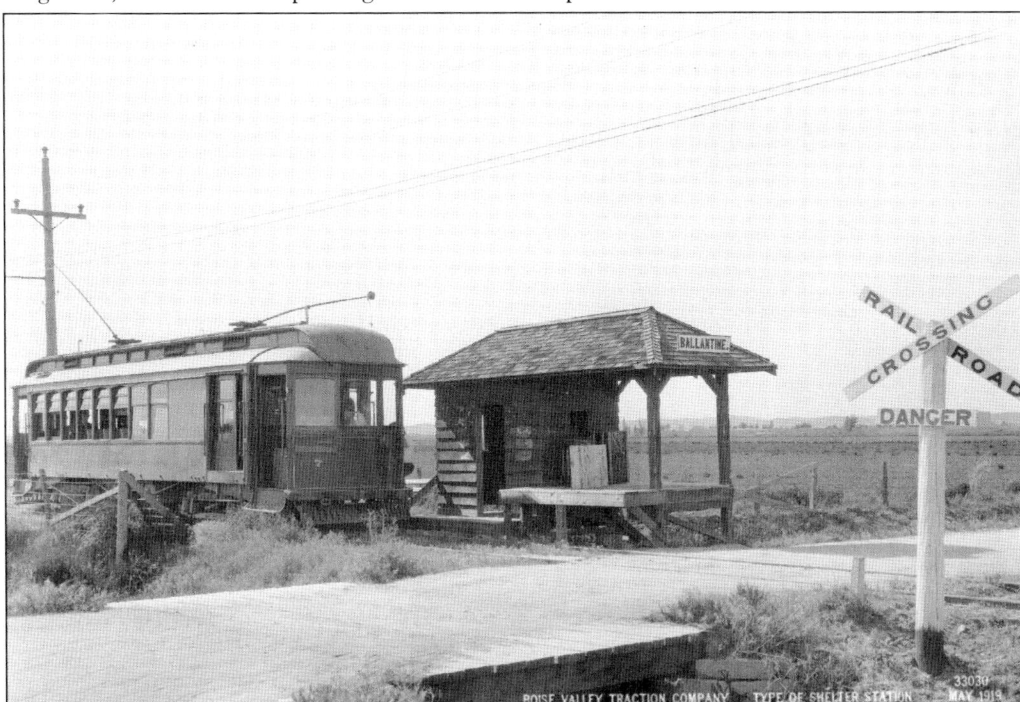

BVTC Car No. 7 waits at the Ballentine shelter station on the northern route in this 1919 photograph. A combination car, it could hold both passengers and freight. (Courtesy of Idaho Power Company.)

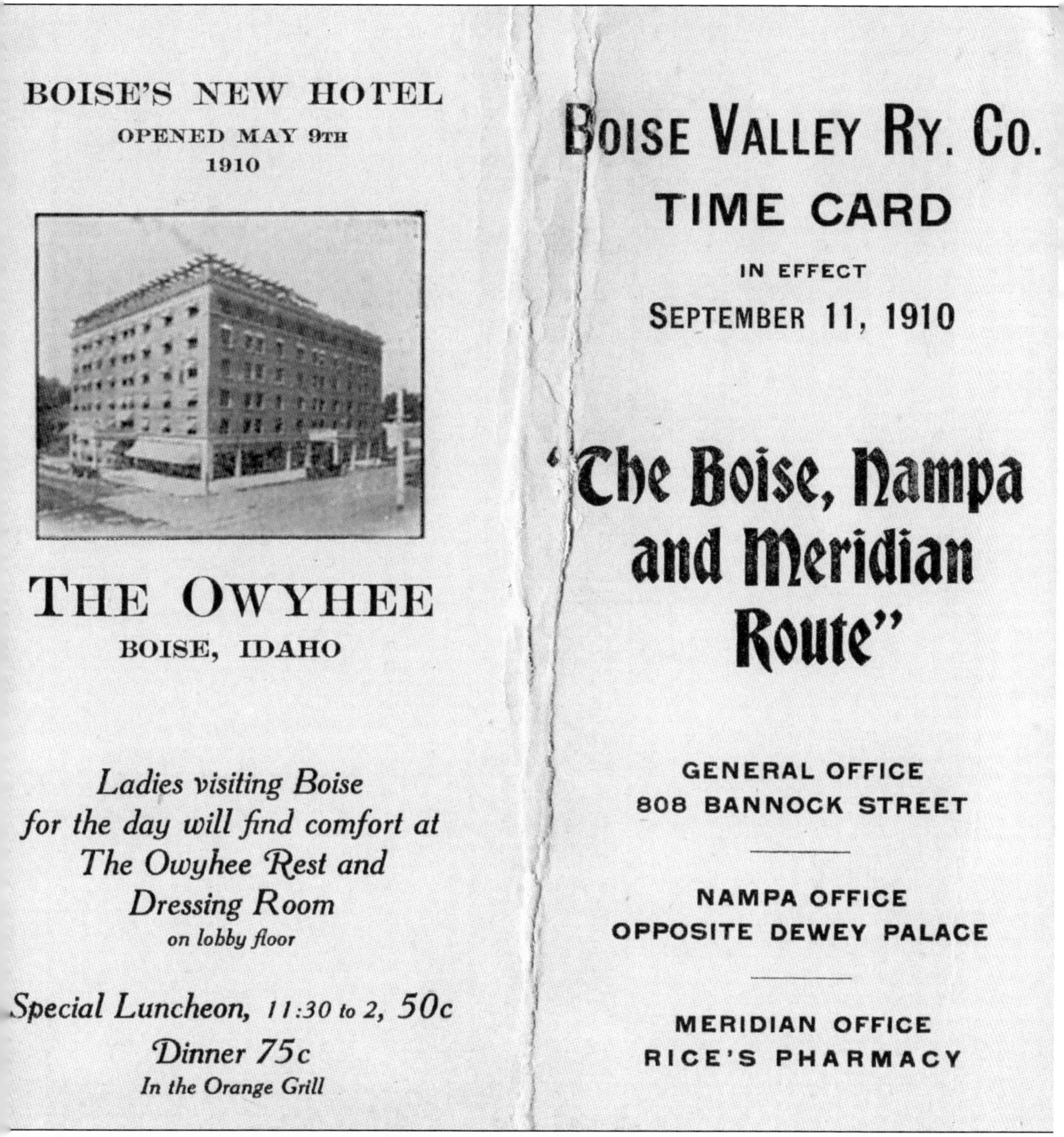

BOISE'S NEW HOTEL
OPENED MAY 9TH
1910

THE OWYHEE
BOISE, IDAHO

Ladies visiting Boise for the day will find comfort at The Owyhee Rest and Dressing Room
on lobby floor

Special Luncheon, 11:30 to 2, 50c
Dinner 75c
In the Orange Grill

BOISE VALLEY RY. CO.
TIME CARD
IN EFFECT
SEPTEMBER 11, 1910

"The Boise, Nampa and Meridian Route"

GENERAL OFFICE
808 BANNOCK STREET

NAMPA OFFICE
OPPOSITE DEWEY PALACE

MERIDIAN OFFICE
RICE'S PHARMACY

The front of this 1910 BVRC timetable has an advertisement for the Owyhee Hotel in Boise. The elegant hotel, which featured a rooftop garden, was popular for many years. Tickets to ride the BVRC were purchased from Rice Pharmacy in Meridian. (Courtesy of John Aguirre.)

BOISE - NAMPA DIVISION

LEAVE BOISE	Leave Eich'berger	Leave Ustick	Leave Yost	Leave Onwiler	Leave Victory	Leave Noble	Leave Co. Ranch	Leave Sugar Fact.	LEAVE NAMPA
	7.55 am	7.50 am	7.45 am	7.40 am	7.35 am	7.25 am	7.15 am	7.05 am	7.00 a
8.30 am	8.55 am	9.00 am	9.05 am	9.10 am	9.15 am	9.23 am	9.30 am	9.40 am	
	10.55 am	10.50 am	10.45 am	10.40 am	10.32 am	10.23 am	10.15 am	10.05 am	10.00 a
11.30 am	11.55 am	12.00 m	12.05 pm	12 10 pm	12.15 pm	12.25 pm	12.30 pm	12.40 pm	
	1.55 pm	1.50 pm	1.45 pm	1.40 pm	1.35 pm	1.25 pm	1.15 pm	1.05 pm	1.00 p
2.30 pm	2.55 pm	3.00 pm	3.05 pm	3.10 pm	3.15 pm	3.25 pm	3.35 pm	3.40 pm	
	4.55 pm	4.50 pm	4.45 pm	4.40 pm	4.35 pm	4.25 pm	4.15 pm	4.05 pm	4.00 p
5.30 pm	5.55 pm	6.00 pm	6.05 pm	6.10 pm	6.15 pm	6.25 pm	6.35 pm	6.40 pm	
	7.55 pm	7.50 pm	7.45 pm	7.40 pm	7.35 pm	7.25 pm	7.15 pm	7.05 pm	7.00 p
8.30 pm	8.55 pm	9.00 pm	9.05 pm	9.10 pm	9.15 pm	9.25 pm	9.35 pm	9.40 pm	
	10.55 pm	10.50 pm	10.45 pm	10.40 pm	10.35 pm	10.25 pm	10.15 pm	10.05 pm	10.00 p
11.30 pm	11.55 pm	12.00 pm	12.05 am	12.10 am	12.15 am	12.25 am	12.35 am	12.40 am	

NAMPA OFFICE--OPPOSITE DEWEY PALACE HOTEL

BOISE - MERIDIAN DIVISION

Meridian Offic
Rice's Pharm

LEAVE BOISE	LeaveEich'berger	Leave Ustick	Leave Yost	Leave Onwiler	LEAVE MERIDI
	6.50 am	6.45 am	6.40 am	6.35 am	6.30 am
7.00 am	7.25 am	7.30 am	7.35 am	7.40 am	
	8.20 am	8.15 am	8.10 am	8.05 am	8.00 am
9.00 am	9.25 am	9.30 am	9.35 am	9.40 am	
	10.20 am	10.15 am	10.10 am	10.05 am	10.00 am
11.15 am	11.40 am	11.45 am	11.50 am	11.55 am	
	12.25 pm	12.20 pm	12.15 pm	12.10 pm	12.05 pm
1.00 pm	1.25 pm	1.30 pm	1.35 pm	1.40 pm	
	2.20 pm	2.15 pm	2.10 pm	2.05 pm	2.00 pm
3.00 pm	3.25 pm	3.30 pm	3.25 pm	3.40 pm	
	4.20 pm	4.15 pm	4.10 pm	4.05 pm	4.00 pm
5.00 pm	5.25 pm	5.30 pm	5.35 pm	5.40 pm	
	6.25 pm	6.20 pm	6.15 pm	6.10 pm	6.00 pm
7.00 pm	7.25 pm	7.30 pm	7.35 pm	7.40 pm	
	8.20 pm	8.15 pm	8.10 pm	8.05 pm	8.00 pm
11.30 pm	11.55 pm	12.00 pm	12.05 am	12.10 am	

CITY CARS: *Morris Hill*—¼ after each hour; first car 6:30 a. m.
South Boise—¼ before and after each hour; first car 7:15 a. m.
An extra car leaves Boise for Ustick at 10:00 p. m. Saturdays.

The back of the timetable names the stations on the route. The main line was rerouted through Meridian after local citizens raised $4,000 to pay for the extension from Onweiler into town and south down Franklin Road toward Nampa. (Courtesy of John Aguirre.)

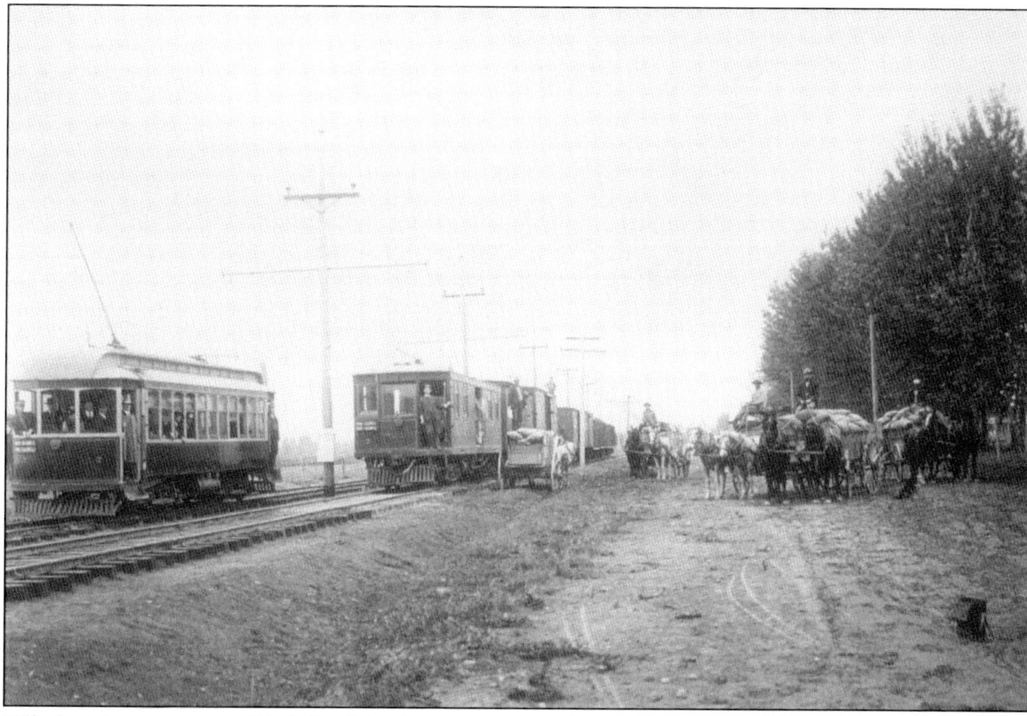

Filled with passengers, B&I Car No. 2 is stopped on the track near Middleton, Idaho, while B&I freight cars are loaded with farm products. The B&I's rolling stock for cargo consisted of freight cars (used for rough bulk freight) and express cars (used for package freight).

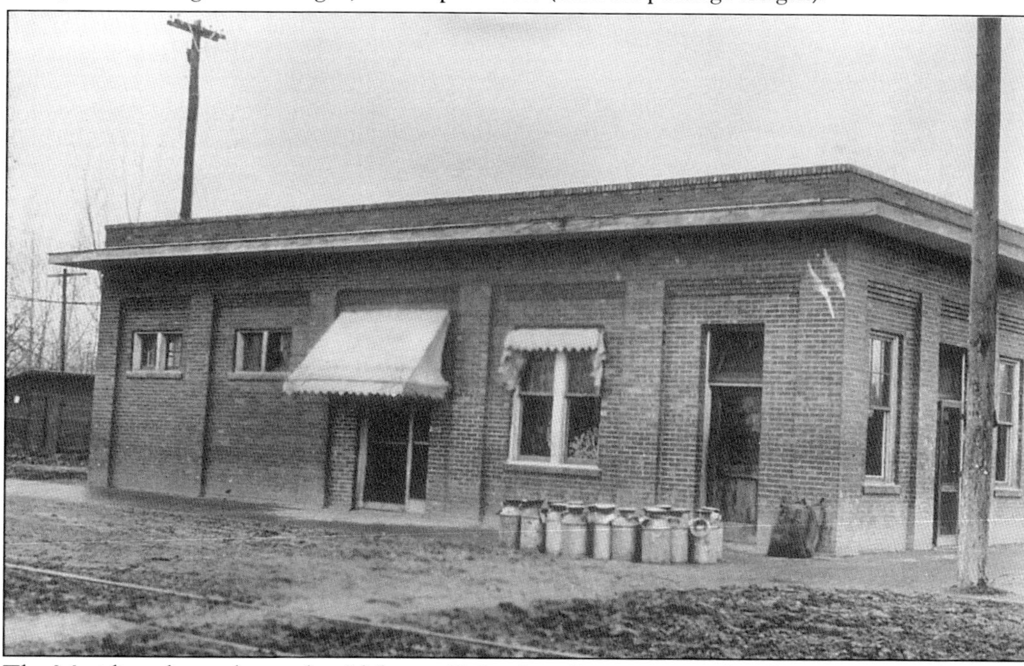

The Meridian depot, located at Idaho and Meridian Streets, opened in January 1913. The depot housed the generator, freight, and ticket offices. Note the milk cans waiting to be loaded on a freight car for delivery.

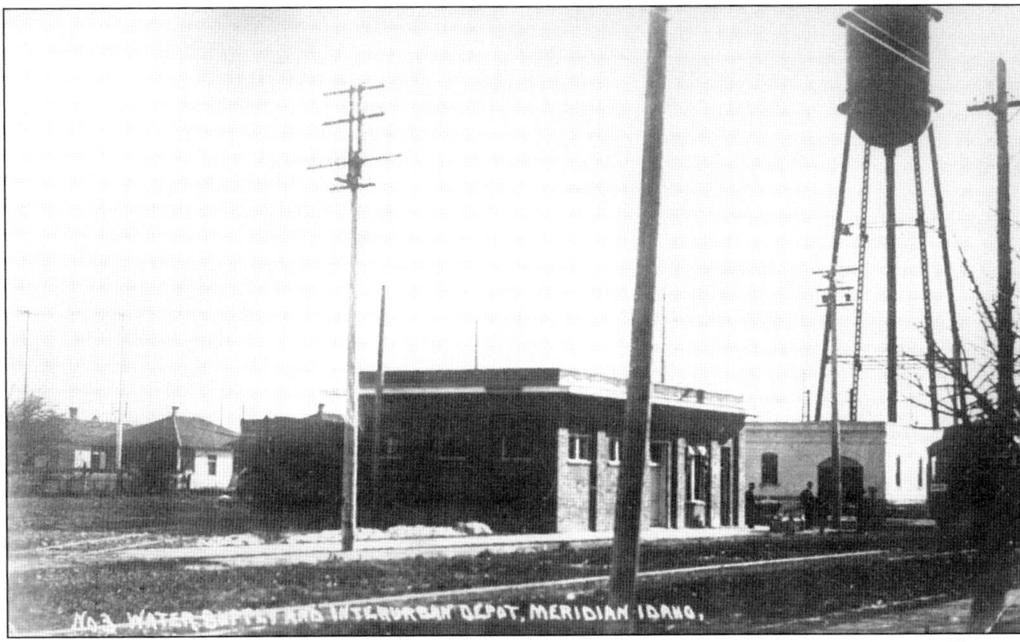

Passengers and freight are being loaded onto a waiting interurban car at Meridian. Following the closure of the BVTC in 1928, the former depot became the home of the Occident Club, a community organization. The structure was later incorporated into the city library building. (Courtesy of John Aguirre.)

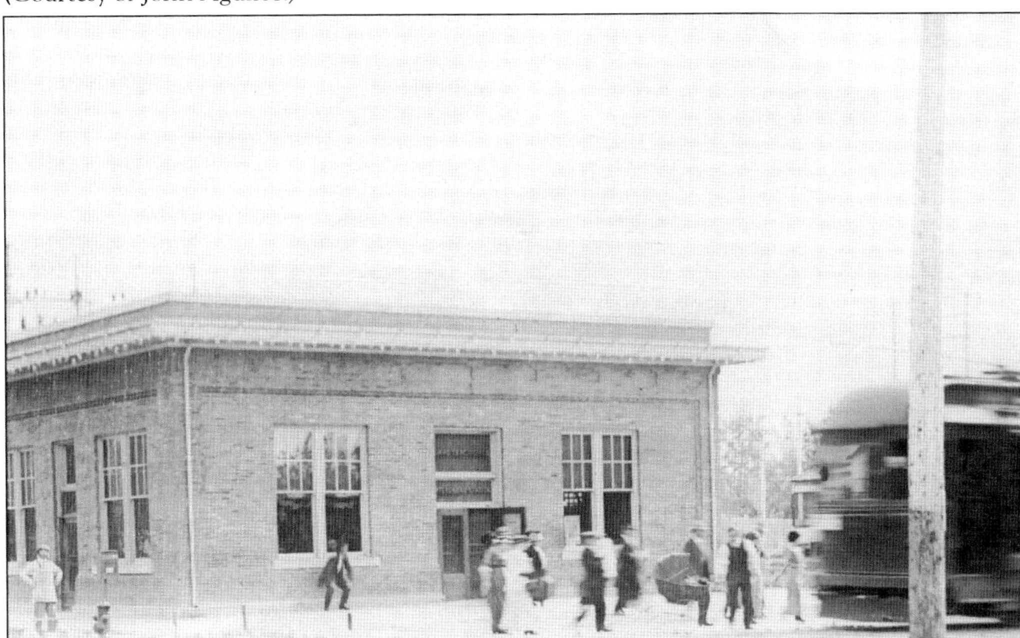

ITC built additional depots and substations at Nampa and Caldwell. In Nampa, the company constructed a substation, light and power office, and passenger depot at the corner of Second Street and Eleventh Avenue South. This photograph, taken around 1917, shows passengers (including a man with a baby carriage) boarding the interurban car. (Courtesy of John Aguirre.)

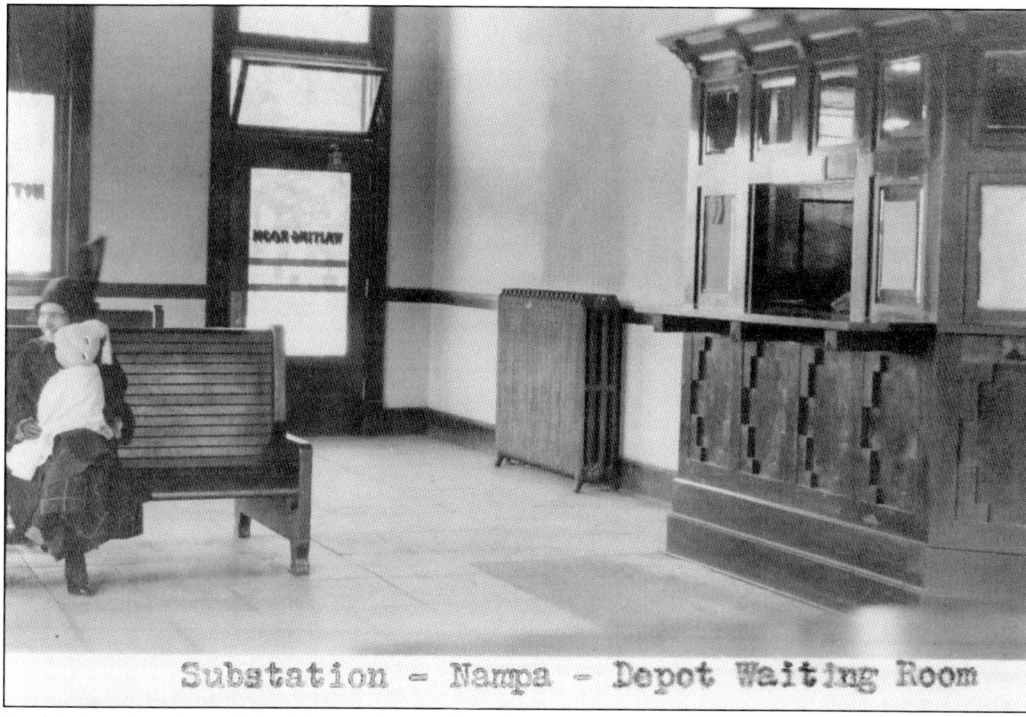

In this interior view of the Nampa interurban depot, a woman and her baby are seen waiting for the interurban. The Cleveland Construction Company designed the plans for the substations and interurban depots. After a disastrous fire in 1909 destroyed much of downtown Nampa, a new depot was constructed in 1912. It came to be considered one of the town's handsomest buildings.

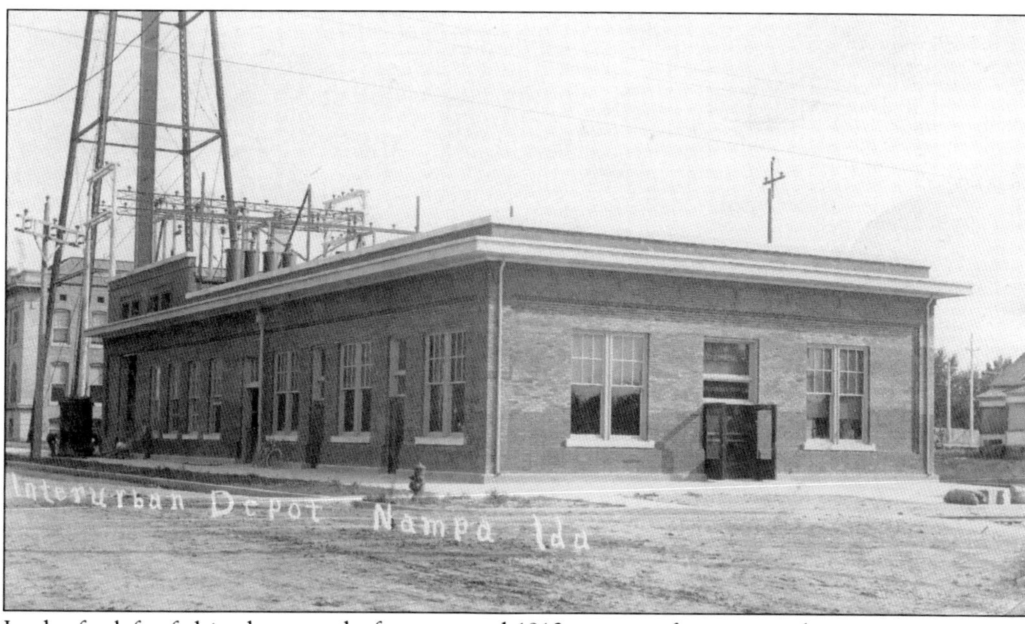

In the far left of this photograph, from around 1913, a crew of men is working on transmission lines of the powerhouse. The open doors at the entrance of the depot suggest that this may have been a warm day. (Courtesy of John Aguirre.)

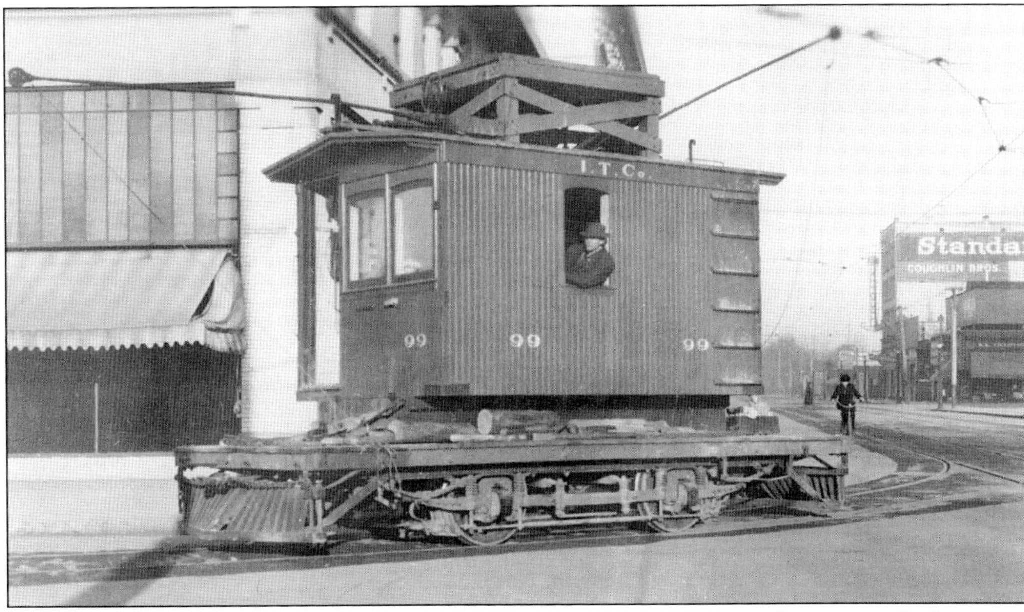

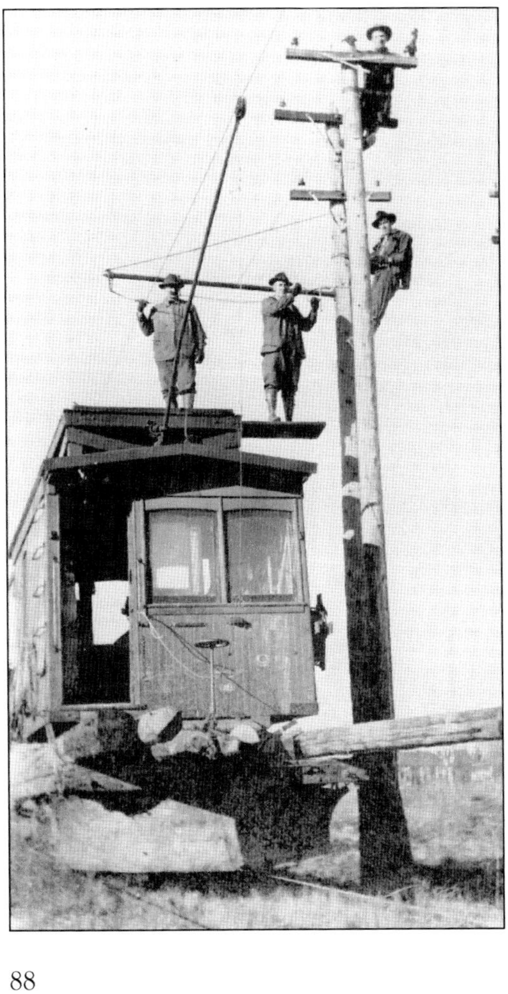

ITC Car No. 99, a work car, rounds the corner from Bannock Street to Seventh Street in downtown Boise. The work car transported crews throughout the Treasure Valley to repair the tracks, poles, and lines of the traction company.

An interurban maintenance crew works from the roof of ITC car No. 99. They are replacing a pole and attaching electric wire to the bracket arm (the pipe extension attached to the pole). The man on the left holds the wire in place as another man attaches it. The typical bracket arm held a horizontal wire at right angle to the track.

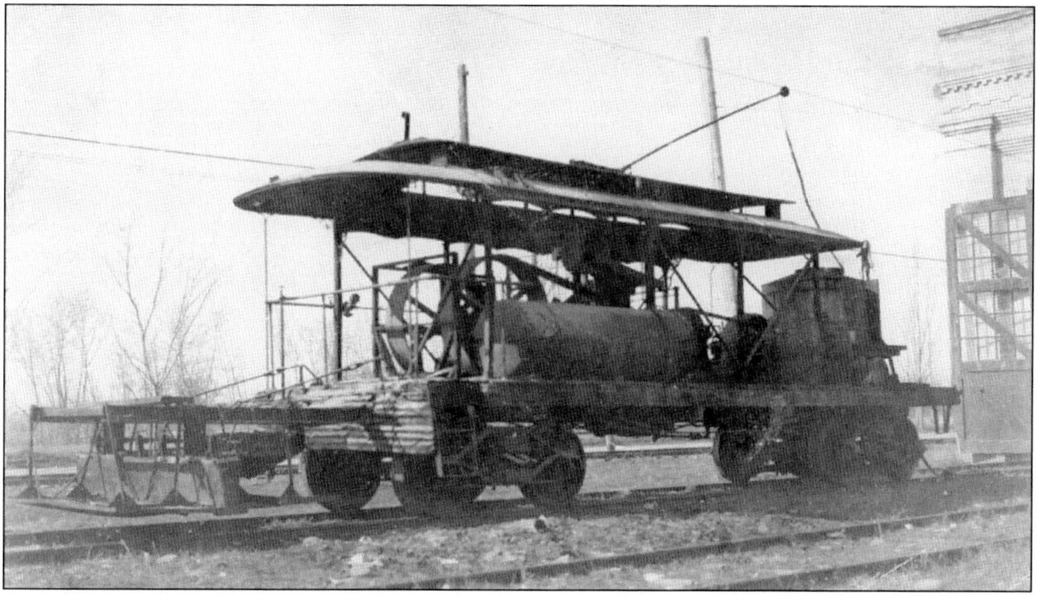

The companies' rolling stock did not just include passenger and freight cars. It was necessary to have maintenance stock to make repairs, move equipment, and burn weeds. Here, a work car with a steam engine is stopped at the Pierce Park carbarn.

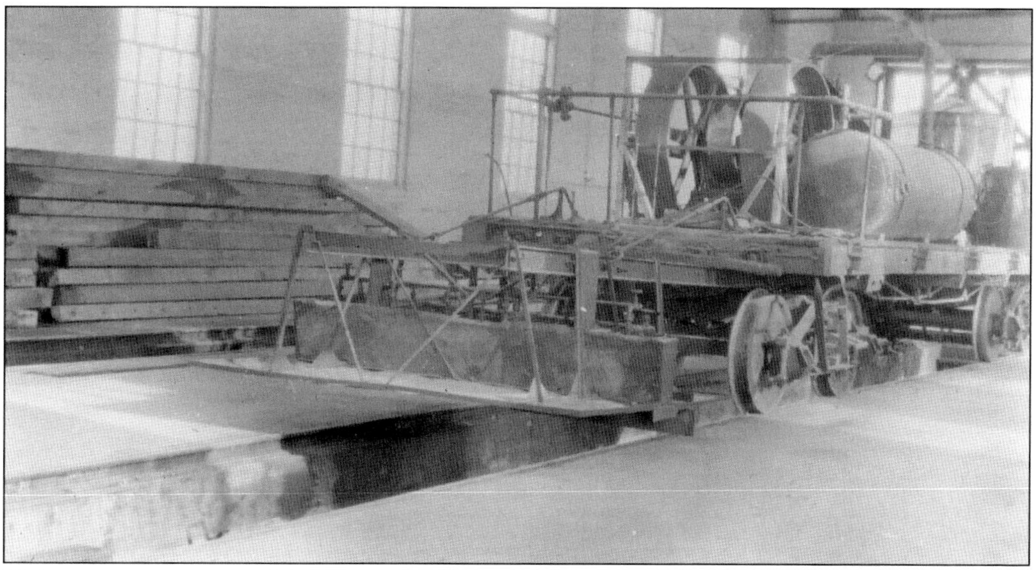

This contraption, a weed burner, was stored in the Pierce Park carbarn. The machine burned weeds and grass on the track, between the rails and two feet to either side. It was mounted on a flatcar, which also carried sand and water to prevent the spread of fire. Grass and weeds in the vicinity of the rails presented a fire hazard, and vegetation growing over the rails could become slick, potentially causing cars to derail.

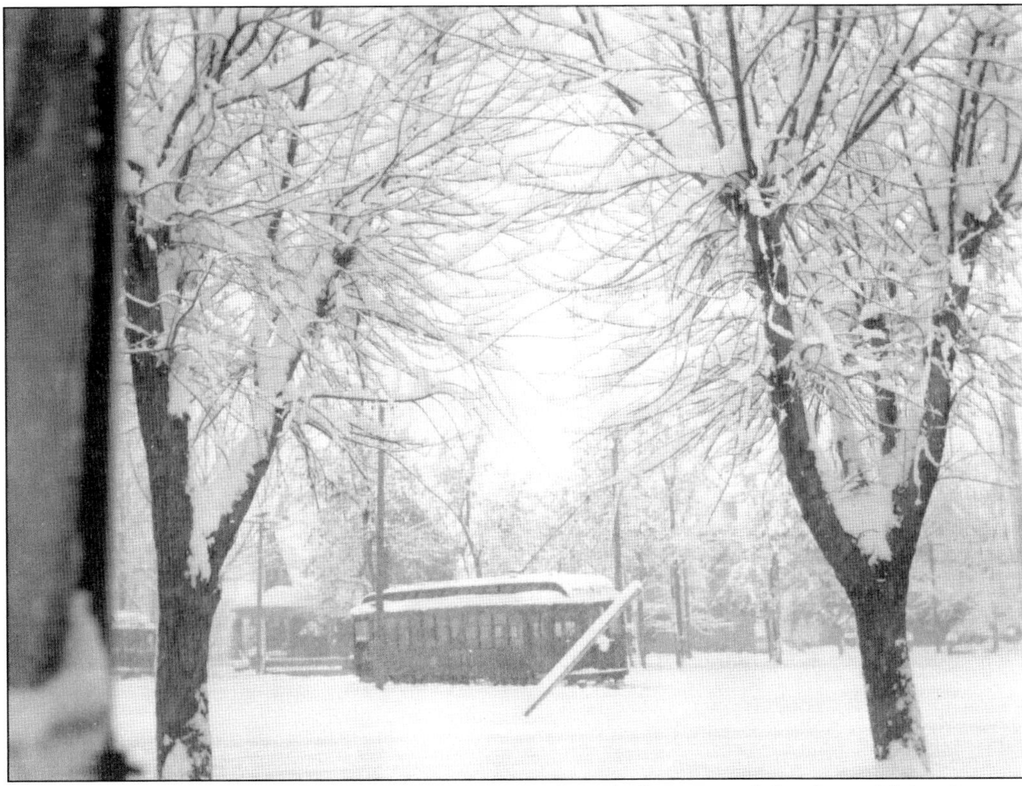

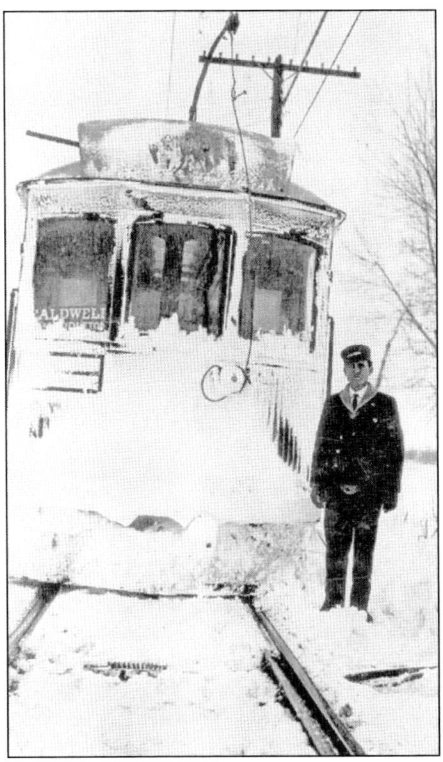

An unidentified city car glides down Idaho Street on a snowy winter day in Boise. Men wielding snow shovels and rotary snowplows attached to work engines helped keep the tracks clear of snow. The electric railway companies occasionally lost power when snow collected on the wires. (Courtesy of TAG Historical Research & Consulting.)

After a winter storm, conductor F.H. Turner poses with his snow-covered car on the line between Caldwell and Middleton. The tracks have been cleared of snow. Dressed in a wool-lined coat and gloves to protect against the cold, the conductor appears ready to continue the trip and pick up passengers.

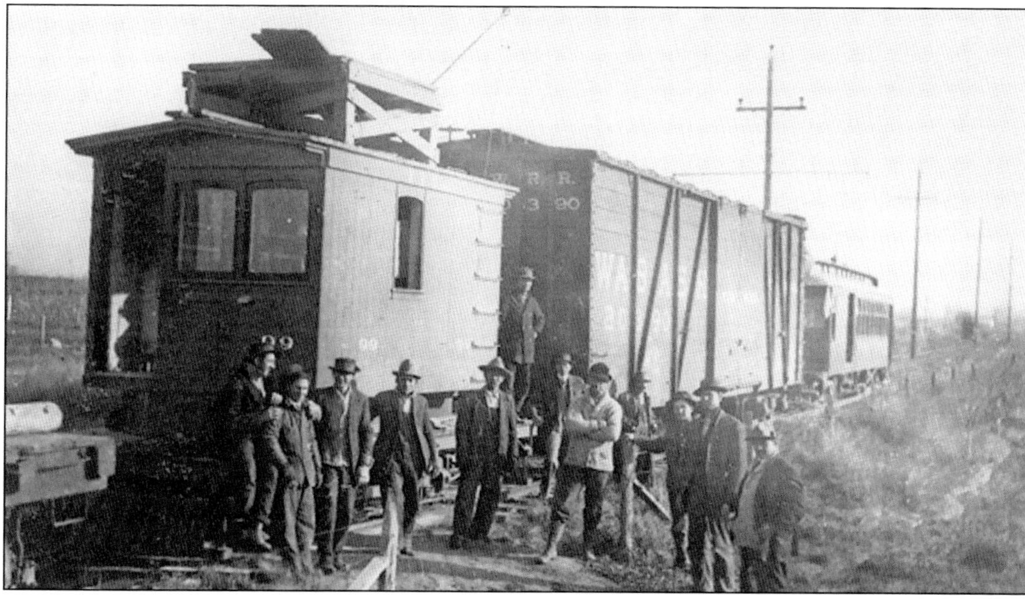

An ITC work crew poses with Car. No 99. Note the Wabash Railroad car placed between the work car and the passenger car at the rear.

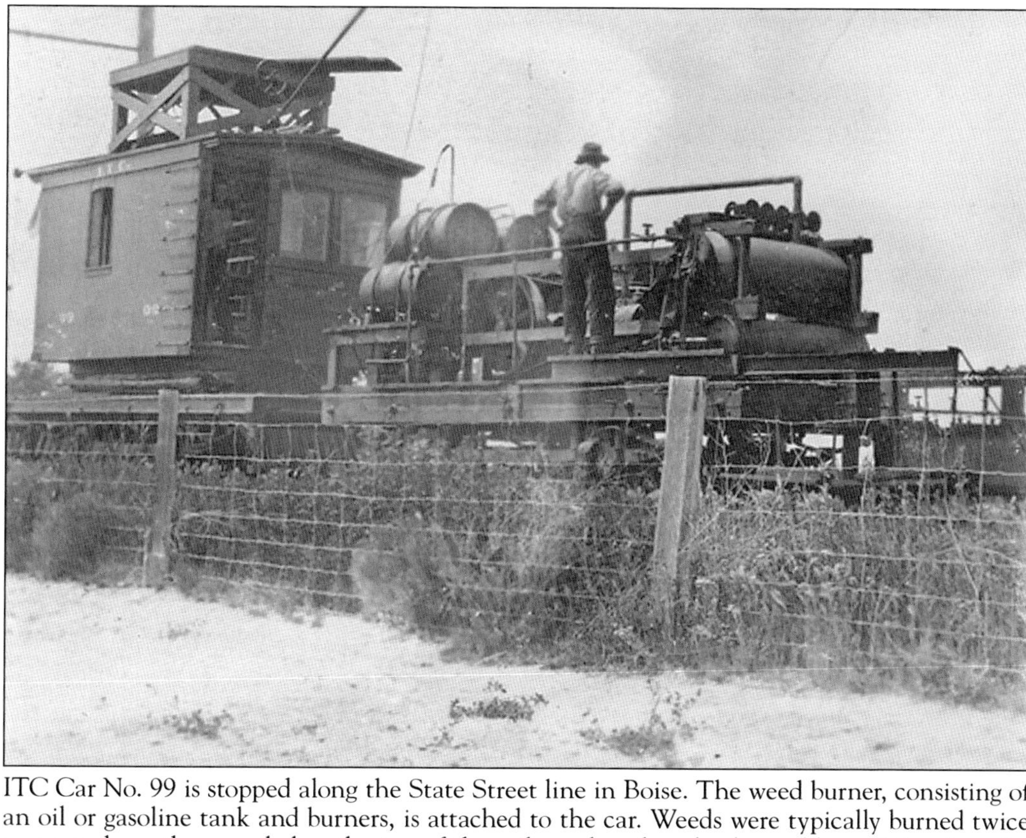

ITC Car No. 99 is stopped along the State Street line in Boise. The weed burner, consisting of an oil or gasoline tank and burners, is attached to the car. Weeds were typically burned twice a year to keep the grass below the top of the rails so that the wheels would not slide when the brakes were applied.

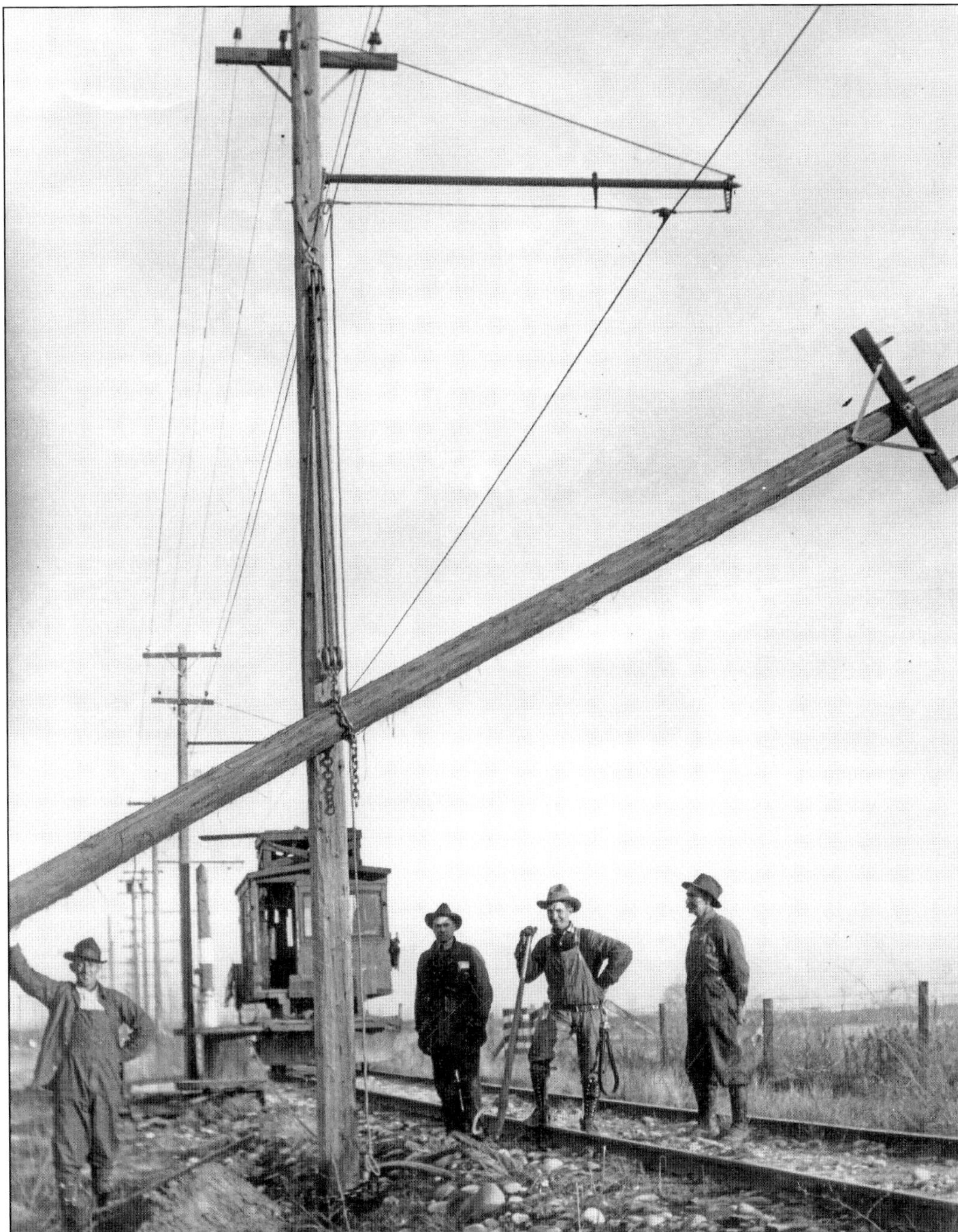

This group of unidentified men is replacing poles along the Ustick line. The man second from the right is equipped with leather boots and a safety belt to climb the pole.

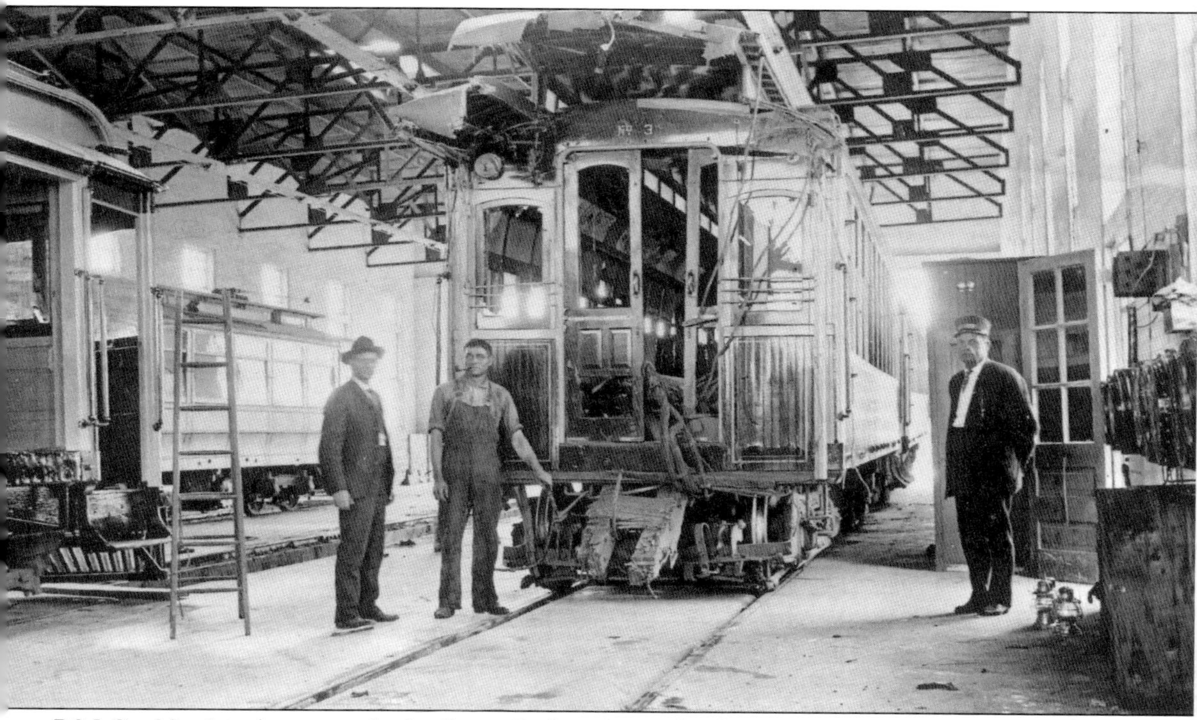

B&I Car No. 3 is shown inside the Pierce Park carbarn after being involved in a collision with Car No.1 near Eagle. A motorman was killed in the wreck.

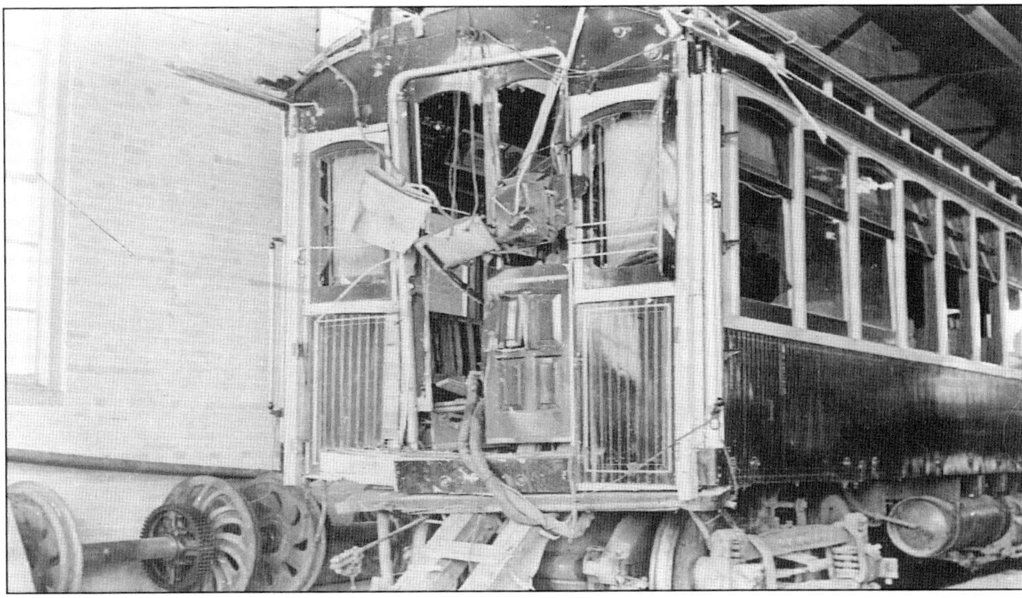

Pictured here is the damaged B&I Car No. 1 after an accident in the early evening of July 20, 1910. Car No. 1, eastbound from Caldwell to Boise, collided with Car No. 3, westbound from Boise to Caldwell. Headlights were required on the cars, but they had not yet been lit when the accident occurred on a dangerous tree-lined curve between Eagle and Boise. Motorman William Earwood was fatally injured, and a number of passengers were also hurt in the collision.

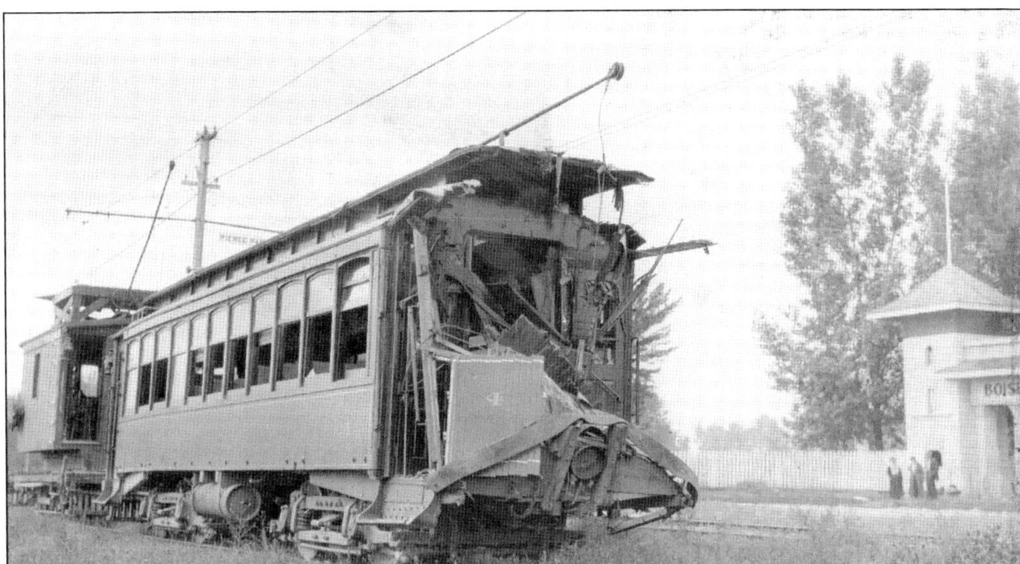

BVTC Car No. 4 is being moved to Pierce Park carbarn after being damaged in an accident. The Pierce Park Station sign is visible on the pole above the car, and the entrance to the Boise Country Club, formerly known as Pierce Park, is visible at the right. The Boise Country Club was formed in 1916 to provide a golf course for Boise. The new golf course laid out on the former park grounds was opened during June, 1917. Hole No. 10 bordered the trolley tracks, and the park dance pavilion was remodeled for use as the clubhouse. (Courtesy of John Aguirre.)

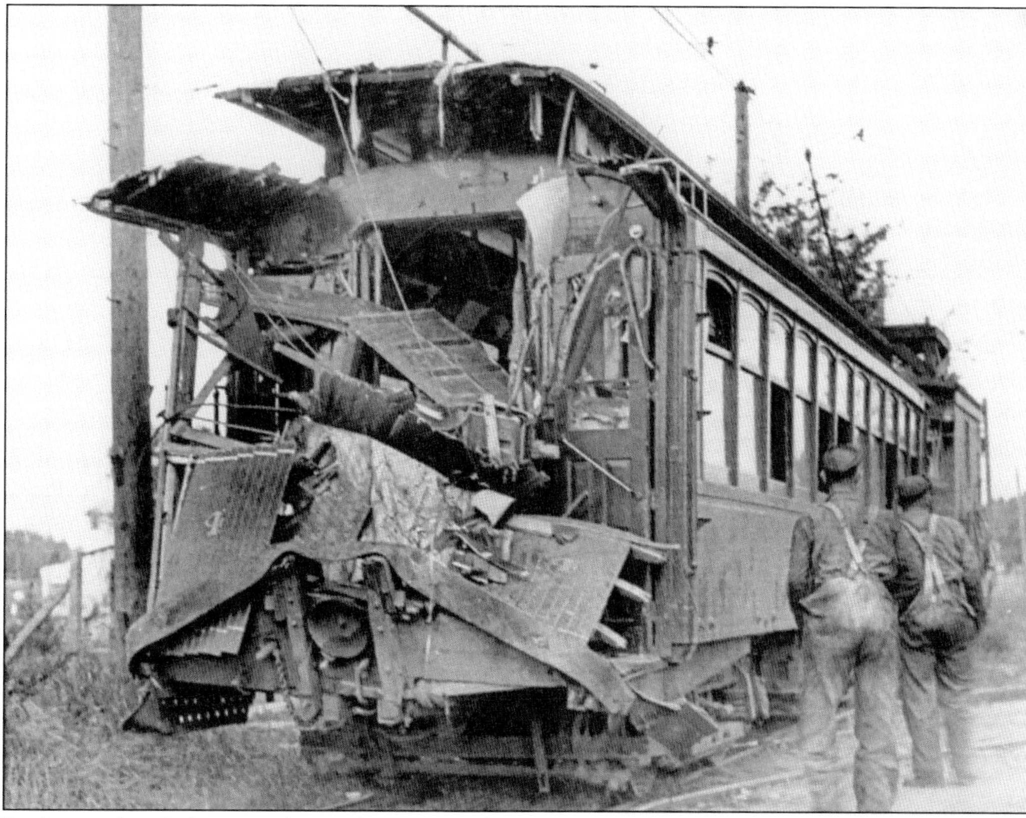

In this undated photograph, mechanics watch as the twisted and mangled BVTC Car No. 4 is moved to a carbarn for repair. Unfortunately, accidents were not uncommon on the interurban line. Damaged cars were repaired, if possible, and placed back in service on the line.

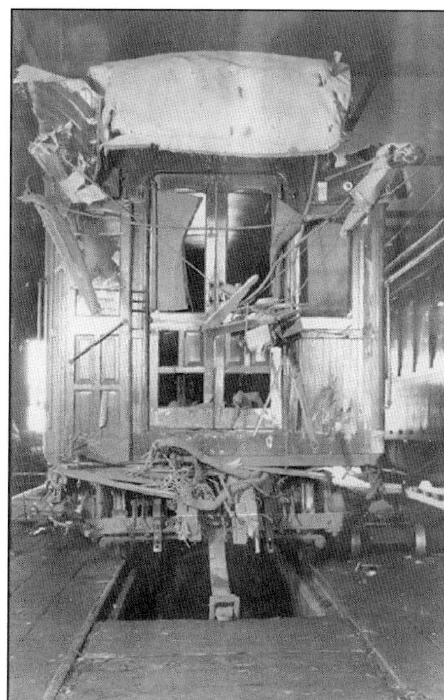

This photograph shows Car No. 4 inside the Pierce Park Car Barn, ready for repairs. Many Treasure Valley men worked for the various traction companies as mechanics and repairmen.

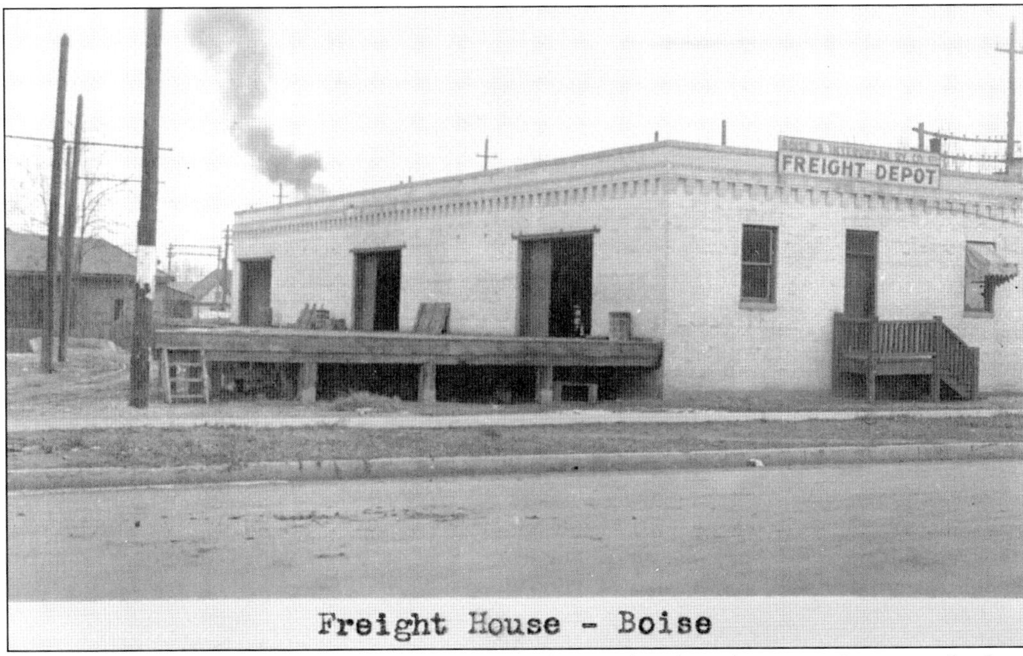

Freight House - Boise

Car barns, depots, freight houses, and other buildings related to the interurban were built in Treasure Valley towns. This is the freight house on Front Street in Boise, originally constructed by the B&I. It eventually became the property of the BVTC.

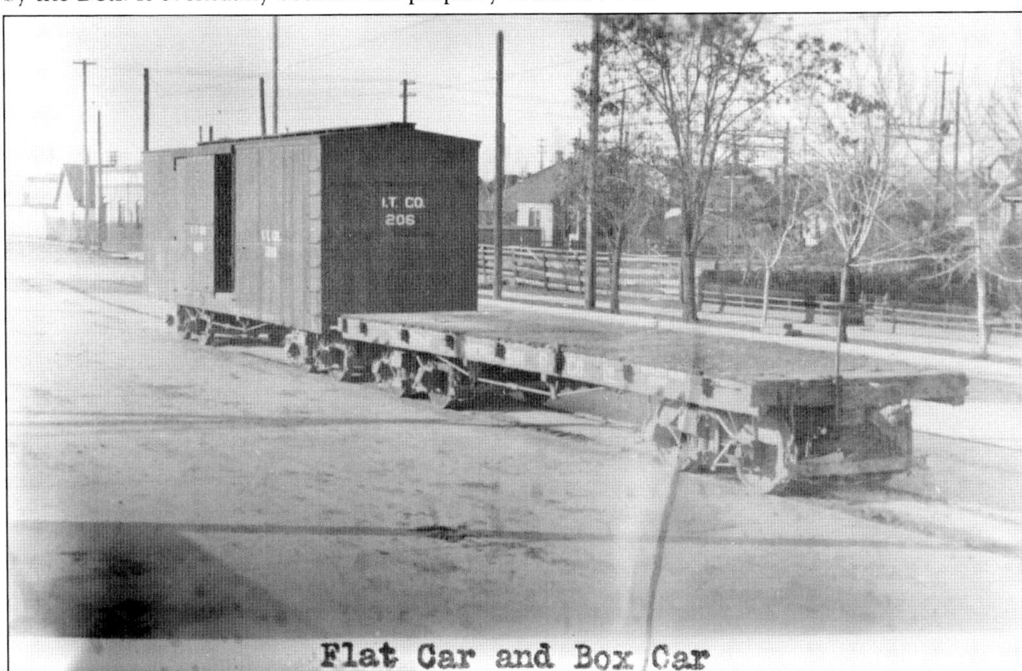

Flat Car and Box Car

A flatcar and a boxcar are shown near the Boise interurban freight house on Front Street between Twelfth and Thirteenth Streets. The B&I constructed this building in 1908 and extended its city line to reach the structure. A line was built from Twenty-eighth Street up Fairview Avenue to Front Street.

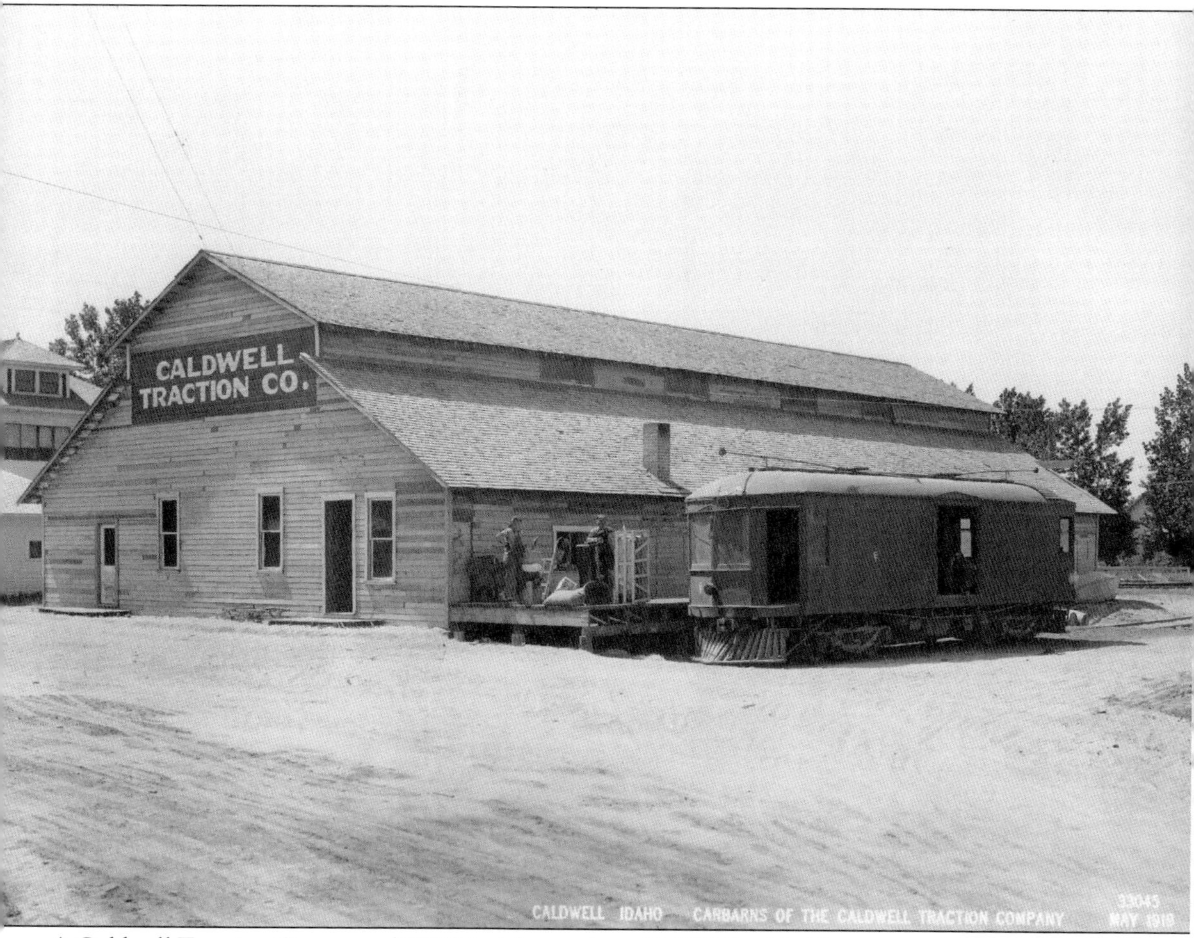

A Caldwell Traction Company (CTC) freight car, later BVTC Car No.73, is stopped at the CTC carbarn in Caldwell around 1919. Railroad photographer and historian Henry R. Griffith Jr. noted that the car was later used as a shanty near the Quinn-Robbins concrete plant in Boise in 1963. (Courtesy of Idaho Power Company.)

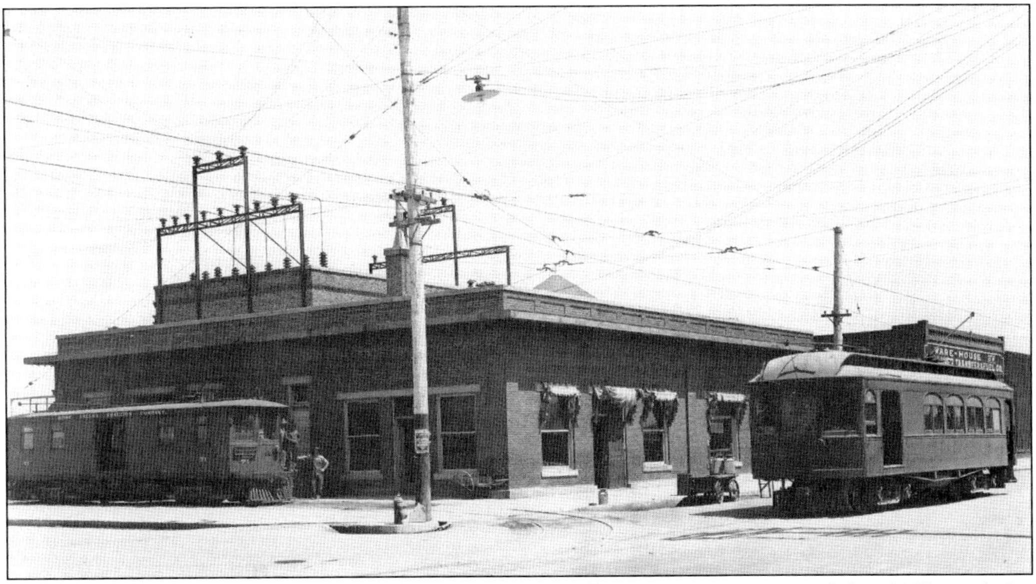

This BVTC car is stopped at the Caldwell freight and passenger station in May 1919, and the freight crew stands next to BVTC Car No.71. Caldwell Station was constructed by ITC in 1912. It was similar to Nampa Station and was designed by the Cleveland Construction Company, contractors for the traction company. (Courtesy of Idaho Power Company.)

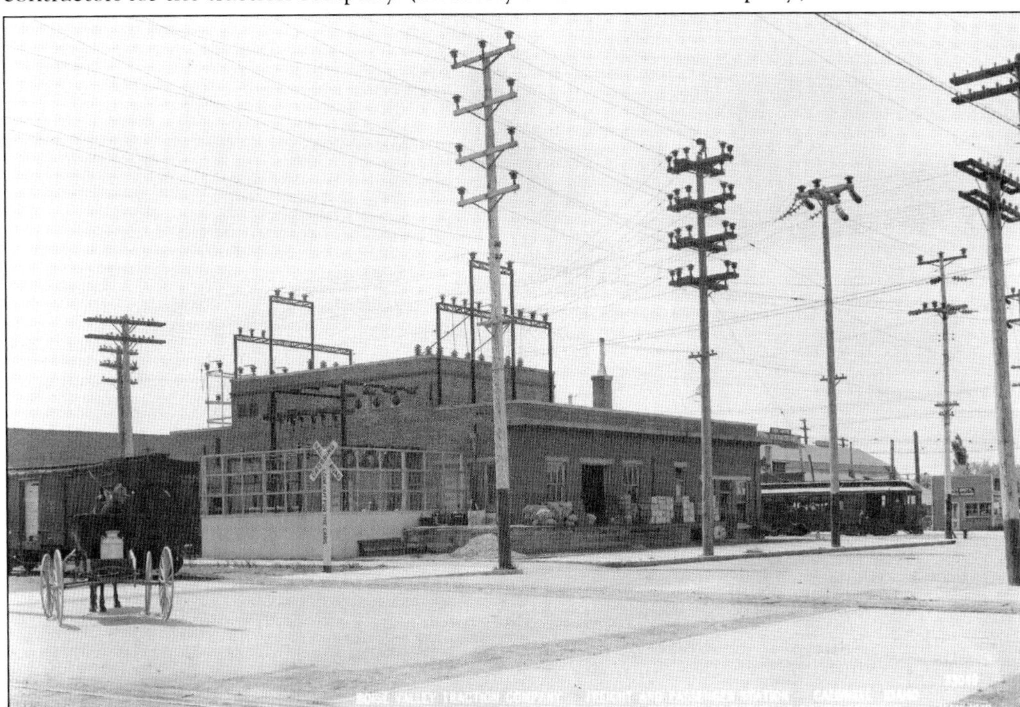

This 1919 photograph shows the Caldwell freight and passenger station loading dock. Bags of potatoes or onions, grain, and other farm products are stacked up for loading. In the background, passengers embark a BVTC car headed to Boise. An unidentified farmer, toting a milk can in his wagon, watches the photographer. (Courtesy of Idaho Power Company.)

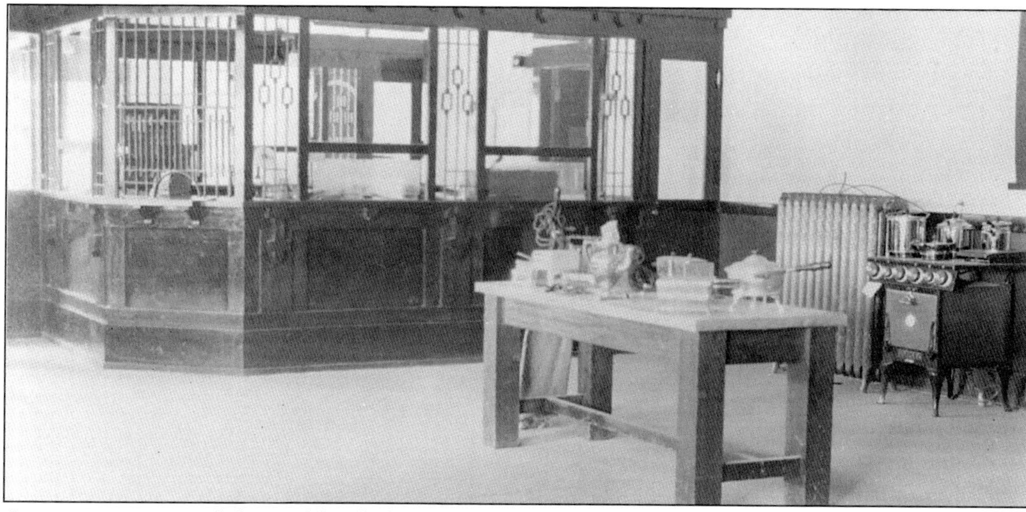

An interior view of the Caldwell depot, around 1919, shows the ticket office and sales room. Power companies of the time often sold electric appliances; items for sale here include an electric vacuum, a variety of cookware, and a stove. The Caldwell depot was also the terminal building for the power company.

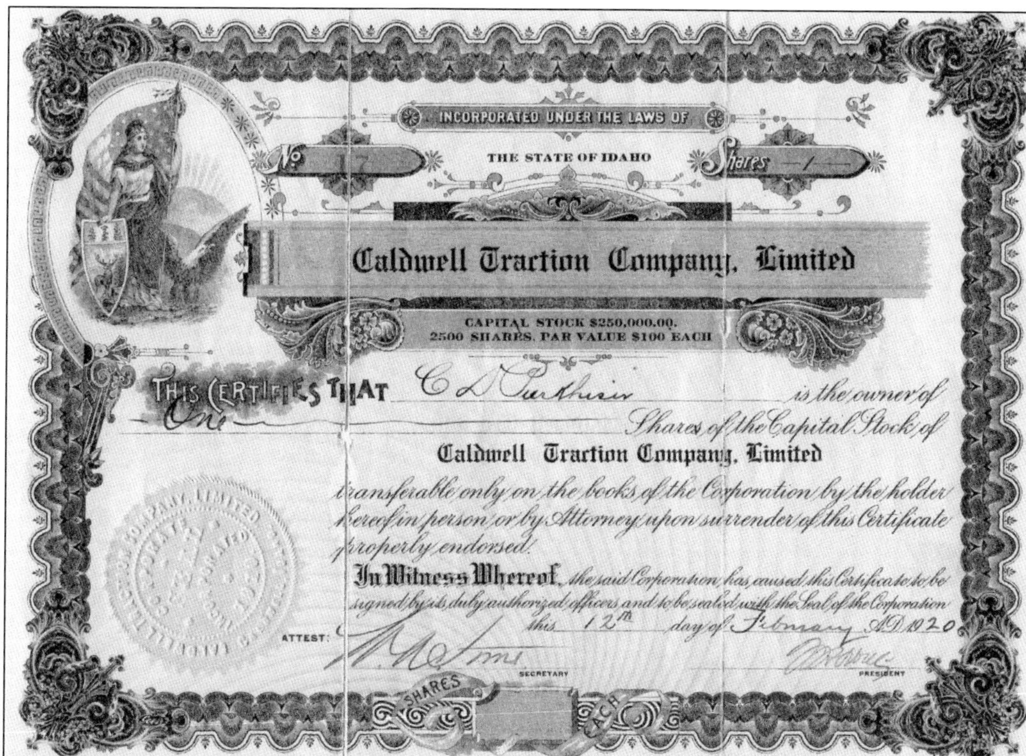

INCORPORATED UNDER THE LAWS OF
THE STATE OF IDAHO
No 17
Shares 1
Caldwell Traction Company, Limited
CAPITAL STOCK $250,000.00.
2500 SHARES, PAR VALUE $100 EACH

THIS CERTIFIES THAT [illegible] is the owner of One Shares of the Capital Stock of
Caldwell Traction Company, Limited
transferable only on the books of the Corporation by the holder hereof in person or by Attorney upon surrender of this Certificate properly endorsed.

In Witness Whereof, the said Corporation has caused this Certificate to be signed by its duly authorized officers and to be sealed with the Seal of the Corporation this 12th day of February A.D. 1920

ATTEST:
SECRETARY
PRESIDENT
SHARES
EACH

Pictured here is a stock certificate for the Caldwell Traction Company, Ltd., dated 1920. The traction company was formed to bring in materials for the dam construction at Deer Flat Reservoir. In October 1918, the company leased the Oregon Short Line steam railroad line to Wilder. The CTC electrified the line and provided passenger and freight service until 1920. (Courtesy of John Aguirre.)

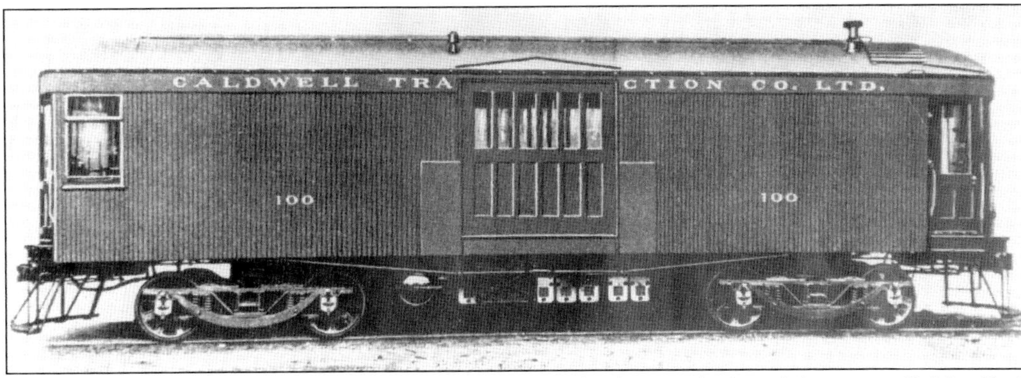

Here, a freight car of the CTC is photographed at the factory before delivery to Caldwell. A variety of products were shipped on these freight cars. During World War I, for instance, Canyon County farmers raised hay for the federal government and shipped it to Caldwell via the CTC, which then transferred the hay to the Oregon Short Line railroad cars for delivery to Kansas City. (Courtesy of John Aguirre.)

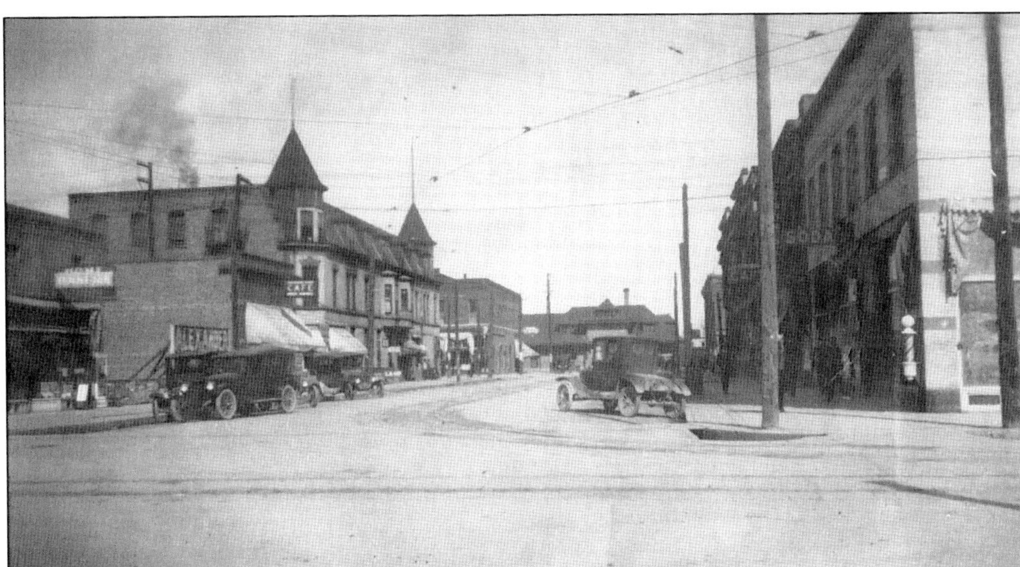

This photograph shows downtown Caldwell around 1923. Tracks of both the BVTC and the CTC are visible in the foreground. The CTC operated until 1924, when service was suspended and the line sold at sheriff's sale. (Courtesy of John Aguirre.)

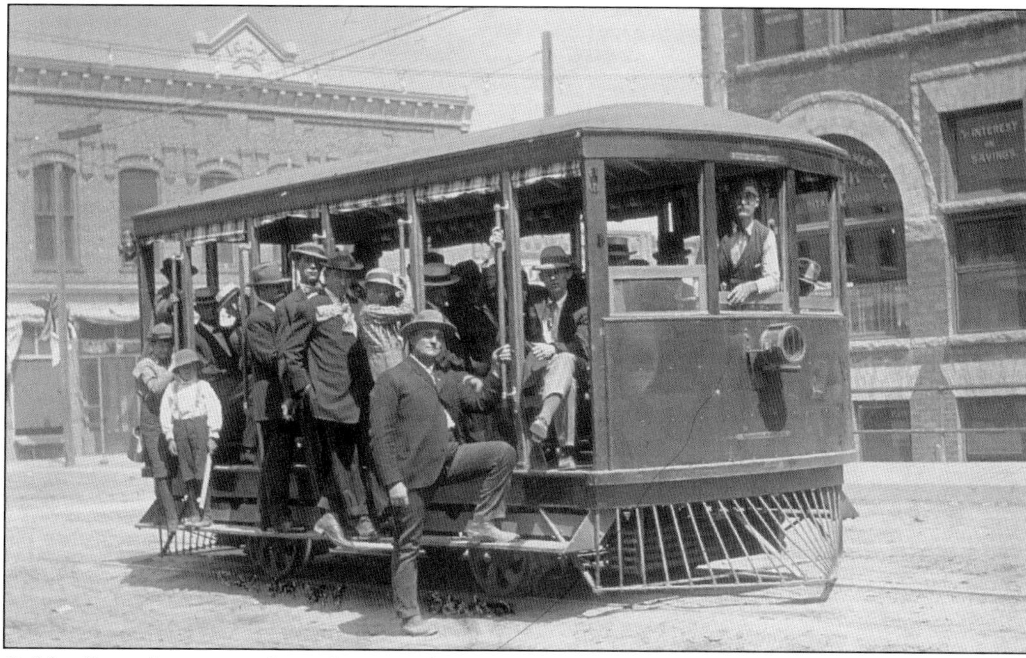

Caldwell residents pose for a photograph on a sunny afternoon. This open-air streetcar was gas powered. Note the striped shades, which could be rolled down to protect passengers from dust.

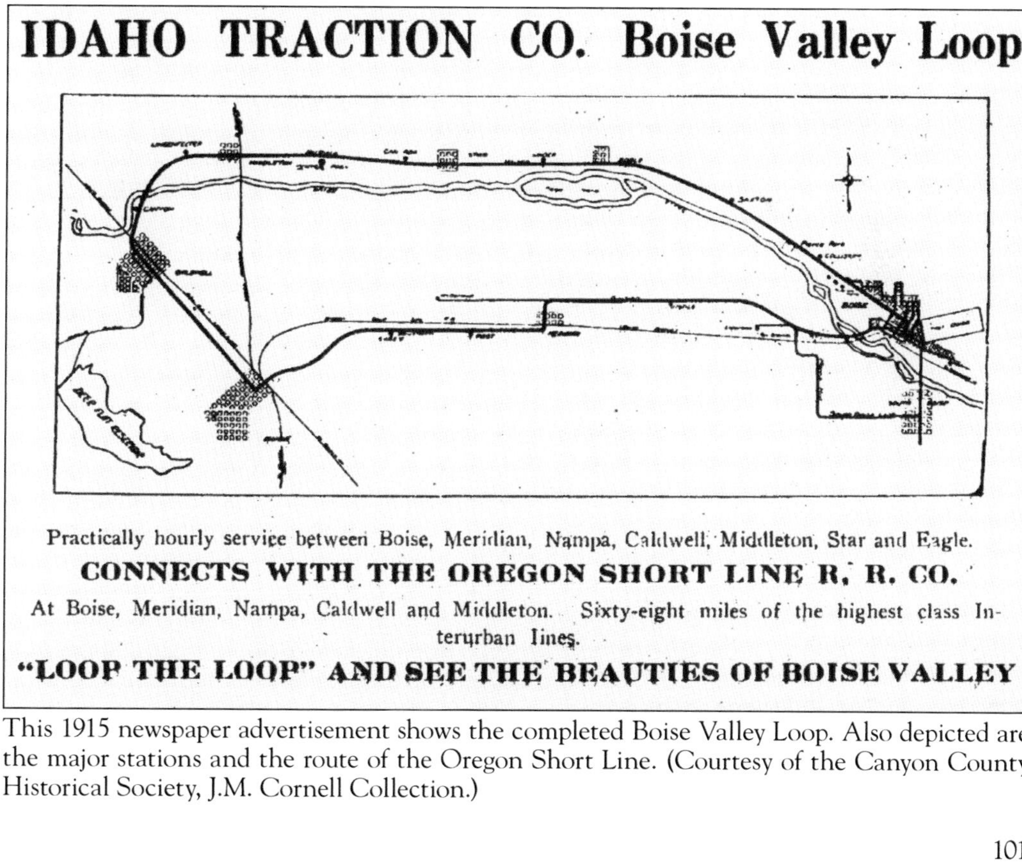

This 1915 newspaper advertisement shows the completed Boise Valley Loop. Also depicted are the major stations and the route of the Oregon Short Line. (Courtesy of the Canyon County Historical Society, J.M. Cornell Collection.)

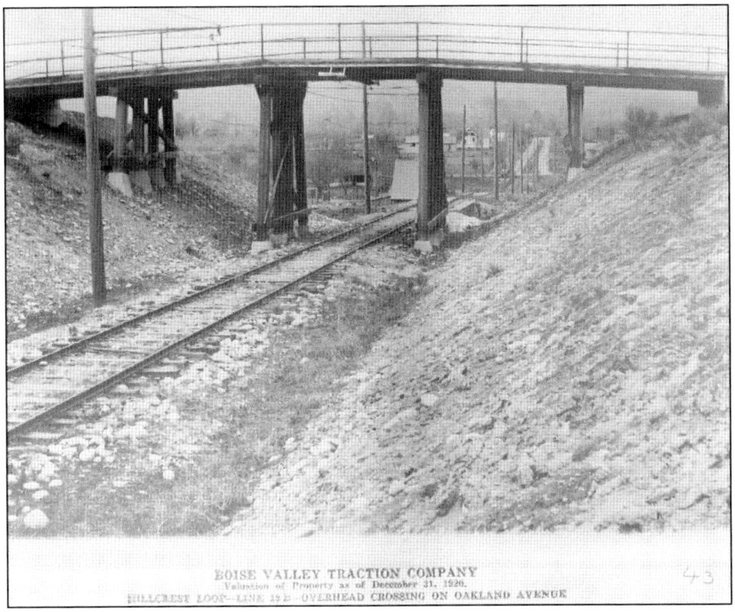

In 1913, the ITC offered a new car service in Boise. The service was started on the new line that ran between Morris Hill and South Boise. Called the "Hillcrest Loop," it provided a connection between downtown and the bench neighborhoods. This northward view toward Boise shows the overhead crossing on Oakland Avenue in South Boise.

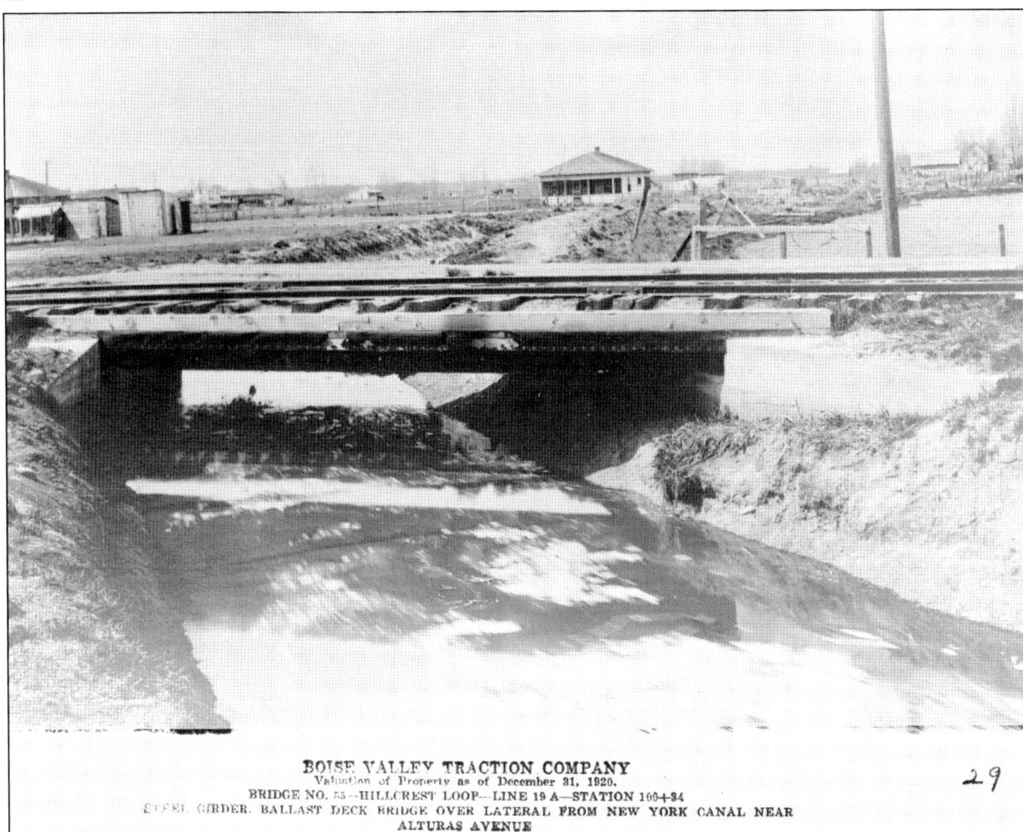

The Cleveland Construction Company, an interurban construction company, designed many of the bridges on the Treasure Valley lines. This is a view of girder bridge over a lateral of the New York Canal in Boise, near Rose Hill (previously called Alturas) Avenue.

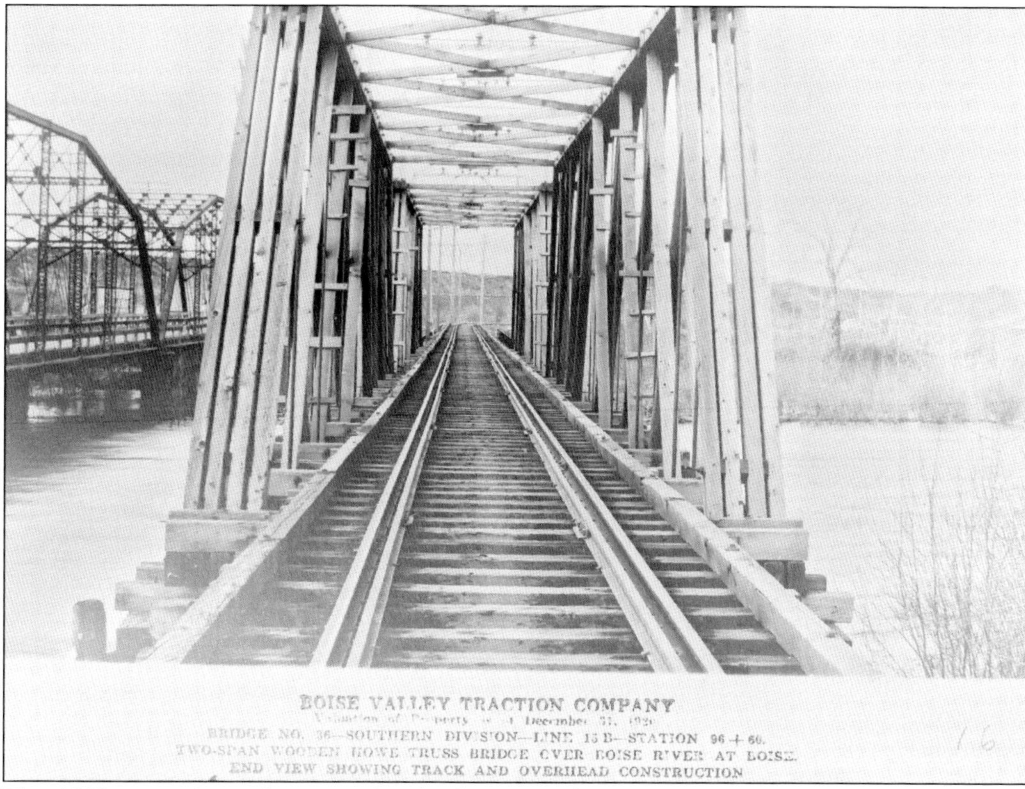

This 1920 image shows the interurban bridge across the Boise River, west of Boise. On the left is the Oregon Short Line Railroad bridge. The photograph was taken in December, although the lack of visible snow suggests that it was a mild winter.

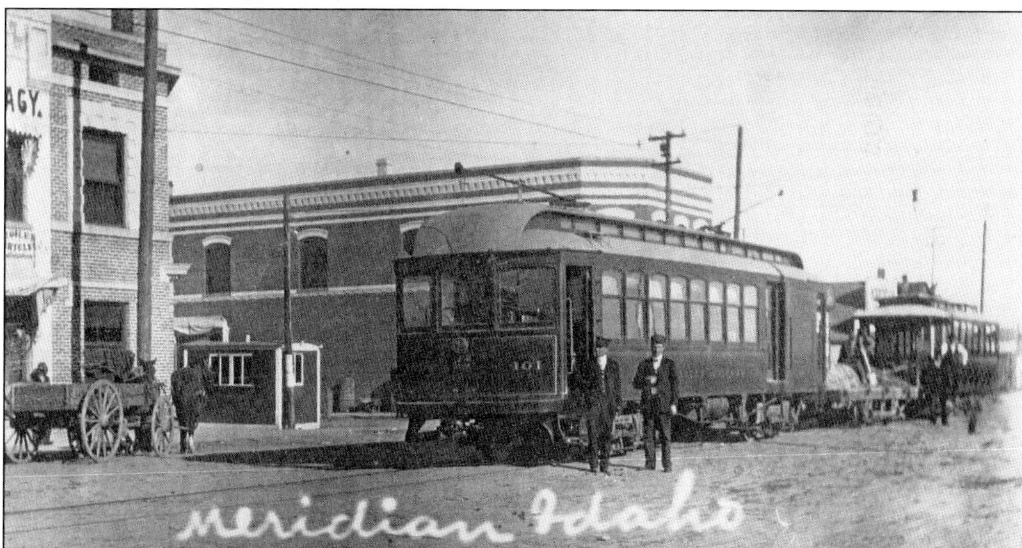

BVRC cars are stopped at Broadway and Second Streets in Meridian around 1910. Cars ran daily from Boise from 7:00 a.m. until 11:30 p.m. The late car stayed overnight in Meridian before returning to Boise early the next morning. (Courtesy of Meridian Historical Society.)

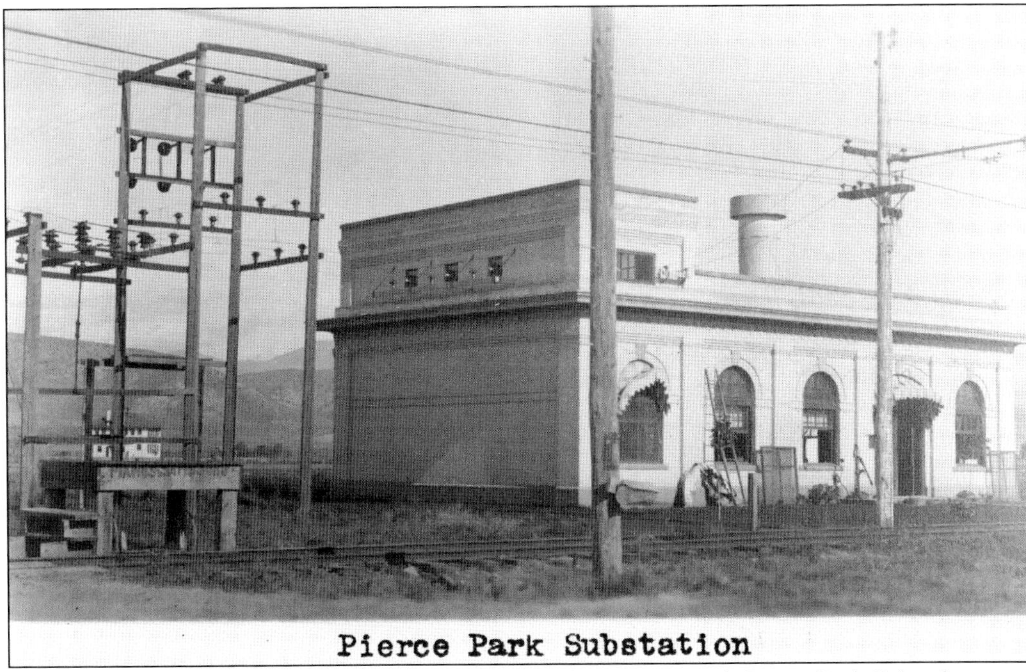

Seen here is the Pierce Park substation, located on the BVTC road. Pierce Park School, named for Walter E. Pierce (a businessman, entrepreneur, and developer) is visible in the background. The interurban tracks can be seen in the foreground.

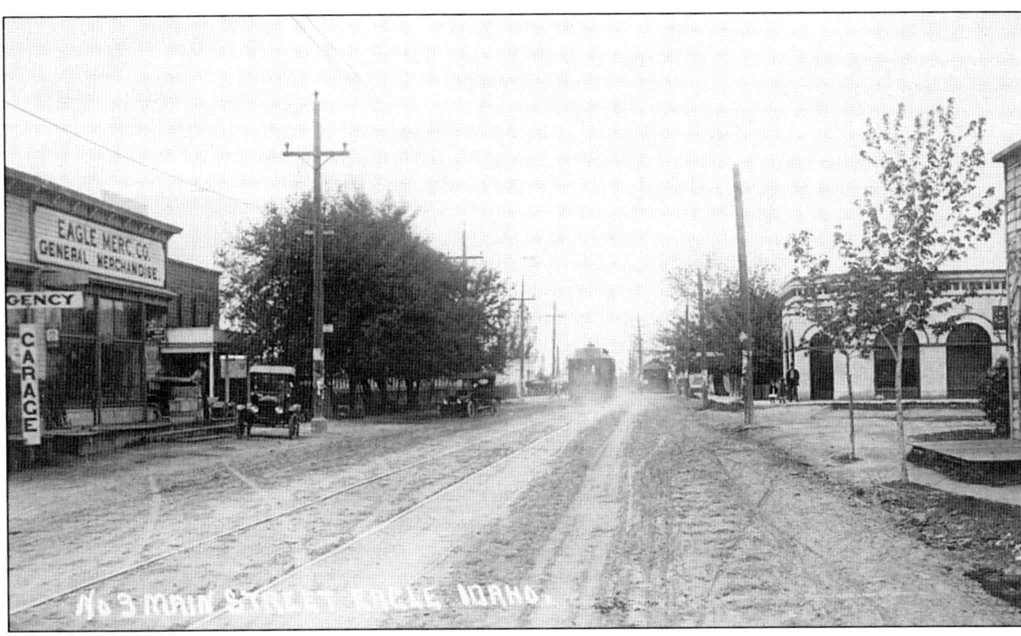

In this c. 1915 view, an interurban car is seen approaching downtown Eagle on Main Street. The Eagle Bank is on the right. The interurban line connected Eagle to other towns in the Treasure Valley and provided an economic boost to the farming community. (Courtesy of Eagle Historical Museum.)

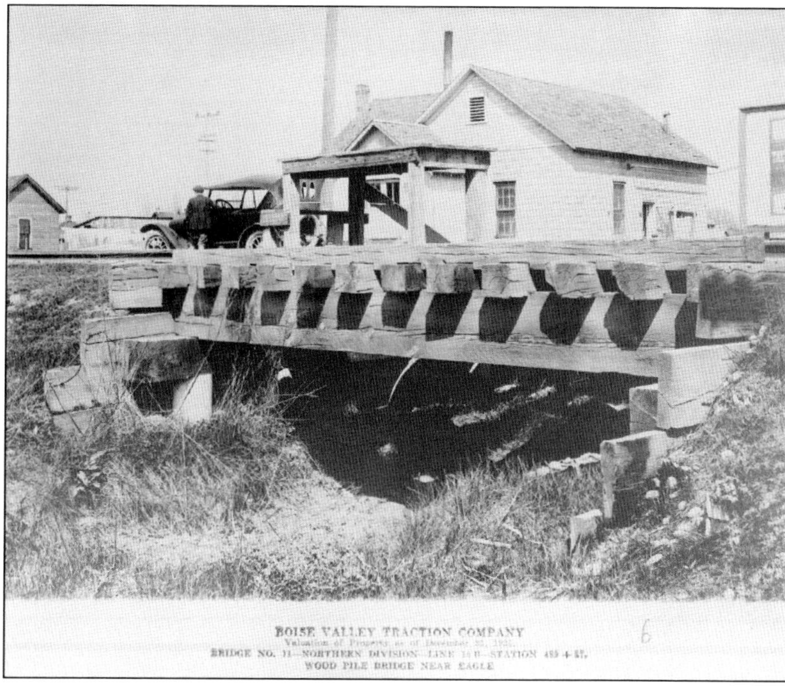

A pile bridge near Eagle is shown in this 1920 photograph. An unidentified man can be seen in the background, getting into an automobile. The BVTC advertised quick express service and prompt and dependable freight service. Interurban service was provided to Eagle between 7:30 a.m. to 11:30 p.m., with car connections every two hours.

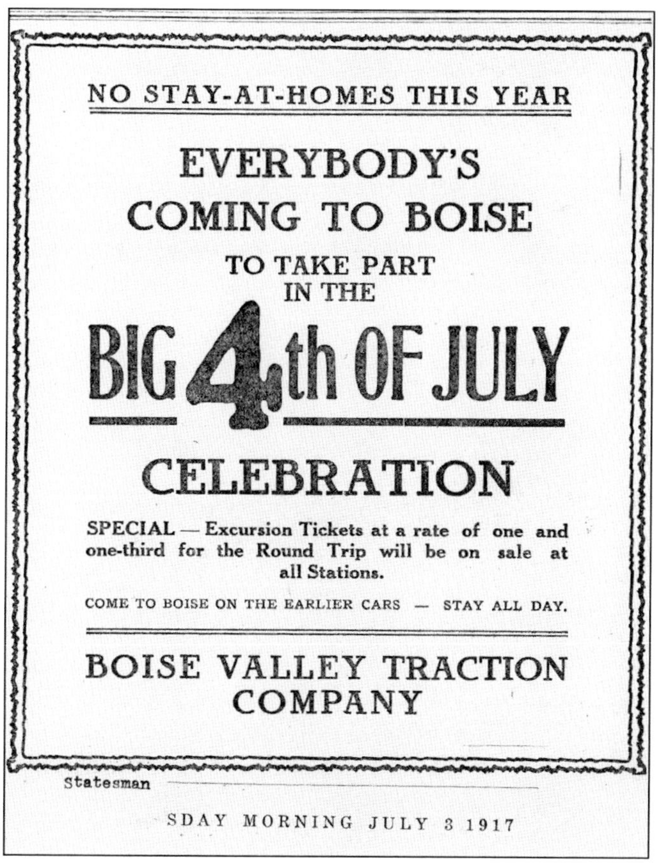

This advertisement promotes a special excursion fare for a Fourth of July celebration in Boise. As automobiles became more affordable and the traction companies began to feel the effects of decreased ridership, the companies continued to come up with ways to attract passengers. (Courtesy of the Canyon County Historical Society, J.M. Cornell Collection.)

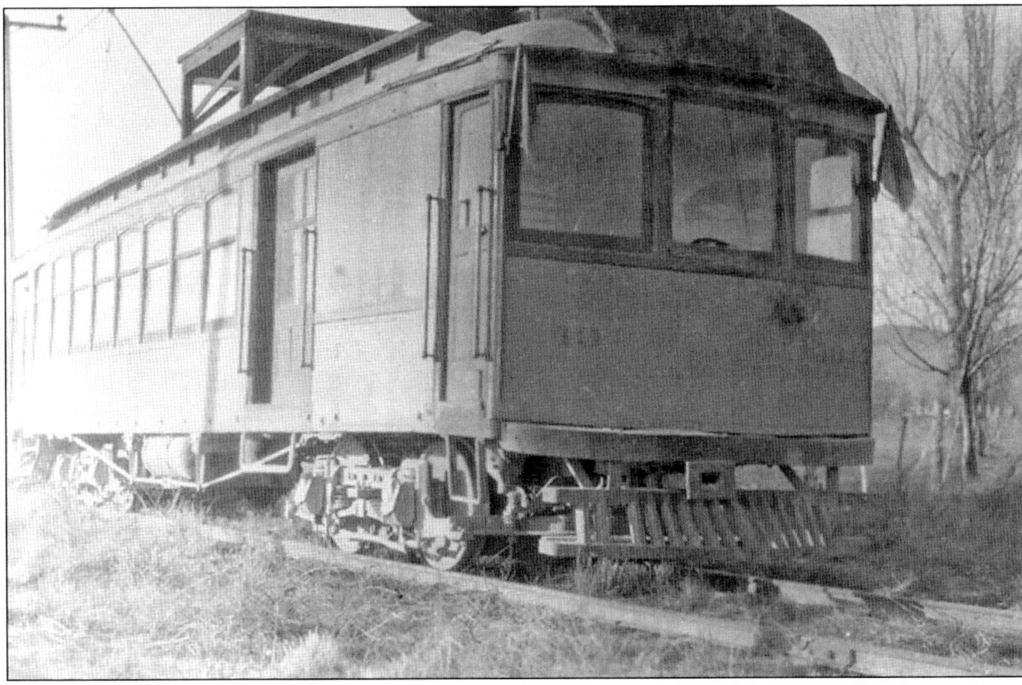

Colored flags were used as signals on the cars. Red flags communicated danger, yellow flags advised caution, and green flags indicated safety. Blue flags were used by repairmen working around the cars, and green-and-white flags were used as signals for passenger and freight trains to stop. In this view, BVTC Car No. 10 has been flagged and stopped.

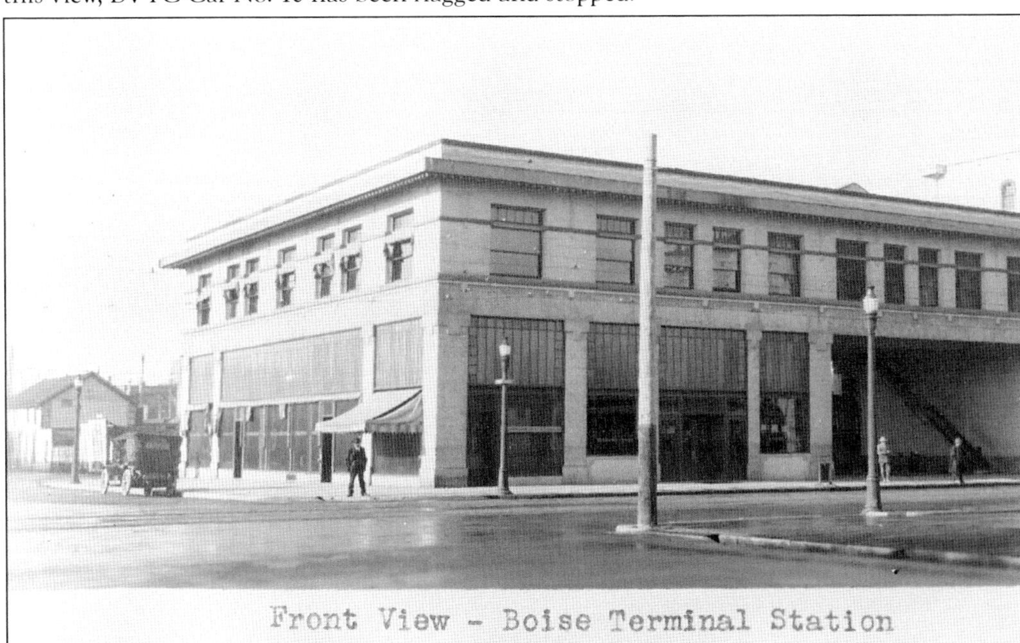

This view looking southwest shows the Boise Interurban depot on the corner of Bannock Street and Seventh Street (now Capitol Boulevard). The front of an unidentified interurban car is visible at the right.

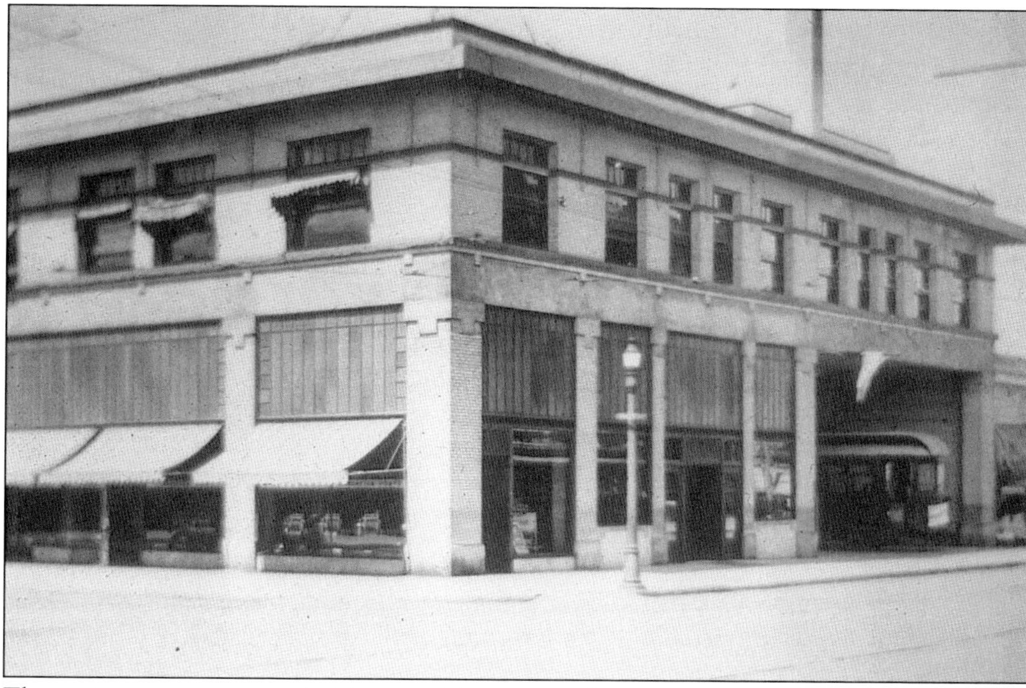

The station was constructed with several features to allow for minor repairs so that cars did not have to be taken to the carbarn near Pierce Park. A track (visible on the right, curving into the station) was built from Bannock Street and circled around the back of the building.

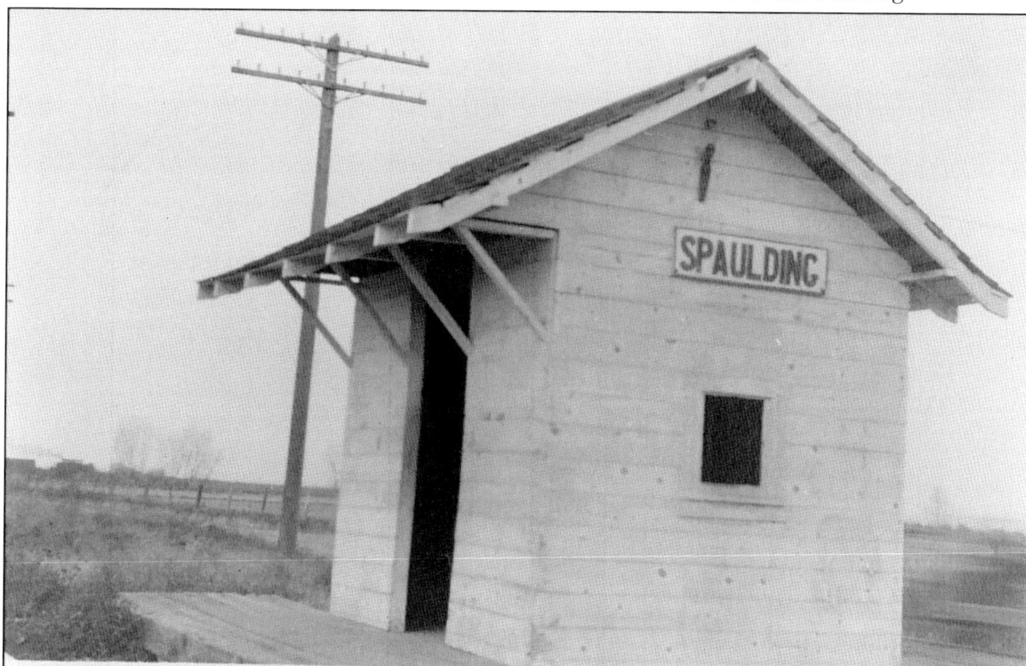

SHELTER STATION AT SPAULDING

Shelter stations were positioned one to two miles apart. This station was located north of Boise, near the Spaulding Ranch (homesteaded in 1896 by Almon W. and Mary E. Spaulding).

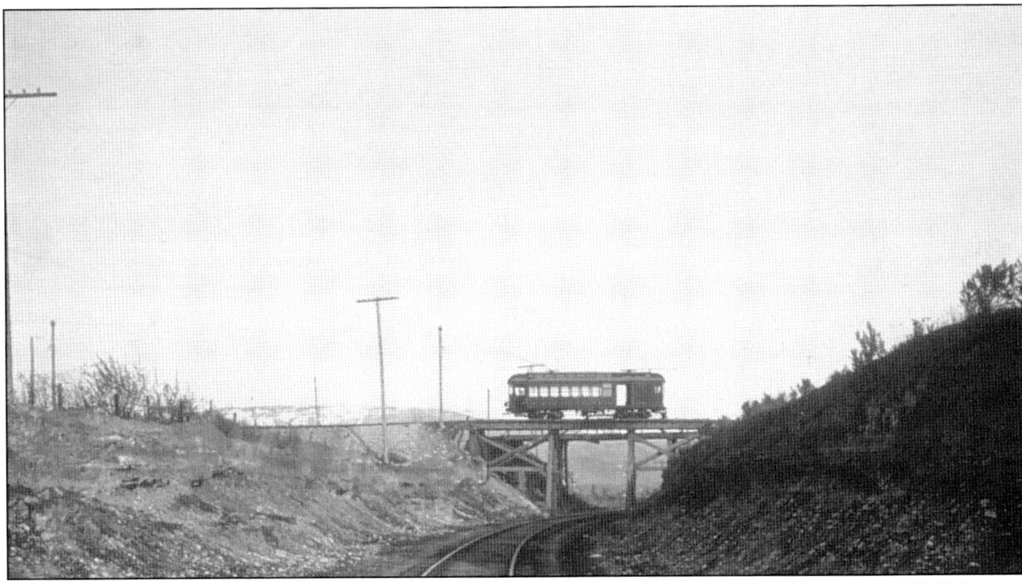

BVTC No. 100 crosses the Oregon Short Line track, southbound on the Morris Hill line in Boise. The line to Morris Hill Cemetery was laid in 1907, and the trestle crossing was built over the Oregon Short Line right-of-way. In 1911, the line was rebuilt and routed up Fairview Hill to the fairgrounds.

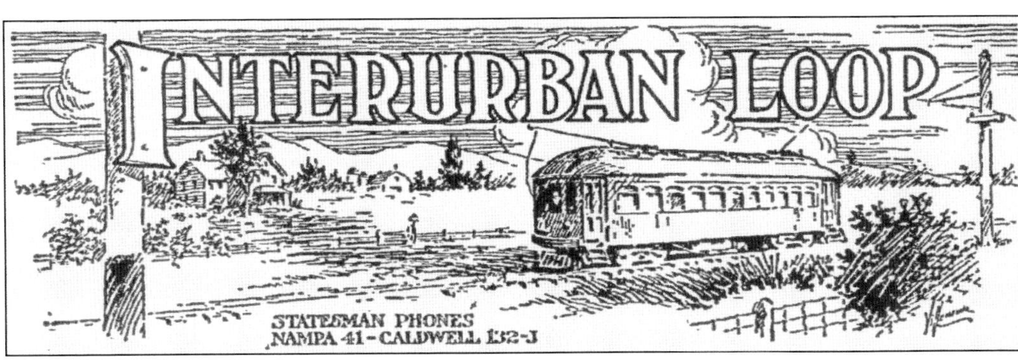

The *Idaho Statesman*, the local Boise newspaper, featured news reported from towns on the loop under this heading. The newspaper employed a reporter who travelled the interurban loop daily, collecting information from the communities, stops, and stations on the route.

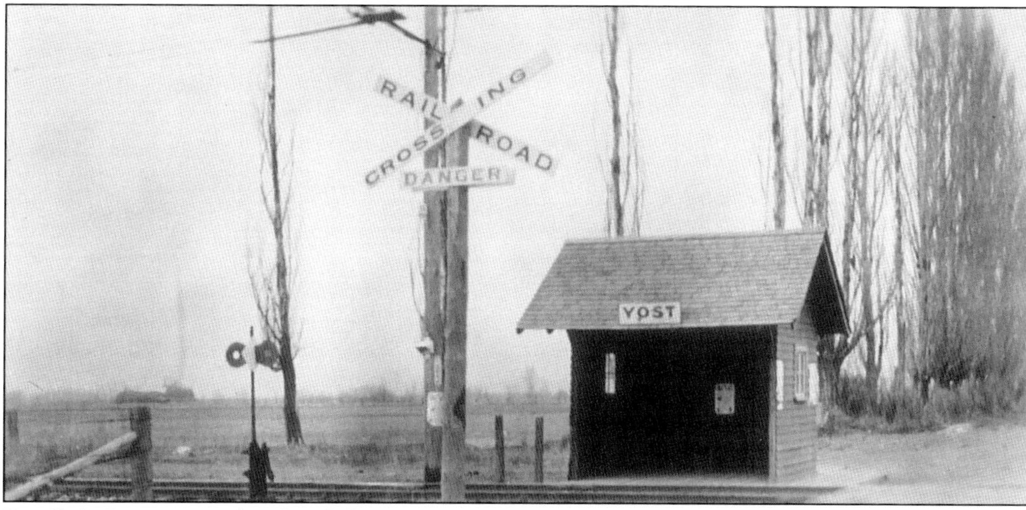

Small shelter stations bordered the interurban tracks and dotted the countryside for miles. After the demise of the system, many of the buildings were moved from the tracks and either dismantled or repurposed. This photograph shows the Yost shelter station located on the southern line west of Meridian.

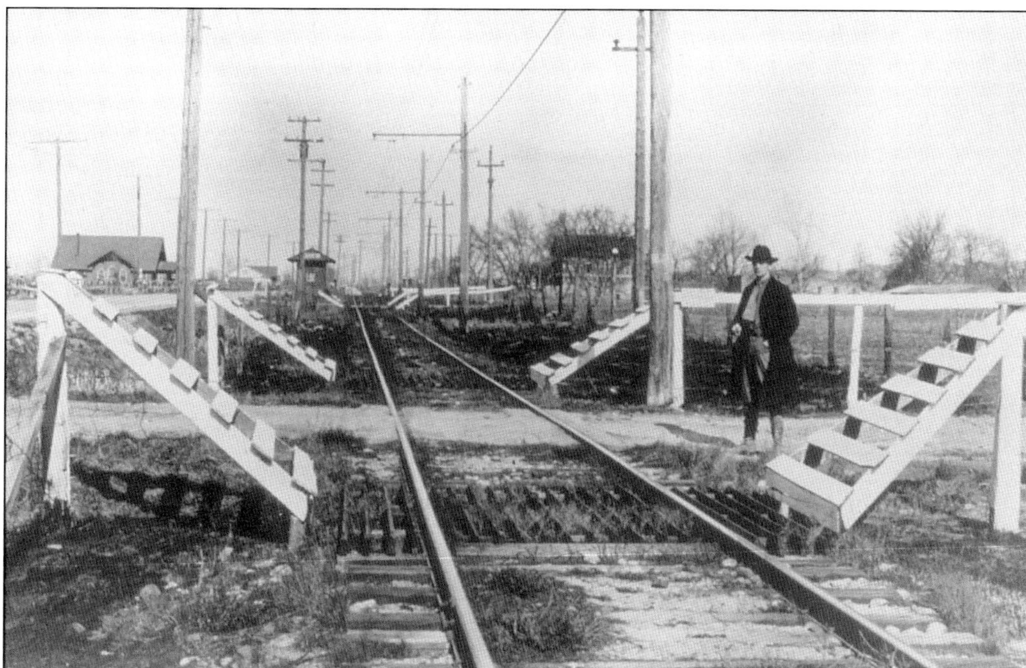

An unidentified man poses by the interurban tracks west of Boise on State Street. Wiley Station is shown in the background. Cattle guards were placed at the crossing to prevent livestock from wandering onto the tracks.

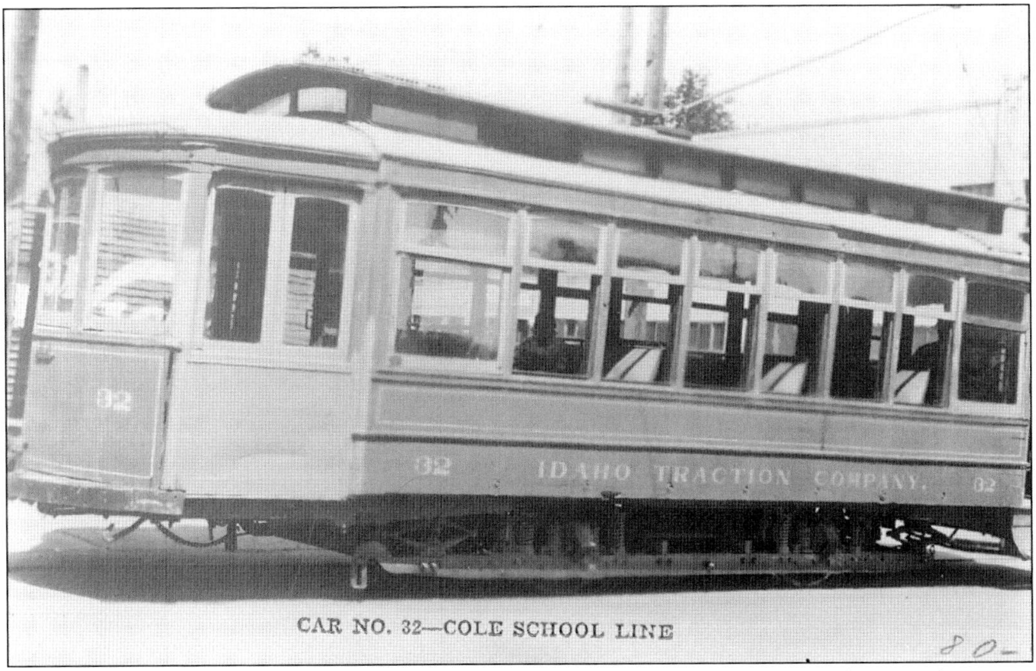

Here, ITC Car No. 32 is stopped near Eleventh and Front Streets in Boise. This may be a pay-as-you-enter (PAYE) car, constructed by the Brill Car Company. In a PAYE car, the conductor did not circulate through taking fares, but stood on the rear platform to collect as the passenger boarded the car. The rear platform on a PAYE car was designed with space to accommodate the conductor. Car 32 was a city car that ran to Cole School, which was located on the bench, southwest of downtown.

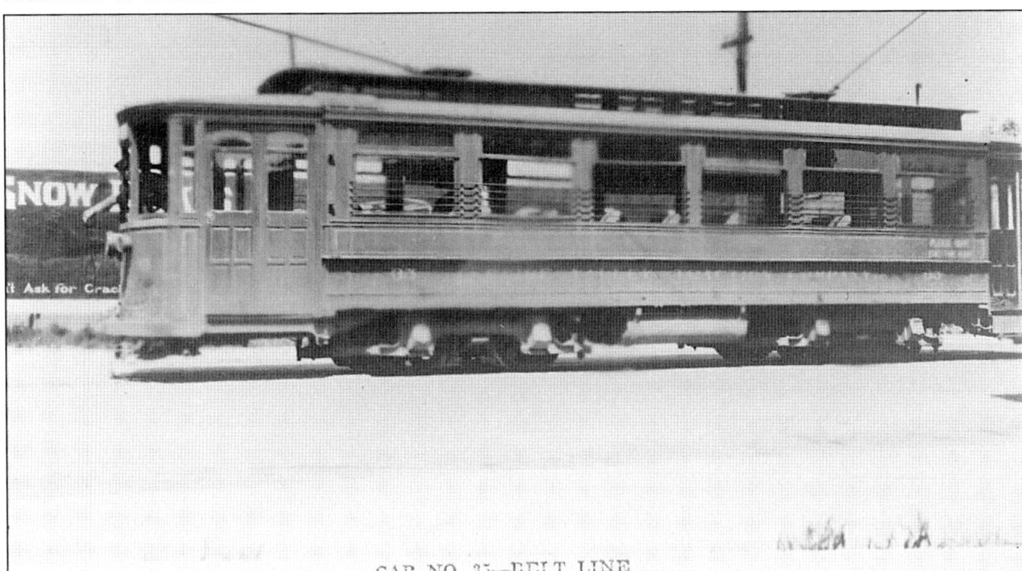

BVTC Car No. 33 is shown on the belt line that traversed Boise's North End, around 1919. By this time, the car lines were facing competition from automobiles for passengers. In Boise, the streetcar companies promoted the system by entreating citizens to "Use the Street Car for Business – Your Automobile for Pleasure."

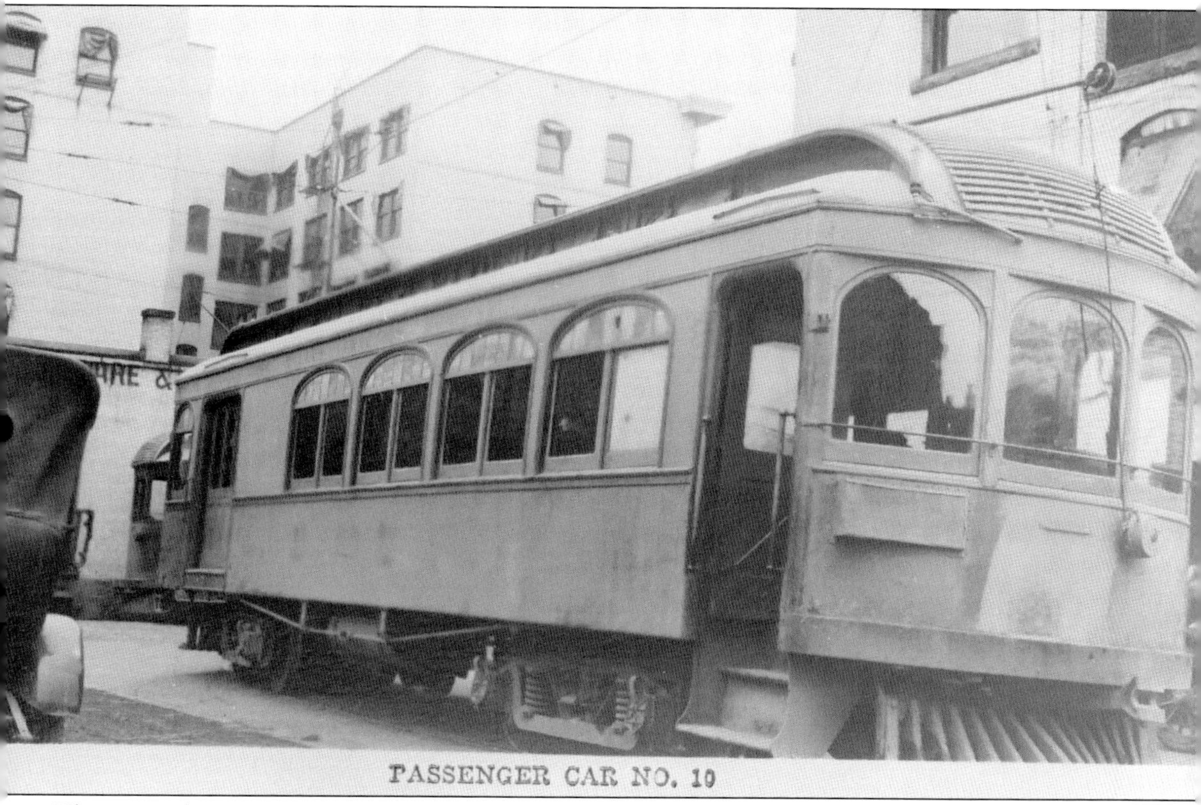

The interurban station at Boise was constructed with room to store cars behind the building. This view shows BVTC Car No. 10 behind the station, with the Idaho Building visible in the background.

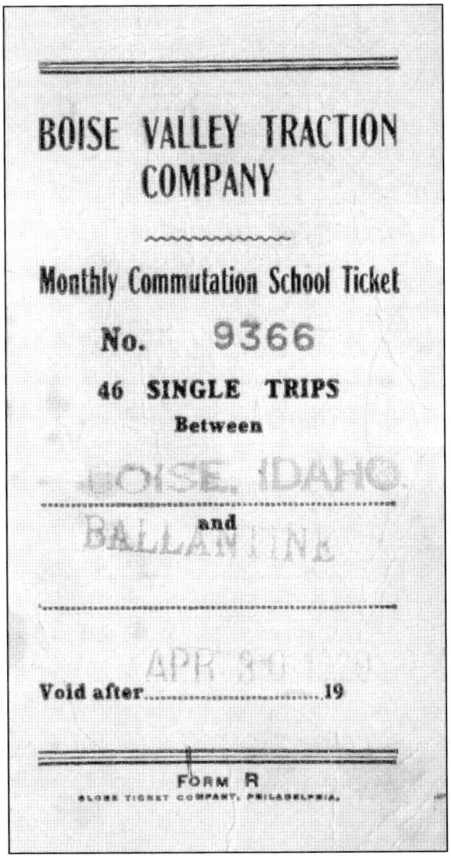

BOISE VALLEY TRACTION COMPANY

Monthly Commutation School Ticket

No. 9366

46 SINGLE TRIPS

Between

BOISE, IDAHO

and

BALLANTINE

APR 30

Void after..............................19

FORM R

GLOBE TICKET COMPANY, PHILADELPHIA.

This 1920 student fare book was used by a child traveling between Ballentine Station and Boise. It was common for children, depending upon their ages, to ride free or to be given a reduced fare without a ticket. The car companies each had its own rates and restrictions for different classes of passengers. (Courtesy of John Aguirre.)

Sidings were constructed at various locations throughout the Treasure Valley. They were used to provide a spot for the freight cars to stop and pick up farm products. This one was located at Cruzen, west of Boise.

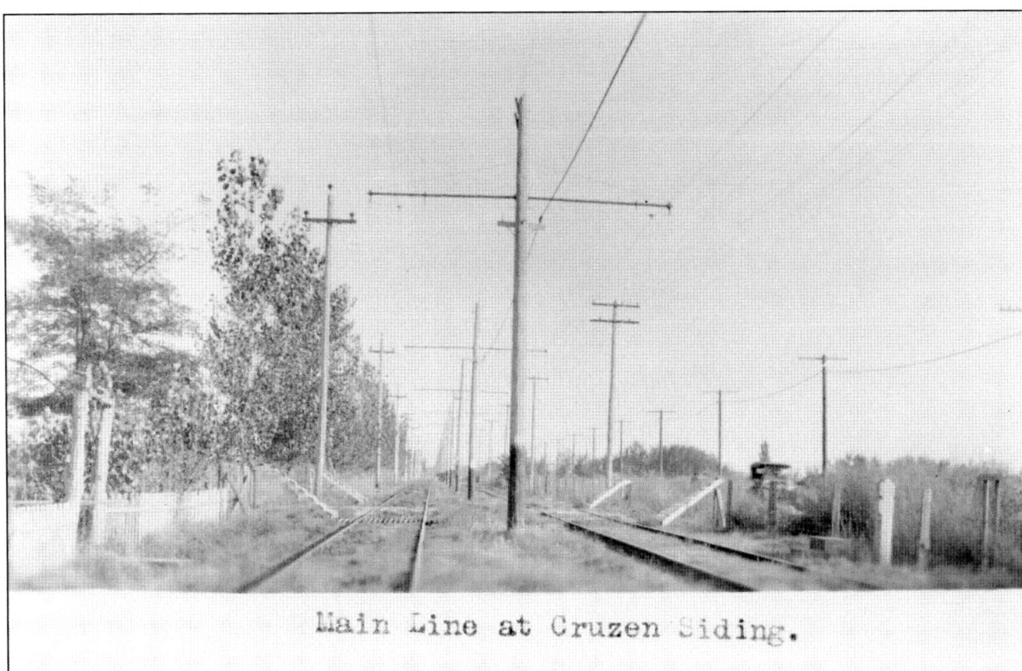

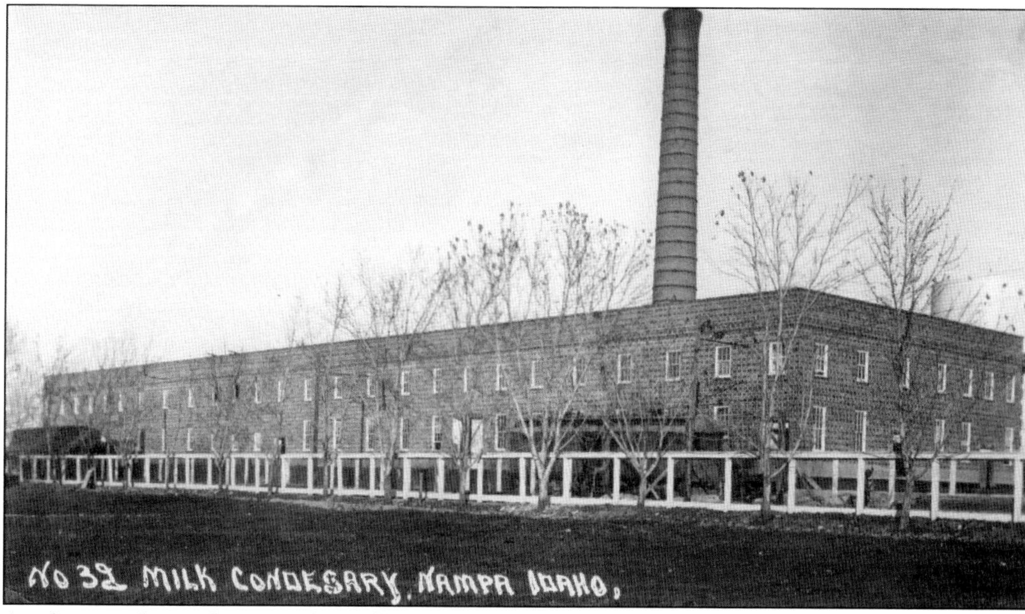

A siding was located next to the milk condensery plant at Nampa. This view shows two interurban cars, stopped for loading. (Courtesy of John Aguirre.)

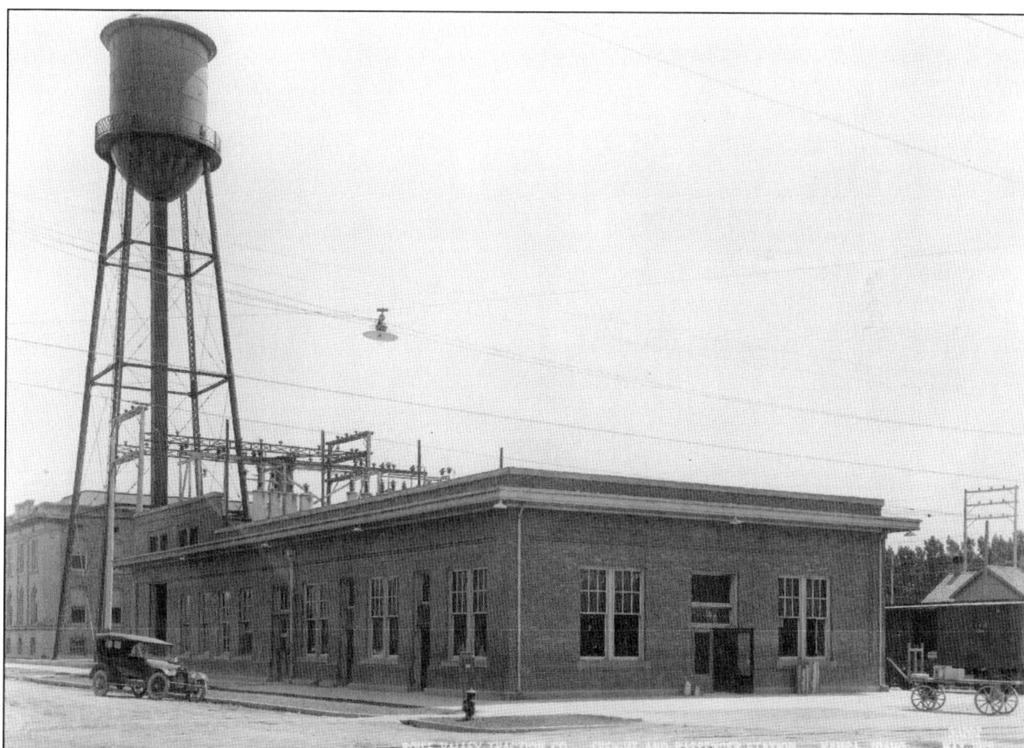

This view, from May 1919, shows the Nampa passenger-and-freight station. At the left, a freight car is being either loaded or unloaded, and milk cans and crates have been placed near the door. (Courtesy of Idaho Power Company.)

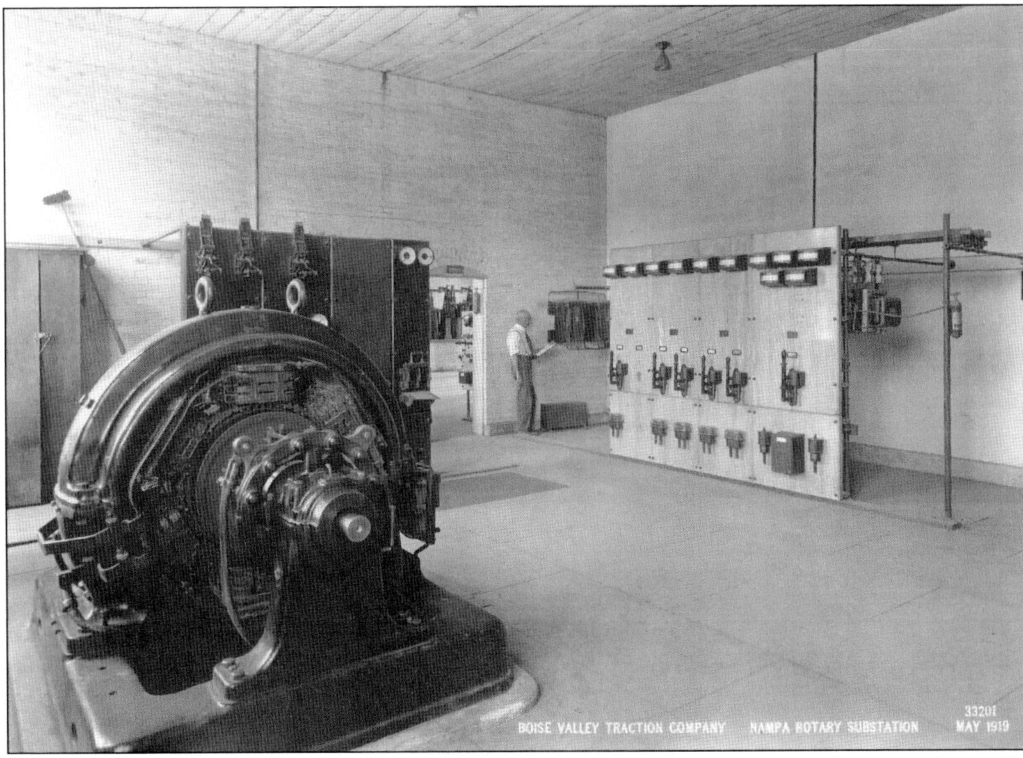

The Nampa substation is directly behind the passenger-and-freight station. This view shows the interior of the substation. (Courtesy of Idaho Power Company.)

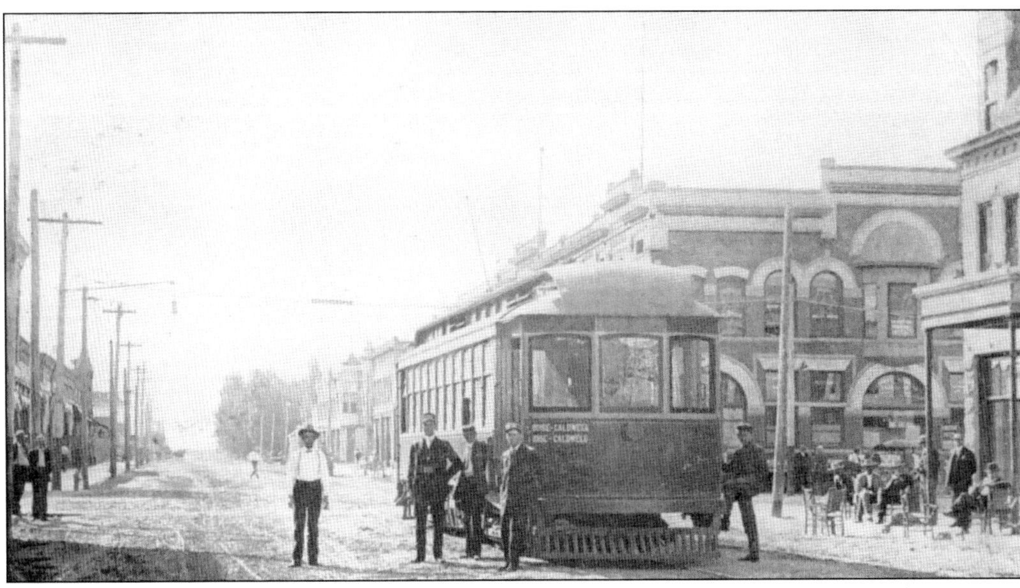

This view of Caldwell, from around 1907, shows B&I Car No. 4 stopped in front of the Saratoga Hotel. It would be five more years before communities in the Treasure Valley were linked by interurban rail.

Six

The End of an Era

On May 17, 1928, the local newspapers reported the end of the electric railway service in the Treasure Valley. Passenger service was discontinued on Boise's Southern and Northern Divisions and in Caldwell and Nampa. According to reports, not everyone was sorry to see the end of the streetcar era; many drivers were tired of traversing the uneven tracks, while homeowners welcomed an end to frequent racket of steel wheels on steel rails.

Some people, however, were dependent on the streetcar service to travel in the city and between the towns. To help cover the loss of streetcars, Boise City passed an ordinance discontinuing rail service and authorizing the use of gasoline-powered buses. The Gem State Transit Company, which operated buses between Boise, Nampa, and Caldwell, added two buses to the city system. The Boise Traction Company, soon renamed the Boise Streetcar Company, which had organized in 1919, began operating local motor bus service on the old streetcar routes. The Boise Streetcar Company changed its name to the Boise Bus Company and continued operating for many years.

A new railway company, the Boise & Western Railway, was formed by local interests and took over the section of abandoned rail lines between Boise and Onweiler (10 miles) and between Boise and Star (22 miles) for freight service only. The company operated until 1931, when the Great Depression finally forced abandonment of the line.

The streetcars disappeared, and the rail lines were torn up or paved over, but many area residents fondly remember "looping the Loop." Their stories were collected and preserved by the Idaho State Historical Society in the 1970s and 1980s. Aside from the oral histories, photographs, and a few timetables and tickets, all that remains of the electric railway are a few scattered buildings, repurposed for modern uses, with nothing to indicate their origins as elements of a vital transportation system connecting the communities of the Treasure Valley before the advent of interstate highways.

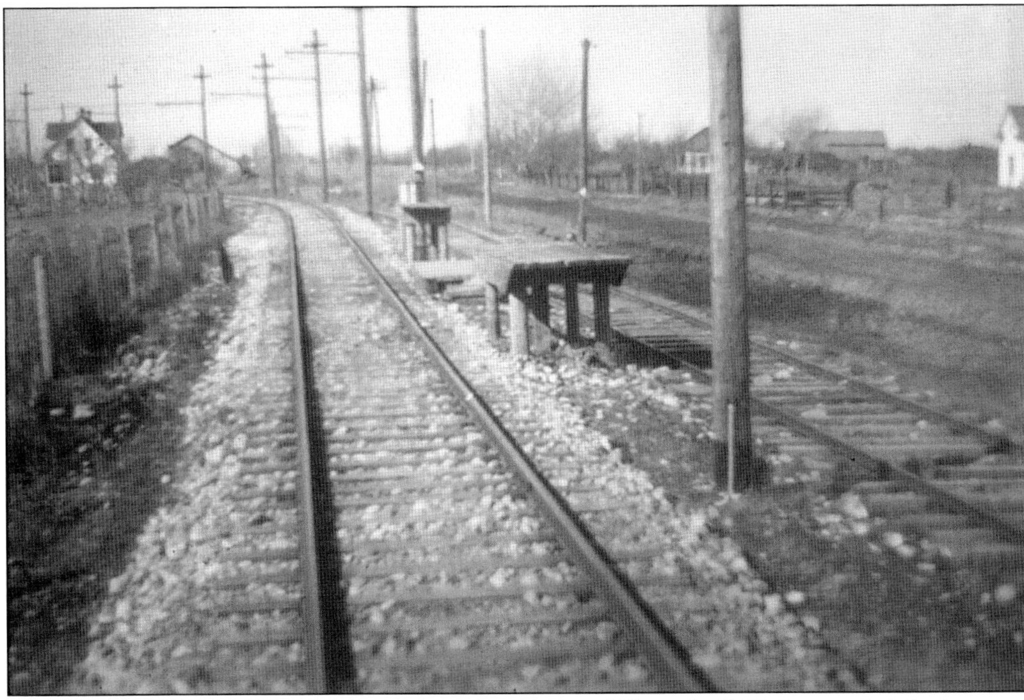

Meridian residents were eager to have interurban service. When the BVRC extended the line west from Ustick, Meridian was passed by. Instead, the original line made a curve south at Onweiler (today Meridian Road), then went on to McDermott Station. In 1908, a line was extended to Meridian from the Onweiler platform station. (Courtesy of the Meridian Historical Society, Jim and Ann Witherell Collection.)

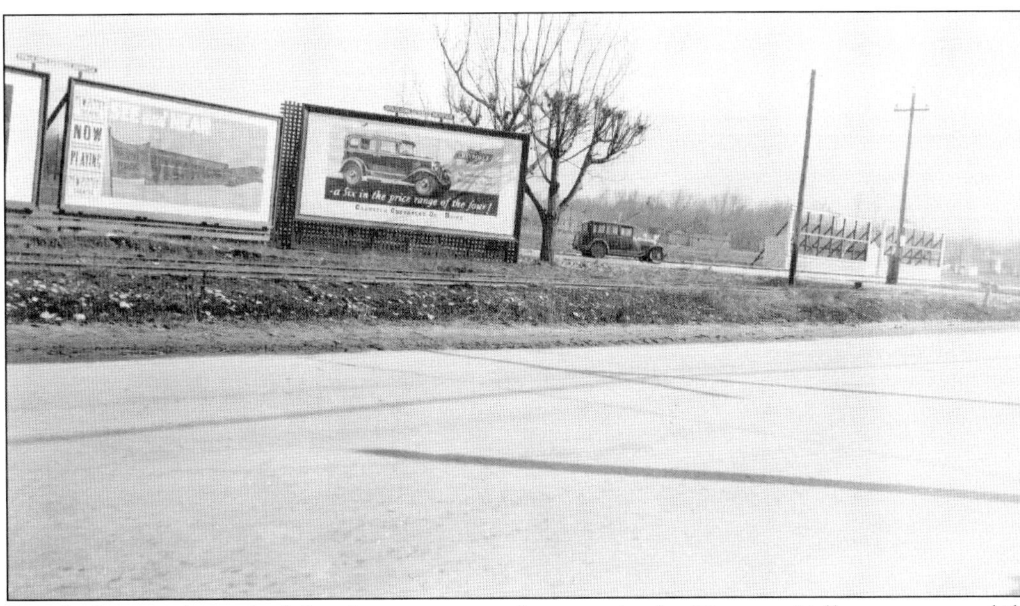

Foreshadowing the end of the electric street railway era in the Treasure Valley, an automobile passes behind a billboard advertising Chevrolet automobiles as it approaches a crossing on a section of tracks in Boise near Twenty-eighth and Main Streets.

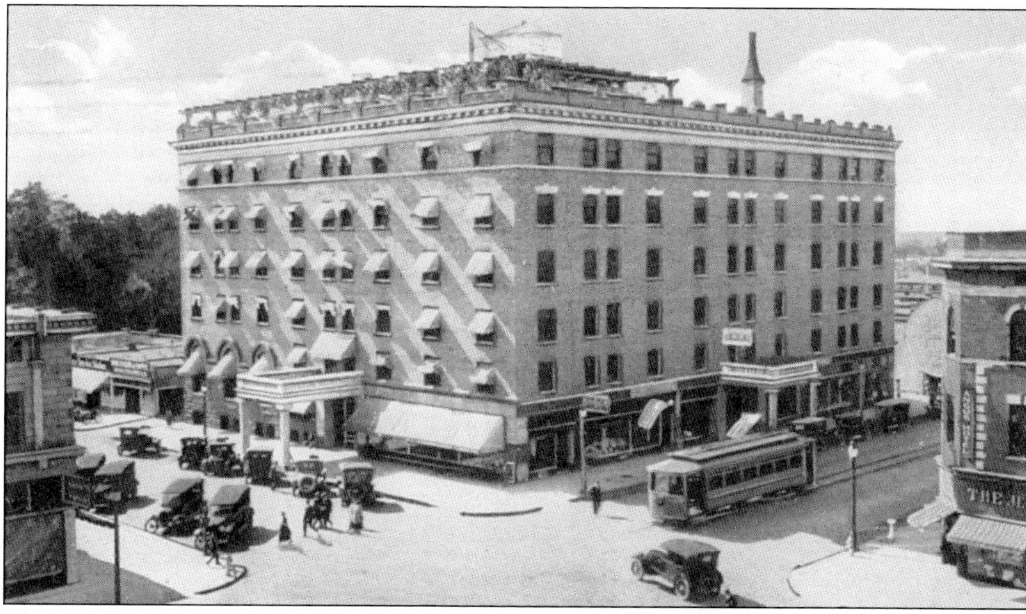

This 1924 postcard view of Boise shows the Owyhee Hotel at the intersection of Tenth and Main Streets, with automobiles parked along the sidewalk. The BVTC car passes in front of the hotel.

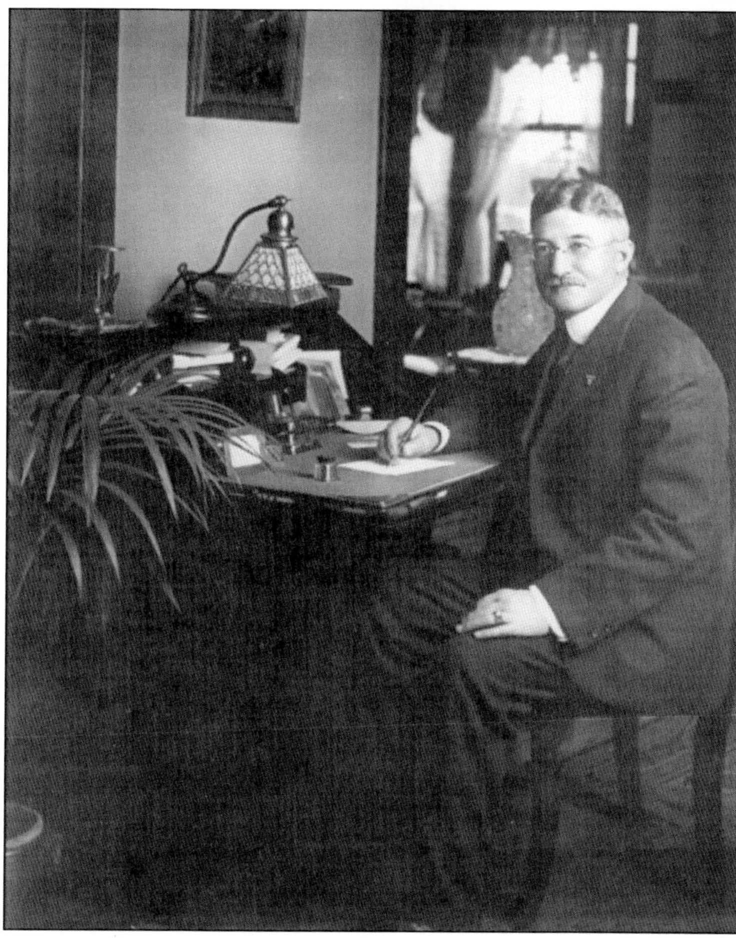

Walter Edgar Pierce was one of Boise's leading real estate agents and developers. He and his partners John Haines and Lindley Cox platted many neighborhoods in Boise and the surrounding Treasure Valley towns. Pierce was well known as the organizer of the B&I, which he sold in 1911. He remained involved in the interurban and streetcar companies.

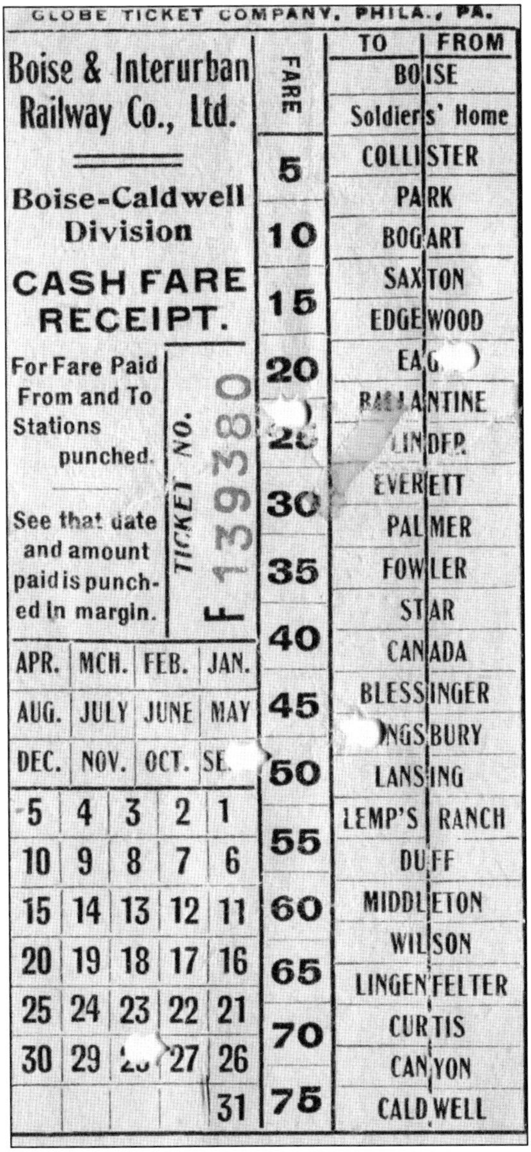

This ticket for the B&I cash fare shows the date and destination of the rider. The wait stations on the line between Boise and Caldwell are shown, as well. The unknown passenger who used this ticket travelled from Eagle, west of Boise in Ada County, to Kingsbury in Canyon County. (Courtesy of John Aguirre.)

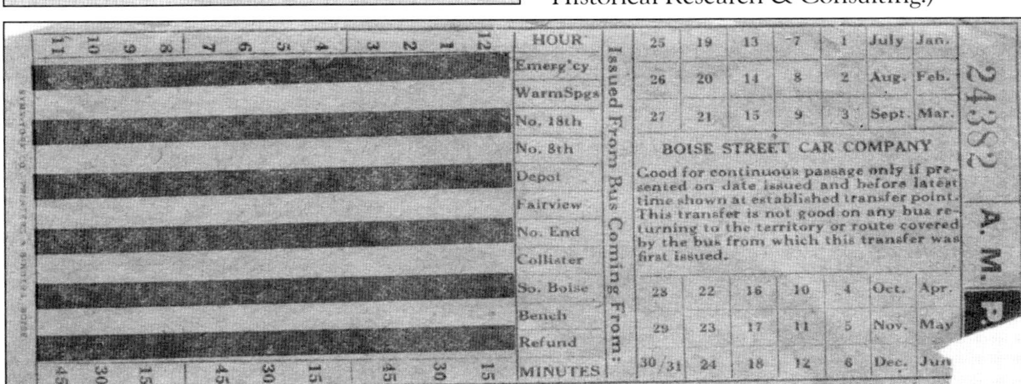

Bus service eventually took over some routes of the city streetcar and the interurban. This unused fare receipt shows the locations of bus stops around 1930. (Courtesy of TAG Historical Research & Consulting.)

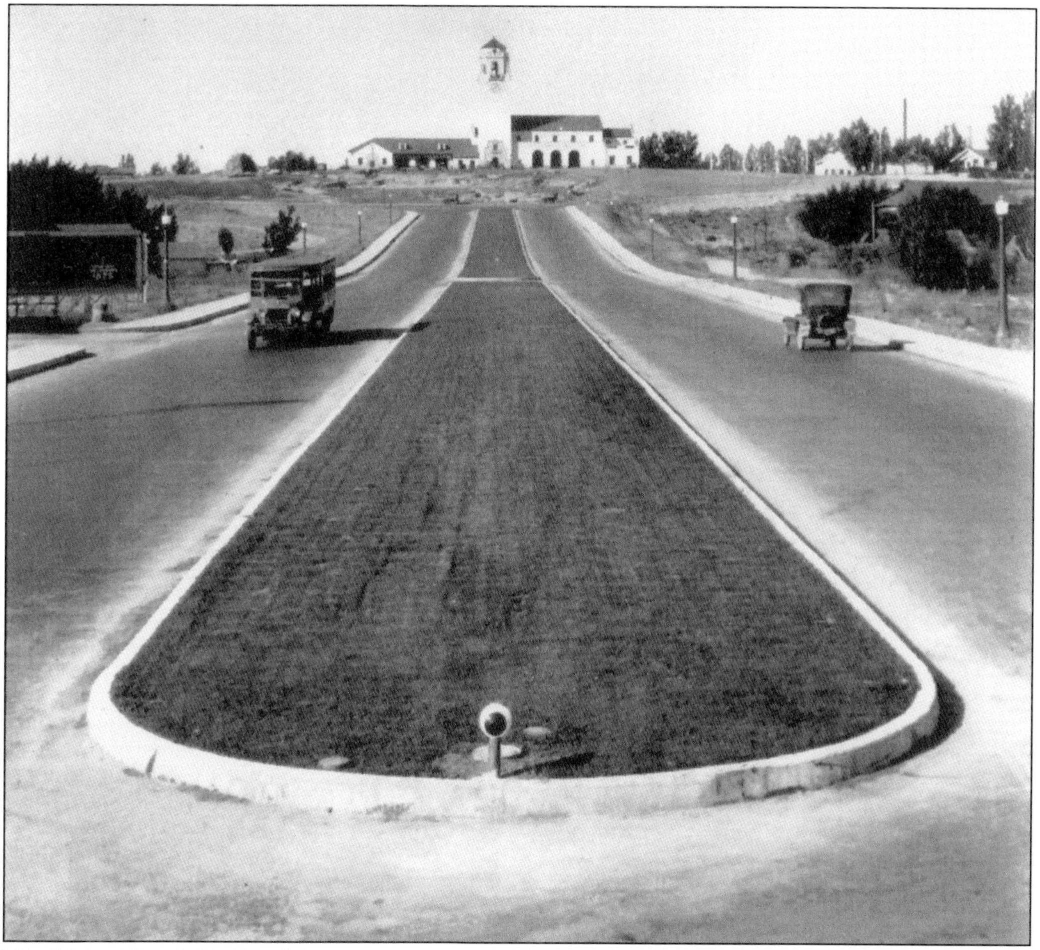

The Union Pacific Railroad depot was constructed in 1925, and Capitol Boulevard, which provided a grand entrance to Boise from the depot, was completed in the 1930s. In this photograph, looking north at the depot from the boulevard, buses have replaced the streetcars.

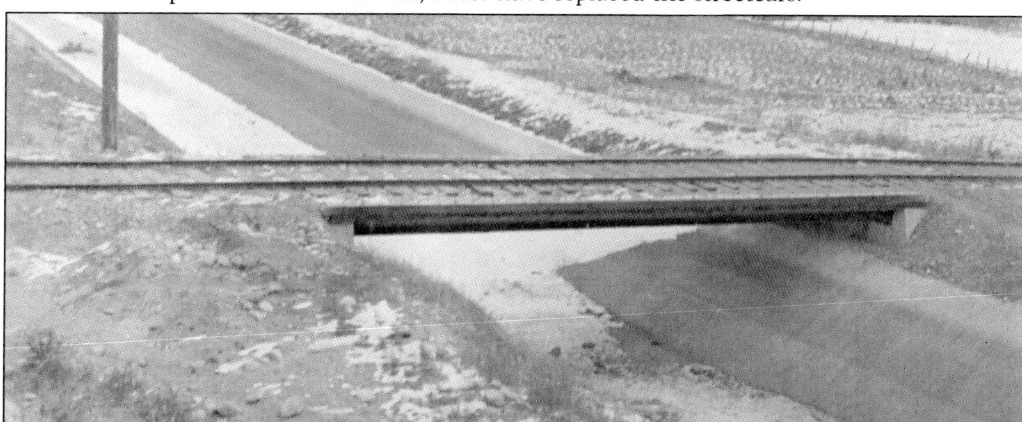

This bridge over the Ridenbaugh Canal, off of Chamberlain Street in Boise, was removed once the streetcar service ended.

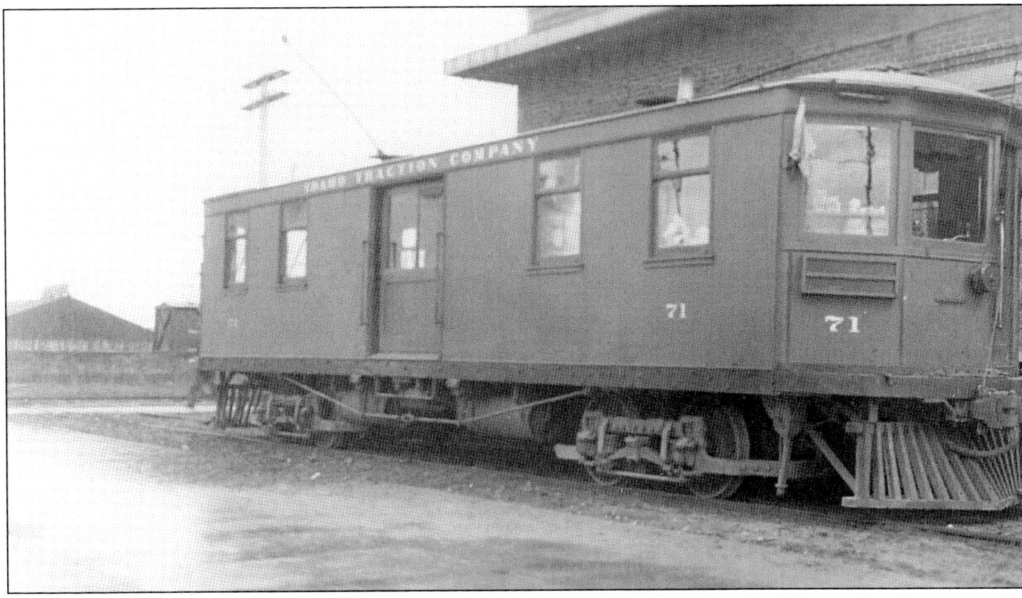

ITC freight Car No. 71 is pictured at the Caldwell depot. Note the double trucks shown under the body of the car. The truck encompasses the entire system of the wheels, axles, and motors supporting the car on the rails. On a double truck car, each truck has two axles and pivots under the body of the car.

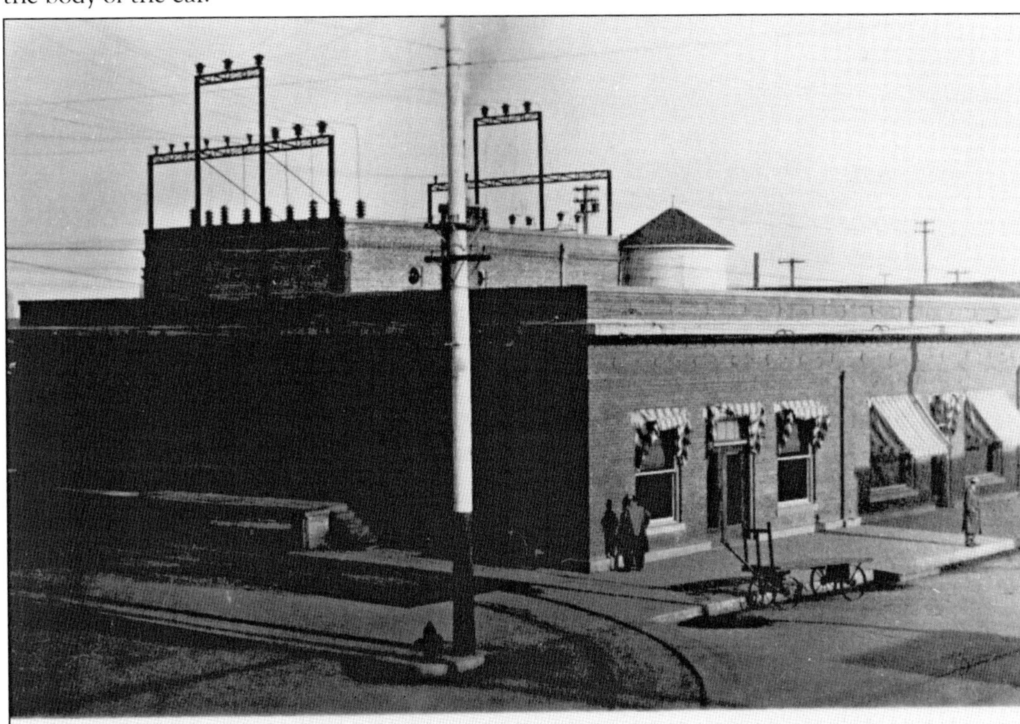

Caldwell Terminal Building

This view shows the Caldwell depot and terminal building. Note the awnings over the window to protect against the sun.

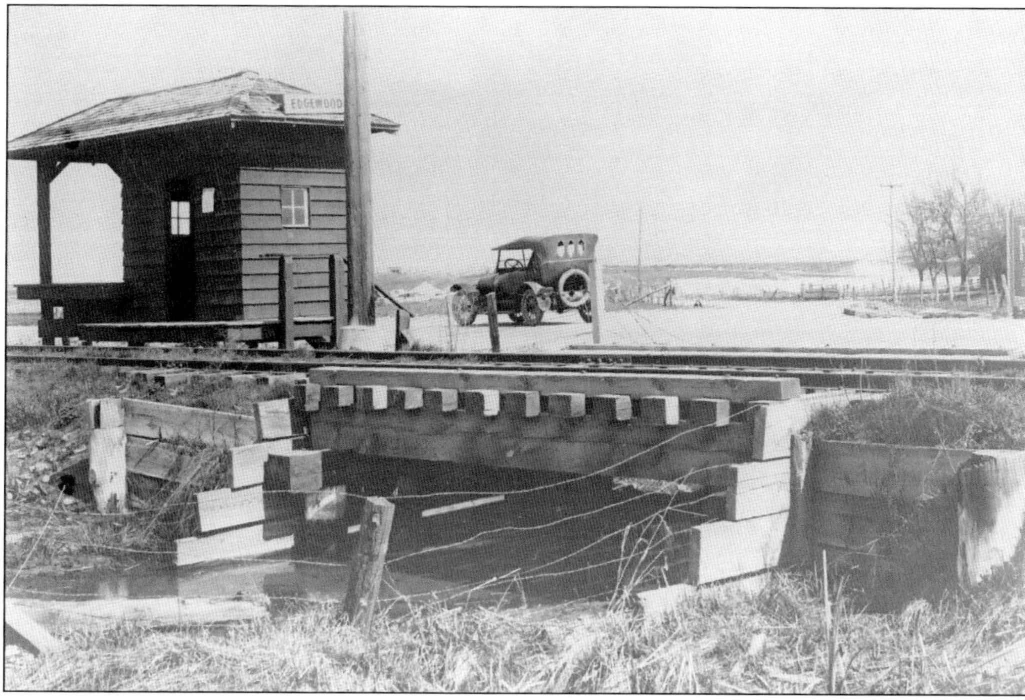

The traction companies provided regular maintenance on the shelter stations as long as their budgets allowed. Window replacement and repainting were yearly maintenance projects. This view shows the woodpile trestle and waiting station at Edgewood, on the Northern Division of the interurban.

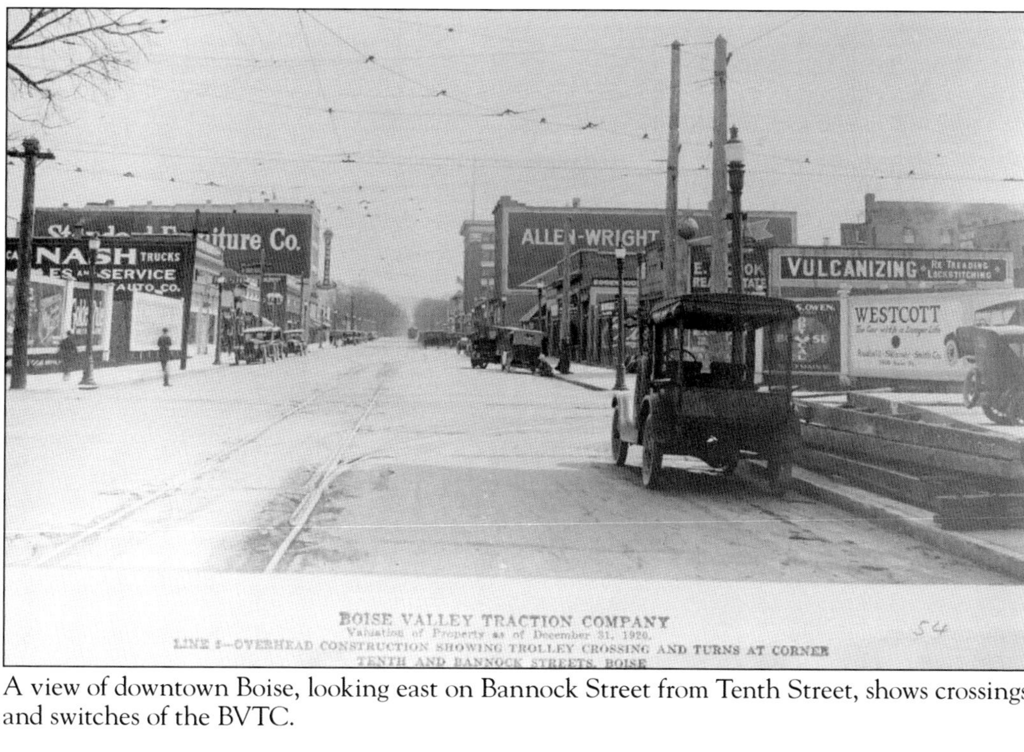

A view of downtown Boise, looking east on Bannock Street from Tenth Street, shows crossings and switches of the BVTC.

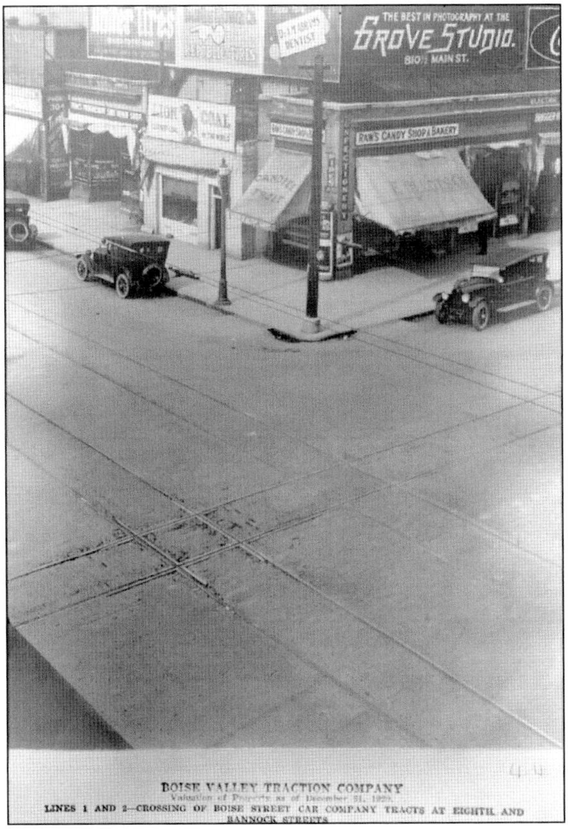

This view shows the northwest corner of Eighth and Bannock Streets, the original location of the BVRC depot. The BVTC tracks crossed the city streetcar tracks at this location.

BVTC Car No. 72 is seen at the materials-storage yard near Twenty-eighth Street and Fairview Avenue, in Boise.

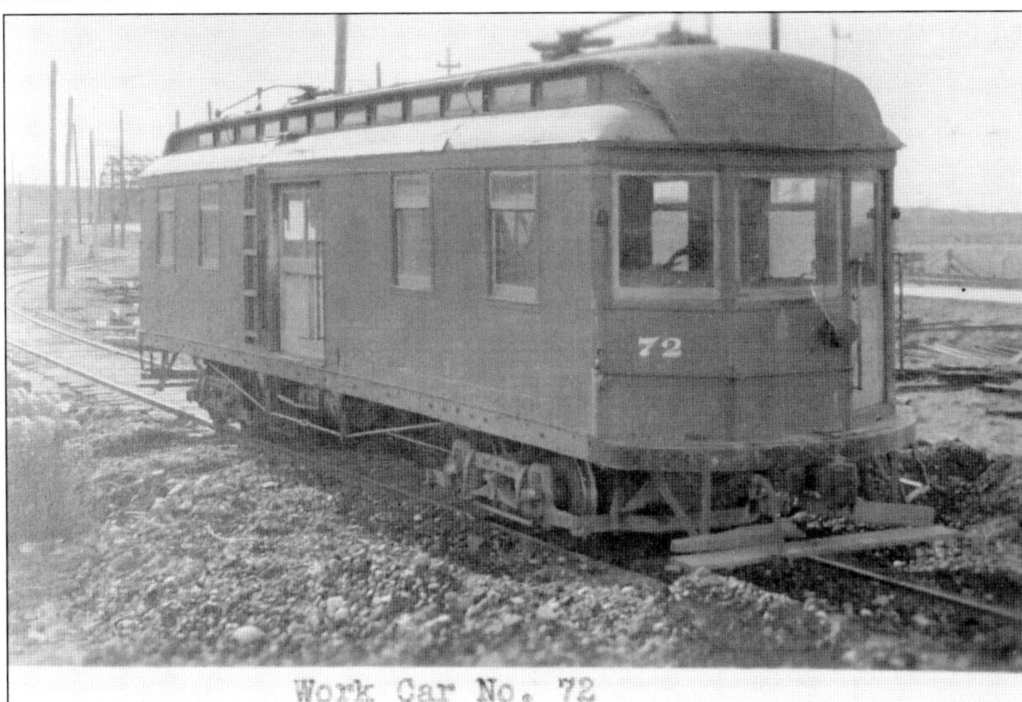

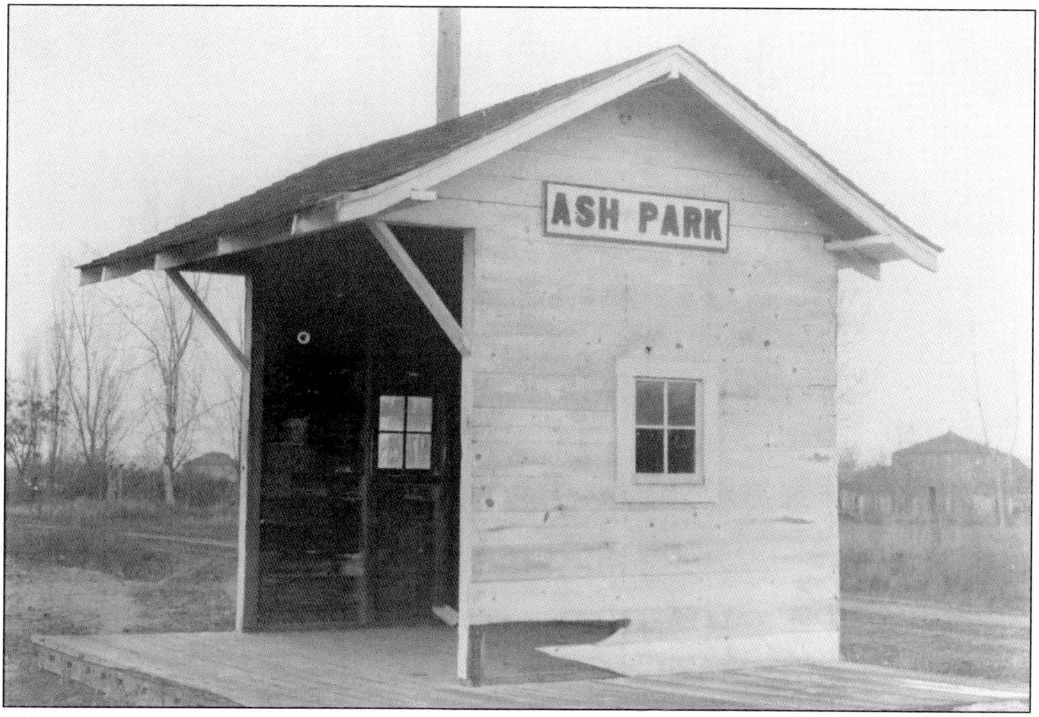

The shelter station at Ash Park, pictured around 1920, was located approximately five miles west of Boise on the Southern Division.

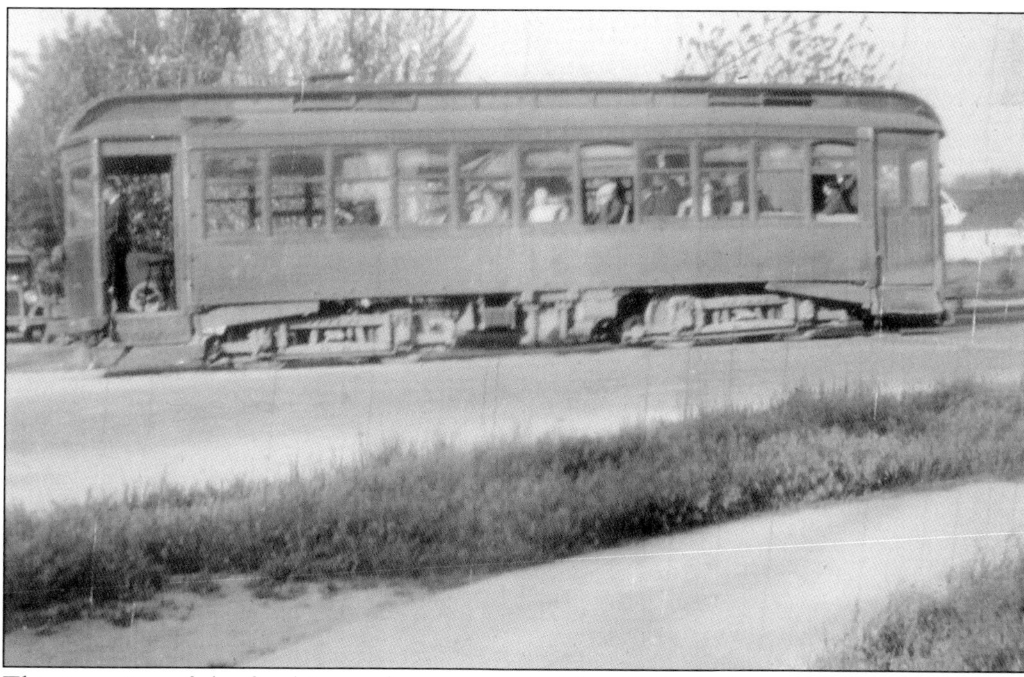

This is a view of the final interurban car run in May 1928. As fewer people rode the cars, maintenance on the tracks and equipment was reduced, schedules were cut, and, one by one, the streetcar and interurban lines were abandoned.

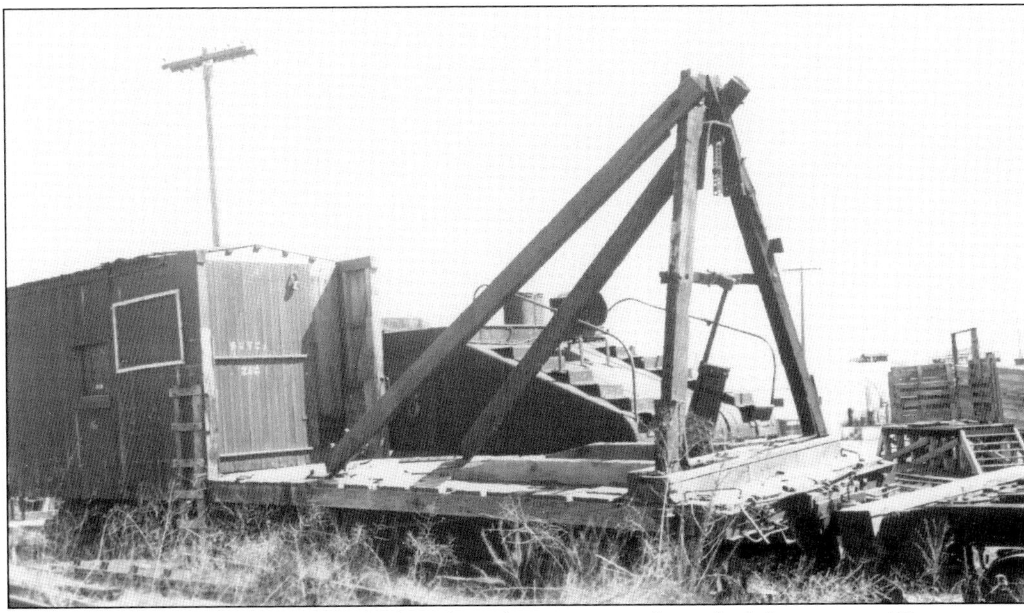

A BVTC car sits, forlorn and abandoned, at an unidentified location. (Courtesy of John Aguirre.)

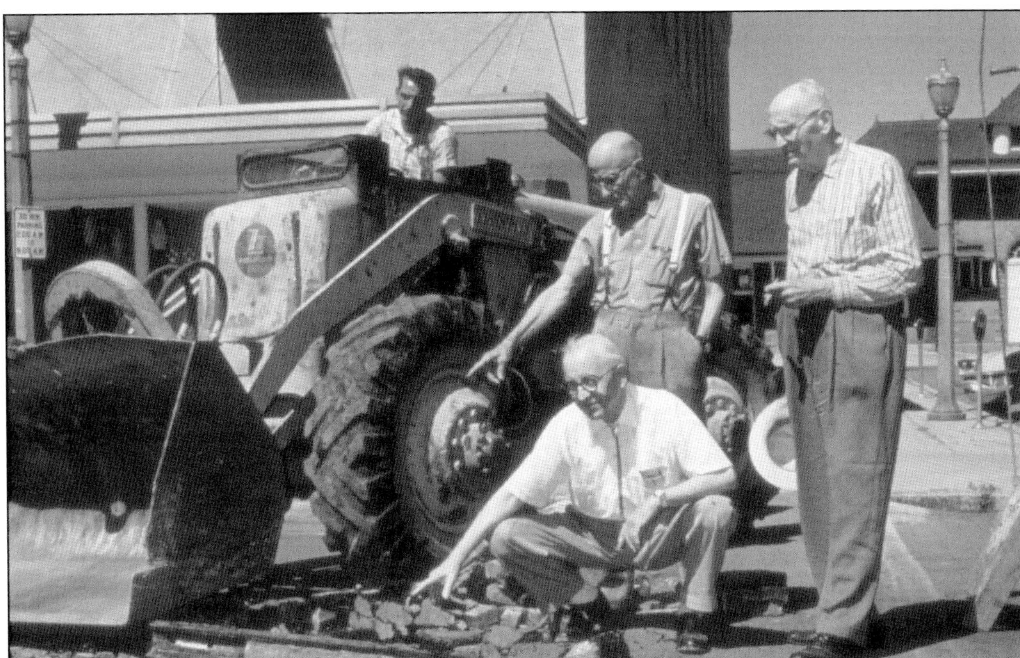

Elated Caldwell residents point to interurban tracks uncovered on the corner of Main and Seventh Streets during road construction in the 1960s. Given the age of the photograph, it is possible that the men pictured here may have ridden the interurban in their youth. The Caldwell depot is shown in the background.

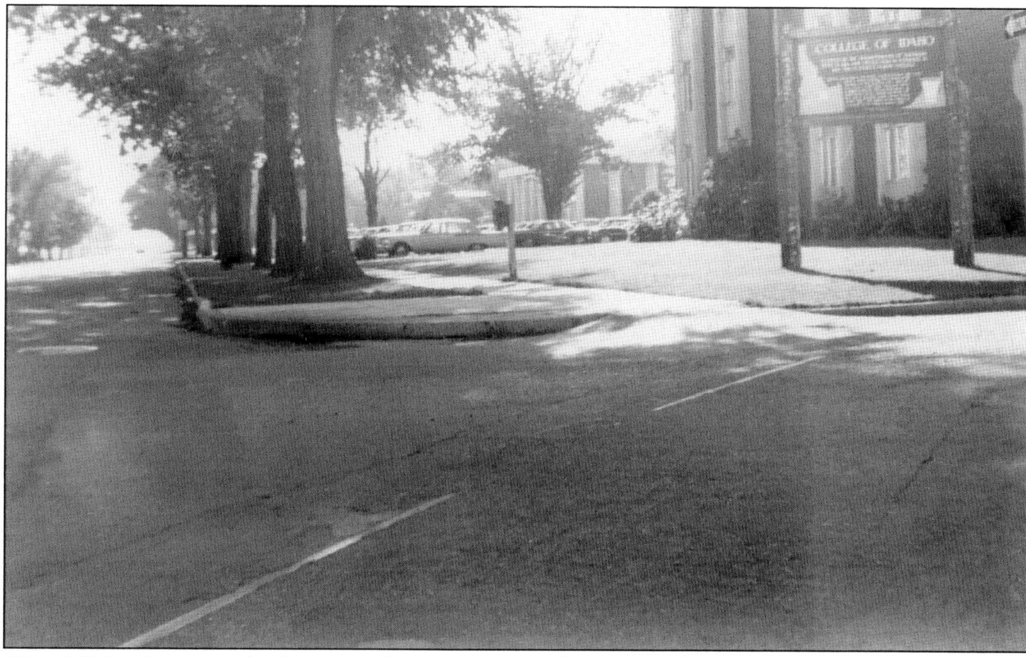

This 1970s photograph shows track remnants of the interurban line that once crossed near the College of Idaho. Over 50 years after the line was torn up, the rails were still visible in the asphalt roadbed.

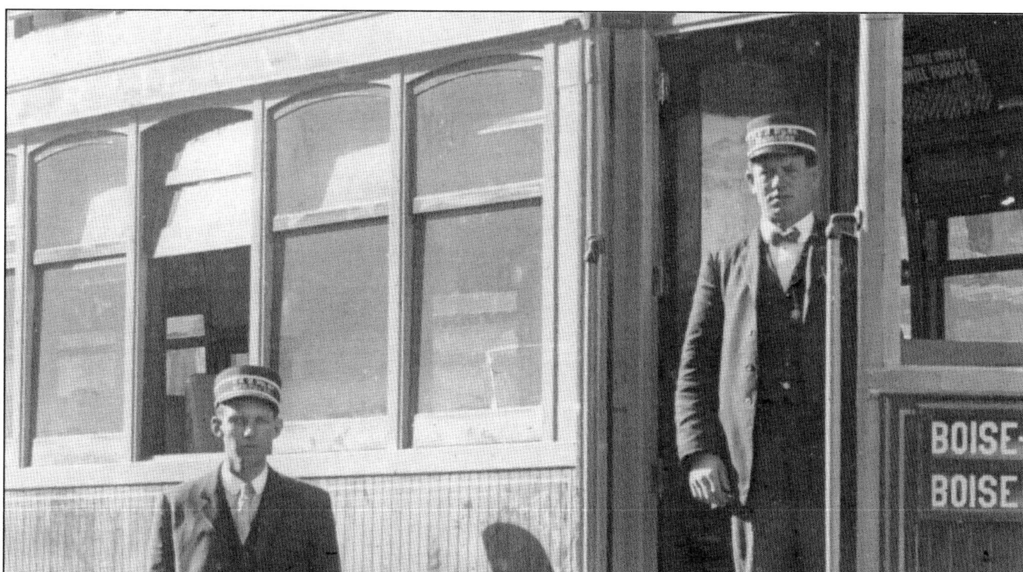

Two employees of the B&I pose with their car at Caldwell around 1908, during the heyday of the interurban. The conductor on the left is identified by the lettering on his cap. The motorman, also identified by lettering on his hat, stands in the door of the car. After the demise of the interurban, many employees went on to work at the power company, in office jobs, or as linemen and mechanics.

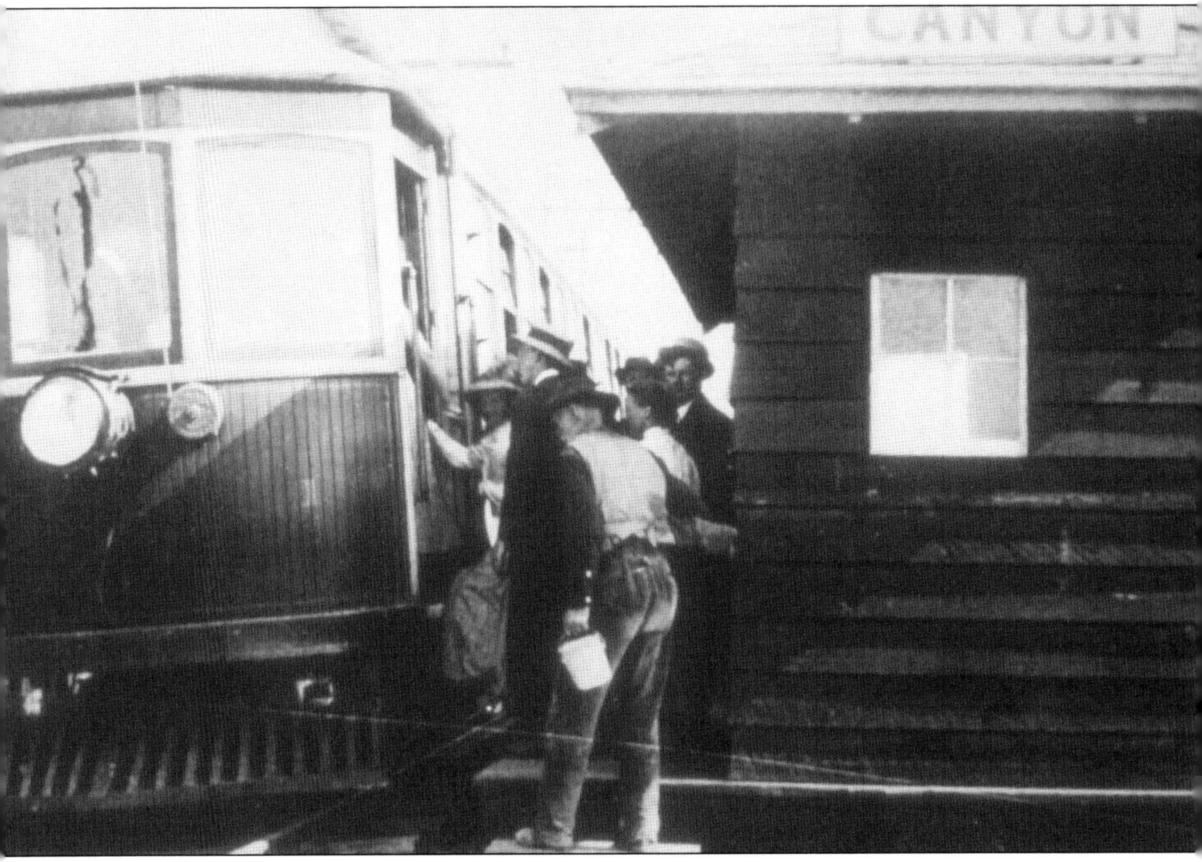

Passengers prepare to board B&I Car No. 1 at Canyon Station. The loop service provided by the interurban companies made travel convenient and linked the communities of the Treasure Valley. Although few traces of the interurban remain, modern bus routes follow routes established by the electric railway.

BIBLIOGRAPHY

Bird, Annie Laurie. *Boise: The Peace Valley*. Caldwell, ID: Caxton Printers, 1934.
———. *My Home Town*. Caldwell, ID: Caxton Printers, 1968.
Brill, Debra. *History of the J.G. Brill Company*. Bloomington: Indiana University Press, 2001.
Casner, Nicholas, and Valerie Kiesig. *Trolley: Boise Valley's Electric Road, 1891–1928*. Boise: Black Canyon Communications, 2002.
Electric Railway Review (American Street and Interurban Railway Association) 15–20 (1906–1908).
Hill, Lila, and Glen W. Davidson. *They Came to Build a Community: A History of Meridian, Idaho and the People Called Methodists*. Meridian, ID: First United Methodist Church, 1986.
Hilton, George W., and John F. Due. *The Electric Interurban Railways in America*. Stanford, CA: Stanford University Press, 2000.
Marion K. Fox Papers. Idaho Historical Society, Boise.
Wells, Merle W., and Arthur A. Hart. *Boise: An Illustrated History*. Woodland Hills, CA: Windsor Publications, 1982.

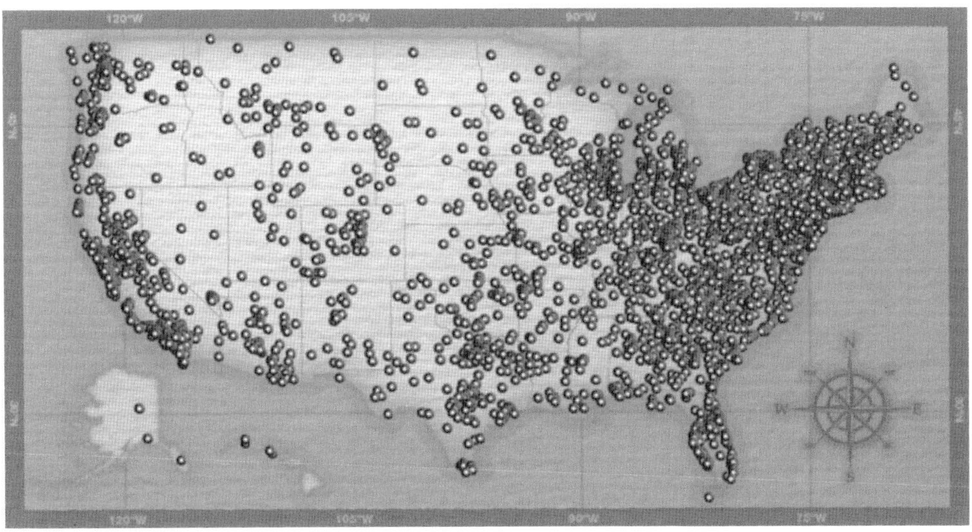